A Craft Collection

A Craft Collection

Compiled by Henry Pluckrose

Evans Brothers Limited London

Published by Evans Brothers Limited
Montague House, Russell Square,
London, W.C.1.

© Evans Brothers Limited 1973

First published 1973

Set in 9 on 11 point Grot. 215 and 216 and
printed in Great Britain by
T. & A. Constable Ltd., Edinburgh

ISBN 0 237 44614 6   PRA 3380

Contents

Introduction

Over the past ten years I have been fortunate enough to teach at two levels. Most of my day is spent with young children aged between $4\frac{1}{2}$–$11\frac{1}{2}$ and, like many another Primary School teacher I never cease to be amazed at the quality of drawings, paintings and models which flow, apparently spontaneously, from their hands. My other level of teaching has been with adults (most of them teachers or teachers in training) who want to understand a little better how to establish situations in which creative activities can flourish.

Now what fascinates me is how similar these two groups are. The seven-year-old on being introduced to poster paint will pick up the tube, squeeze it gently, open it, examine the paint—perhaps even smelling it, or smearing a spot over a sheet of paper to "test" the colour. The 27-year-old behaves exactly the same—as does the 57-year-old close to retirement. Give clay to any group of teachers and before any activity starts it will be prodded, smoothed and talked about, just the response the nursery assistant would expect from five-year-olds. Of course, the similarity of response to materials by different age groups should come as no surprise. Both adults and children are human beings and curiosity is not the perquisite of the young.

It is here that my art activities begin, for whether I am working with teachers or children I find in the materials the point from which, together, we can move forward.

The materials themselves present the challenge, each having their own behavioural pattern. What I can do easily with crayon I find difficult to do with pencil and impossible to accomplish in paint. A process that is acceptable with clay, fails when applied to plastic modelling materials or plaster. Thus groups discover that the materials that are available largely determine the techniques employed and that the mastering of techniques *as ends in themselves* have very little value.

Let me illustrate this with one example drawn from my own school days. Instead of learning to handle wood—by using it in constructions, its natural forms in sculpture, its shavings in collage—I was given instruction on how to make a joint, a joint to unite two poor scraps of wood that were fit for nothing but kindling. The directions were clear, the unspoken implications understood. Make the joint well and, all things being equal, I could employ my new found skill to make a pipe rack, a toothbrush holder or a pine matchbox case. Failure merely meant being marooned on a desert island of kindling wood until success came—and for me success came so slowly as to be almost imperceptible.

This book then, aims at providing you, the reader, with a starting point much less sterile than the one that drove me inexorably from plane, chisel and work bench. Each of our main contributors was invited to begin by examining a material and, by concentrating upon its own peculiar properties show how these peculiarities indicate and determine the technique which we need to master and handle them.

Having decided that this was to be a collection of crafts which stemmed from experiments with materials it was comparatively easy to select those to feature. As this is essentially a book for home, school and club, it would have been pointless to include materials which are expensive, difficult to obtain or which require sophisticated tools and equipment to process. Thus to follow A Craft Collection you will need little more than some colours, a needle and thread, card, paper, scissors, glue—and a pair of hands.

Inspiration, which many adults feel they need before embarking on any art activity, is deliberately omitted from my list. Involve yourself with the material and, like as not, something will come. All art contains much that is accidental.

Allow yourself that accident—who knows where it may lead?

H.P.

February 1973

Using wet colours

Using wet colours

Water—the magic ingredient

All young children enjoy a visit to the beach. The occasion can be especially exciting if the tide has just turned and the loose, dry sand, which 'doesn't do anything', is transformed into a firm surface capable of providing a sports arena for the older children and an imaginative art workshop for the very young.

That magic ingredient *water* turns the dull, dry sand into a giant piece of drawing-paper capable of being enriched with linear patterns etched into its surface with spades, driftwood and fingers, Fig. 1. These designs can later be adorned with all manner of beach flotsam to become giant collages. The three-dimensional possibilities of carved and moulded sand are endless, Fig. 2.

The appeal of wet sand lies in its flexibility. It is capable of being shaped, modified, destroyed and re-shaped, all in one exercise. These are the qualities that we should expect from the earliest wet-media we offer to our children.

Finger-paint

Finger-paint and wet sand have much in common, offering as they do, a flexible and tactile surface, with the former having the extra appeal of colour, Fig. 3.

We have all seen babies enjoying themselves in the action of spreading their unwanted cereals across the smooth, plastic surfaces of their high-chair tables. Their delight in making patterns with the fingers is a very

Fig. 1. Wet sand—an imaginative art workshop for the young

natural, and surely unpunishable, action.

Many teachers, play-group and nursery supervisors mix their own brand of finger-paint by combining liquid or powder tempera colour with various 'thickeners' such as cellulose-paste, cornflour or boiled starch. These home-made finger-paints do have certain disadvantages when compared with the commercially manufactured product. After considerable time and effort has been expended in their preparation, the resultant paint is often too liquid, too lumpy or too weak in colour. These mixtures must also be used up at the earliest opportunity as they tend to sour with keeping.

The qualities to be expected of an industrially prepared finger-paint are:—

1. A smooth, grit-free liquid with pleasant handling qualities.

2. A strong charge of colour, which should be translucent enough to produce a wide range of tone and to allow good colour mixing and overpainting.

3. A completely non-staining, water-soluble, non-toxic mixture capable of being easily removed from hands, furniture and clothing.

Fig. 2. The dead warrior, built up in sand with seaweed and pebble decoration

Fig. 3. Children delight in experimenting with marks made with different parts of their hands

Fig. 6. Pieces of card can also be used to make different marks

Fig. 4. Taking a mono print

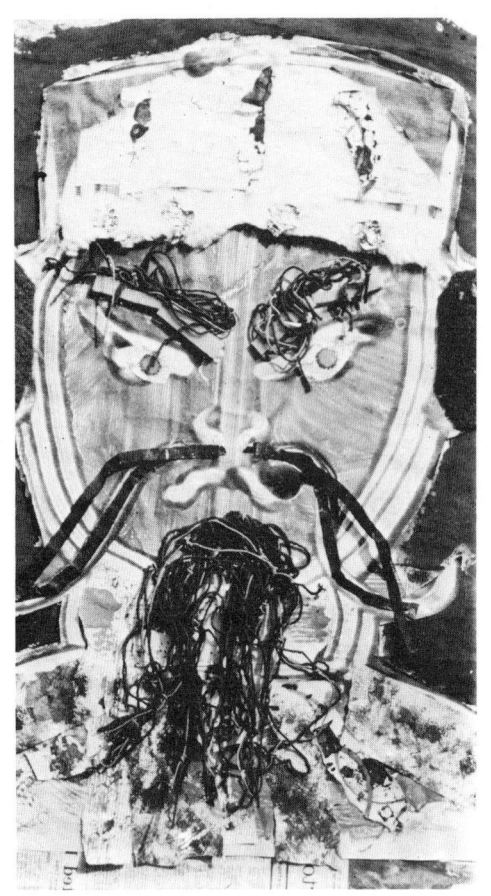

Finger-painting

Although finger-paint can be worked into the dampened surface of a paper specially manufactured for this activity, it can also be manipulated on any smooth surface such as Formica, polythene, painted hardboard, linoleum etc. From these surfaces, prints can be made on to the thin lining-paper, Fig. 4. These prints can often provide the starting-point for three-dimensional or large-scale, collage activities, Fig. 5.

Early experiments with finger-paint should be concerned with creating all manner of patterns and marks by using the hands and arms in a variety of movements both delicate and bold. Designs can be done with finger-tips, palm, side of the hand, nails, knuckles, wrist and forearm. Sponges, lolly-sticks, cardboard 'combs', bottle-caps and other scrap-materials can also be used to produce different lines and marks, Fig. 6.

Thin cardboard coated with a thick layer of wax-crayon, makes a very good base on which to finger-paint, with the crayon colours enhancing every mark made into the paint surface.

Fig. 5. A mono print used as the basis for a collage

Fig. 7. Finger-paintings have been used as a background for this mural

Fig. 8. Forcing the printing ink through the screen with a piece of card

Fig. 9. The finished print

Apart from the fact that surface prints taken from finger-paintings can provide exciting backgrounds for large-scale friezes based on such topics as Neptune's kingdom, primeval jungles, deserts, enchanted gardens, etc. Fig. 7, they can also be used to decorate boxes, display boards, book-covers and Christmas cards.

Not just for infants

Finger-painting need not be the preserve of the pre-school or infant child. Its therapeutic value with timid and handicapped children is well known but there is no reason why it should not be used by older children or even adults.

In considering the whole range of water-soluble paints we must rightly be aware of the particular needs of the child at the different stages in his or her physical development. For example, the demands of acrylic painting might excite a thirteen year old but to a younger child with a lesser degree of manual control, they could prove to be very frustrating. However, whilst it is important to provide the right material at the right time, there is the danger of assuming that once a particular media has been explored it need never be considered again. This is obviously untrue. Because a child has enjoyed using finger-paint at the age of seven, there is no reason why he should not consider its potential again, when he is fifteen or older. Any medium will express the experience and ability of the user.

Finger-paint as a printing ink

We have considered finger-paint as a means of introducing the idea of printing to young children however, the thick, jelly-like nature of this material, makes it equally suitable for use by older children as a screen-printing ink.

Making a simple printing-screen

Making a printing-screen from a wooden frame covered with bolting-silk or organdie often demands facilities and finances beyond the reach of schools but as can be seen in Fig. 8 simple screens can be manufactured from box-lids or cardboard-plates. A rectangular window is cut out of the improvised screen and over it a piece of nylon or terylene-net fabric is stapled. Masking-tape is used to seal the edges of the window to prevent the ink from subsequently creeping under the frame during printing.

The ink

Finger-paint is used as a printing ink and it is forced through the mesh of the screen with the edge of a stout piece of cardboard (squeegee).

The printed images

Simple paper-stencils or doilies were laid under the screen to produce the printed images, Fig. 9. Drawings can also be made directly on to the mesh of the screen with glue or P.V.A. medium, in order to block the interstices. These images, when dry, will resist the paint that is pulled through the net producing, as a result, stencil-like prints. Printing over chalk or wax-crayon areas can produce exciting colour effects.

Tempera colour

Tempera powder colour is still the most popular medium in general school use. Again, the addition of that magic ingredient —water—can result in a thick, opaque paint. More water will produce a transparent colour with the consistency of an ink.

Storage of powder colour

If powder colour is to be an economical consideration for general classroom use, careful thought must be given to its storage and handling. It must, obviously, be kept in a dry place.

Although powder colour has the advantage that it can be mixed to any desired consistency, infants generally find the mixing tedious, hampering as it does, their desire to quickly put their experiences on to paper. Invariably, in their haste, they resort to watery, innocuous colour. This problem can be eliminated by providing a few pre-mixed colours—red, yellow, blue, green, brown, black and white, which can be poured into plastic cartons or baby-food jars and placed inside a suitable box, a cigar-box is ideal. Space can be left in the box to accommodate the water-container. This type of paint-box eases the problem of distribution as it can be placed within reach of a small group of children and it also eliminates the likelihood of spillages. Colour mixing can be done on old saucers, plates or ceramic tiles but the children must be shown how to rinse un-wanted paint from their brushes and how to dry them with a paint-rag before returning them to the paint jars.

Tables

Tables and desks should be covered with newspaper before painting takes place. Even though a table might have a laminated-plastic top capable of being wiped clean with a damp cloth, covering it with paper will speed the final clean-up and will help the children to be tidy.

Painting-easels are not essential. Most children prefer to stand up when painting, with their pictures laid on a table top. In this way the frustration of running paint which is to be expected when painting on a sloping surface, can be eliminated, Fig. 10.

Fig. 10. Most children find it easier to paint standing up, resting their picture on a table

Brushes

Whilst it is important to provide the children with a selection of good bristle and hair brushes, some early experiments in making a brush should be considered. Improvised 'brushes' made from rolled-up newspaper, drinking straws, rope, string, sponge, etc., can be used to explore their own particular mark-making characteristics.

Ways of working

All children are eager to paint and to use colour creatively. They should not, however, be shown 'how to paint'. Instead, they should be allowed to find out for themselves in an atmosphere which encourages experimental attitudes.

Stories, poems and particularly their own experiences provide the necessary stimulation. Illustrations, posters and colourful designs can suggest suitable activities. A film, a trip, a visit to an art gallery may prove to be an inspiration. The first fall of snow may bring a flurry of excitement worth capturing in paint. The world of the imagination is limitless—'Flowers and insects from another planet', 'Creatures from a nightmare', 'Lost cities', 'The four seasons', 'Halloween', 'Carnival time', these are just a few of the subjects which excite all young children.

The broad limits of any theme should be established by the teacher, with the children suggesting ideas and possible ways of

Fig. 11. Several mono prints have been cut up and used in this collage

working. The time spent on this discussion is often repaid in considered and beautiful work. The emphasis should be on the children painting their own pictures that are quite different from their class-mates. Telling the children to produce a picture of their own choice, often produces the most negative response, with many of the children falling back on images of derivative and doubtful origin. A sketchy background might suffice for artistic children, who are full of their own ideas but the majority of children need the stimulus of lively discussion.

A painting vocabulary

As we saw in the section on finger-painting, if the children are to get the best results from a material, the possibilities and limitations of that medium should be fully explored in order that a vocabulary of ways of working can be acquired. With the pre-school and infant child the matter of manual control has also to be considered. A brush is a sophisticated instrument, its secrets are not revealed on first acquaintance especially to a five year old.

A good exercise in developing brush control is to simply let the infants paint irregular scraps of wood, cardboard rolls and boxes, plastic bottles etc., with a few pre-mixed colours. They will learn much about the handling of a brush when painting these awkward surfaces and they will produce some very colourful building material which, used in conjunction with toy soldiers and motor cars, will be a valuable addition to imaginative play activities.

In the infant class, a demonstration is needed on:—

how to hold the brush;

how to dip in the paint to avoid spilling;

how to remove excess paint on the side of the jar;

how to avoid scrubbing and damaging the brush;

how to rinse the brush clean before returning it to the jar.

Since the care of materials is most important, procedures and the location of supplies should be fully explained.

Early exercises in paint are best confined to design rather than picture. The children can learn paint rules and the feel of the brush without the added challenge of realism.

A few basic exercises

1. Cover the paper with curving lines.
2. Paint wide stripes in straight or curved lines. Decorate these with paint dots, after they have dried.
3. Overlap straight and curved lines, then fill in the resulting shapes with solid colour.
4. Dab many colours on to a paper to produce a merging effect. Paint over this effect with shapes using a dark line.
5. Paint many different shapes. When dry outline them with other colours.
6. Cover a paper with patches of colour. When dry, produce different textures on each patch using dots, lines or dry-brush marks.
7. Paint patches of light colours over patches of dark ones and vice-versa.
8. Cover a paper with 'hot' colours.
9. Cover a paper with 'cold' colours.
10. Use a black line round patches of bright colour to simulate stained-glass.

Liquid tempera paint

Many schools are now using tempera paint in its liquid form. Its deserved popularity lies in the fact that, apart from eliminating the time-consuming chore of mixing, it is easy to distribute from flexible plastic bottles which are transparent and offer instant colour recognition. If we are to expect the children to play an essential and active role in the distribution of materials before the lesson and their subsequent storage and care, the matter of instant colour recognition is very important.

Tempera blocks

Solid blocks of tempera colour might appear to offer convenience from a storage point of view but they do have their working-limitations. If the block is a particularly hard one, the children soon tire of scrubbing at it in order to pick up the desired charge of colour. In this case, the wear and tear on brushes is considerable. If, however, the block is of the semi-soluble type, it tends to wear away in the middle, leaving a hard ring of paint in the palette, which has to be used up with some difficulty, before being replaced.

Additives

A number of additives can be used with liquid or powder tempera colour in order to enhance their handling and creative capabilities.

Paste

Cellulose wallpaper paste or cornflour can be added to tempera colour to produce a mixture suitable for paste-combing with notched cardboard. As mentioned in the section on finger-painting, this type of mixture must be used up quickly or stored in airtight containers, as it soon deteriorates.

Detergent

A bottle of liquid detergent can serve more than its obvious use in any classroom. A small drop of this liquid mixed with tempera paint breaks down the surface tension of the mixture and allows it to be brushed on to any shiny surface. With this mixture, plastic bottles can be painted to produce decorative totem-poles, colourful skittles, puppets, robots, etc. It can also be

Fig. 12. Thin washes of paint can be painted over a dried India ink drawing

used directly on to glass to simulate stained-glass effects. Heavily wax-crayoned surfaces can be given a covering coat of a soap/paint mixture which can be scratched into with a suitable stylus to reveal the bright crayon colours. This technique can be used with great effect in any picture or pattern exercise. It is important to note, however, that any brushes that have been used in a soap/paint mixture must be thoroughly washed afterwards if they are to be used with weaker solutions of paint over wax-crayoning to produce the effect known as 'wax-resist.'

Acrylic media

A bottle of acrylic-polymer can be a useful addition to the art room stock. The combination of powder or liquid tempera paint and the thick, creamy acrylic medium results in a heavy-bodied paint of an oil-like appearance. The resultant liquid is capable of being applied to any surface such as paper, hardboard, cardboard, fabric, newsprint, canvas, plaster, etc., and it is quite flexible. Left to dry, within a day, it will harden into a durable and waterproof surface capable of being used on exterior sculpture, murals and posters.

Three-dimensional effects can be achieved by embedding stones, shells, wire, string and matchsticks into the paint surface which, thanks to the acrylic medium, has strong adhesive properties.

In its wet state the acrylic paint mixture can be easily removed from brushes or other equipment with water but if they are accidentally allowed to harden they can be re-softened in methylated spirits and then rinsed in hot water.

A dry, thick layer of acrylic paint applied to a sheet of glass can be removed as a transparent skin, once the glass has been soaked in warm water. The semi-transparent skin can then be attached to a wood or card frame and illuminated from behind.

Acrylic-polymer medium, although having a milky appearance, dries out to a clear, transparent glaze or varnish. It can, therefore, be diluted with water and applied as a protective coat over drawings, book covers, models, puppets, etc.

An acrylic medium is an excellent aid when the activities of model-making and painting are combined.

Inks

Because of the permanence of inks, particularly India ink, their use in the infant class should be discouraged. Careful handling by children over the age of nine, however, will produce fine results. The ink may be distributed in small bottles on tables that have been suitably covered. If the ink is not to be used individually but merely at a group location for a final wash, perhaps over a crayon drawing, then it should be in a larger bottle or container capable of holding a number of larger brushes.

Drawing

Drawing with a pen on a hard-surface paper can result in very effective pictures, particularly if a slow intricate technique is used. A quick, sketchy quality is not as attractive. Before a picture is attempted a few introductory exercises in producing various line textures should be undertaken. These could be drawn in chalk on a blackboard and interpreted by the class in ink.

Ink and crayon

Ink may be brushed over crayon to produce a resist effect in the same manner as tempera. Before brushing over the crayon, the work may be crumpled, dipped in water and flattened out again. The cracks produced by crumpling will be penetrated by the ink to produce a unique surface quality similar to the spidery network of lines seen in batik-decorated fabrics.

Ink and paint washes

A dried India ink drawing may be painted over with thin washes of paint, Fig. 12. The paper can even be soaked with water and the dried ink line will not run. Regular water-colour techniques may be used and the drawing will still show through.

Diluted washes of India ink can be applied to a pen-drawing to produce a monochrome effect. Each layer of water-diluted ink applied over a subsequent layer that has dried, will produce a darkening in tone. This effect can be explored by simply covering a paper with curved or straight brush-strokes of diluted ink, allowing it to dry, then crossing these lines with others and observing the change of tone at the intersections.

Ink scraperboard

White crayon applied thickly to a piece of cardboard can be covered with a layer of India ink to produce an inexpensive scraper (sgraffito) board, capable of being scratched with a nail, old ball-point pen or a variety of pointed instruments.

Watercolour

Watercolours, are more popular in American schools than in Britain. Perhaps this is mainly due to the fact that the small cakes or tubes in which it is usually sold, demand a more intricate technique in contrast to the bolder approach found in the use of opaque tempera colour; an approach that is considered by most teachers to be psychologically more rewarding.

Watercolours, however, do have the unique quality of being comparable with coloured glass in that layers of different colours applied after each has dried will create different colours. Yellow over magenta will produce orange.

There is no white in true watercolour. Any white area must be the white of the paper and, therefore, not covered. Adding more water to paint will allow the paper to show through more and will create lighter colours. Since watercolour is thinned with water, it tends to run. If this quality is not desired and a crisp effect is wanted, care must be taken for an area to dry before painting next to it. It is this sort of problem that might be gladly tackled by a fourteen year old but which could, on the other hand, prove quite frustrating for a five year old.

Watercolours and acrylic medium

If acrylic medium is applied to paper, canvas or board with brush or palette-knife and allowed to dry, it will result in a thick, clear glaze. Watercolours can be flooded on to this glaze with a large brush resulting in colours and textures of unique luminosity.

Mixed media

Although we have considered the various wet-colours being used in schools under separate headings it should be apparent that these materials are quite compatible, simply by virtue of the fact that they are all water soluble. Combinations of various media never fail to excite the imaginations of children and often the introduction of crayons, chalk, detergent or acrylic medium into a painting lesson can stimulate imagination or revitalise a child's approach to his artwork. In Fig. 13 we see a delightful portrait of an eastern princess painted by a ten year old girl. Many ways of working have produced this very colourful picture, including combinations of liquid tempera colour, metallic powder colour, melted wax-crayon and ink. The various media have produced the perfect means to an end.

Fig. 13. An example of the use of several media in one picture

Painted stones and bottles

The following form of art is both exciting and inexpensive and can be achieved whether children live on the moors, by the sea or in the middle of a large industrial city. A variety of different and unusually shaped stones and pebbles can be collected from gardens, waste land, or the beach.

Decorated stones make splendid doorstops, bookends, paperweights and when mounted on polished blocks of wood they can be displayed as elegant sculptures in the house or garden.

Having found a suitable stone it is best for the children to discover its basic shape and then to examine it from different angles to see what its form suggests. It might look like an Indian chief, a space monster or a pre-

A display of painted stones

historic creature. Leave it to the child's imagination!

It is first necessary to thoroughly clean the stone with scouring powder or detergent and when it is dry rub it lightly with fine sandpaper, then dust.

Having completed this operation the surface is now prepared for painting. With a brush or pen and India ink sketch directly on to the surface without going into too much detail. Some children, if they are using flat pebbles, may trace a design first and then work over it with India ink.

When the ink is dry apply bold exciting colours (either oil, acrylic paint or even gloss and emulsion) to the stone and then leave to dry. Painting may have to be carried out in several stages to avoid colours running.

When the paint has dried cover the stone with a good quality varnish and it is now ready for mounting which is a very important part of the operation.

Blocks of wood should be selected for their colour and grain and polished wood further enhances the finish. I have also used small blocks of white Portland stone. Balance is also important in order that the stone will not topple over.

A bed must now be gouged from the top of the mount into which the stone's base must fit securely, then a strong impact glue is spread on to both the base of the stone and also into the gouged-out bed of the wooden block. Allow twenty-four hours for the stone to set and then give both stone and wooden block a final light coat of varnish.

When this project is completed, and it can be enjoyed at all age levels and abilities, good use can be made of the mounted stones in lessons of creative English where children can pretend their stones have a story or secret to tell them and they can record either in prose or poetry the life history of their respective stones or pebbles, noting especially whether or not the stone is pleased with its new design and setting.

Finally, great fun can be had if the class give names or titles to all the stones in the class and then votes can be taken to choose the most suitable caption for each stone.

A technique not dissimilar to that of stone painting, is that of bottle painting. The children may have found odd shaped bottles washed up on the seashore, if not they will be more than willing to bring jars and bottles from home. The bottles have first to be thoroughly cleaned with white spirit or washing soda before painting can begin. It is preferable that an undercoat be first applied and left to dry for a day or two before painting the final pattern. Allow one colour to dry before applying a second, otherwise the colours will run together. The more delicate the pattern attempted, the smaller the brushes will have to be.

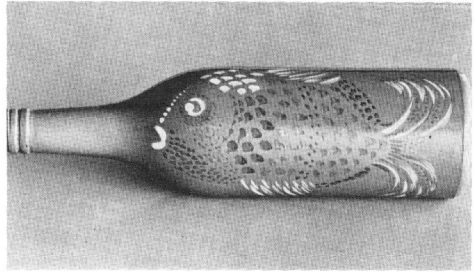

Illustration from "Painting Bottles and Glasses", published by Search Press Ltd.

Paint a line

The introduction of line into painting may often be regarded by artists as a final stage of work, when shapes are brought together or related directly by means of careful drawing. To most "young" children observations or ideas set down in colour take the form of statements in coloured line before areas are filled in.

It is possible to introduce a training that will reverse this process of thought so that areas of colour are seen simply. These may become lines in themselves but are related or joined in various experiments to form arrangements of larger coloured shapes.

Discovering

My eleven year old pupils spend their first term making personal discoveries and observations using a simple line and graphic basis. This is developed later so as to introduce colour and the children may print straight lines with small pieces of scrap wood and matchsticks using powder colour with PVA binder as a medium. They are encouraged to use the colour in as many different ways as they can by introducing overprinting and texture; the stimulus of this "appetiser" usually motivates further thought and discussions on the origins of colour. Having explored sources of colour in prisms, rainbows and oils, the children then relate these empirically. Experiments with complementary colours using straight coloured lines follow from the use of colour circles and may lead to diagrams and models being constructed from cut strips, printed forms and coloured straws.

We find it valuable to spend a few minutes at the end of each session looking at the work of recognised artists who faced similar problems of colour research and comparing their findings with the children's own results. The aim here is not to instil an immediate understanding of art history into children but rather to feed visual experiences and provide further stimulus.

The original enthusiasm motivated by discovering colour may now be stimulated further by the introduction of new ideas. Once this enthusiasm is aroused and the pupils begin to enjoy using colour, projects or exercises may be introduced, according to the wishes of individuals. The observation of natural forms stressed in other design work may be re-introduced with some justification at this point. This makes it necessary for personal observations and collections of as wide a variety of reasonably suitable natural forms to be made by the children, who thus note their colours. Grasses, stems, bark, leaves, seed pods, hair, feathers and small stones are arranged into designs using lines. Others are then stuck down side by side so as to show progression of natural colour.

An understanding of the use of the subtleties of colour may now be pointed out and work can begin with, for example, hot and cold arrangements. This certainly adds to the colour vocabulary of the child. Another method of using line is by painting strips in limited colour and interweaving them to form grids or shapes.

Experimental studies

Sometimes the children experiment in the same way with as many different coloured lines as they may wish to include. Personal discoveries will make this highly successful and the smaller pieces of completed work may then be stuck on to a larger sheet for display. Each child will then see the work developing, a pattern of thought that they have laid down visually.

Coloured raffia provides excellent material for further coloured line studies as the work progresses. This may be purchased ready coloured or in bundles of its natural colour to be dyed by groups in the classroom. Taking natural camouflage in animals as a starting point, so as to add extra cohesion and relevance to the progression of exercises, the children may be encouraged to stick strips of coloured raffia on to paper or card. These will begin to form shapes and many small experiments may be conducted on one sheet by an individual pupil, or as part of a group project.

The final painting

Suddenly what began with coloured linear exercises takes on the form of an arrangement of coloured shapes, a collage or painting, call it what you may. The fact that this point is reached through a direct process using colour experiments and discovery makes it of relevance to the child. He is now able to tackle unaided, and with confidence, the highly intellectual process of grouping coloured masses to form visual statements.

Below. These linear experiments can then lead on to painted arrangements of shapes

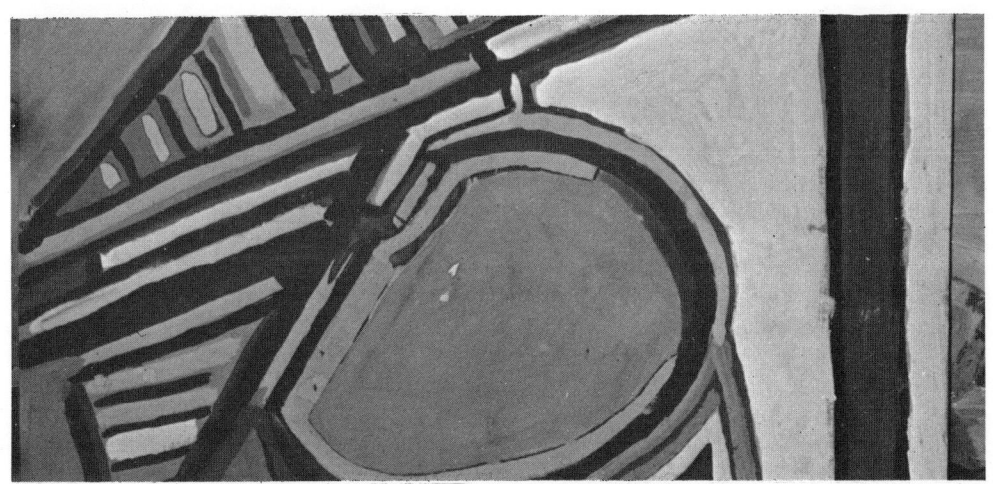

Scribble a line

This year my class has consisted of very young children, most of them coming in September as four-and-a-half year olds. It has been a particularly exciting opportunity for many of them were at the 'scribbling' stage when they arrived, and those who were drawing people were recording large heads and tiny arms only. Having the children from so early a time has enabled me to watch the sometimes slow or rapid development of line and control in many aspects of their work. Tracing simple patterns and pictures has been popular with many of the class and although it has only played a minor part in the school day nevertheless it has indicated a child's willingness to persevere with the problem. Control has developed considerably and on the rare occasions when these tracing cards are still used the children can clip their own paper clips on.

Lines in finger-paint

There is a never diminishing queue of children eager to use the finger-paint. It comes in various bright colours and we apply it directly to a plastic laminated table which is easily cleaned. We often take prints of patterns and pictures made in this way. It makes a lovely smooth surface which can be constantly drawn on and smoothed out. Initially, the texture of the material was explored by the children perhaps using the whole hand to push, squeeze and glide the paint about the table. The children explored the patterns produced by just using an index finger, or perhaps using both hands rhythmically to produce almost symmetrical designs. The "lines" produced in this manner have often been beautiful and were certainly executed with maximum enjoyment. Perhaps this method has done more than many other approaches to draw children's attention to linear rhythms.

Links

"Line" is not only confined to the classroom and aspects of art work, for it is constantly being extended in our movement sessions. The children are gradually gaining much more control over the lines and patterns they make; complicated rhythms like skipping they find difficult, but they can all manage and enjoy floorwork such as slithering and sliding under, through and round the hall and apparatus. A recent hot spell of weather made the children very restless (a supply of nursery beds and a nice verandah would have been very welcome at this time)

"Line" patterns in finger paint

28

so we had a "happening"—it was really a version of follow my leader. We all pretended to be crawling through a deep, tangled, dangerous jungle. We had to keep to an exact linear path for who knows what dangers lurk in the tall jungle grass? We must have looked an amusing sight crawling past the headteacher's office—one long woman followed by thirty-eight cautious small children all on hands and knees.

I suppose most of us have used music as an inspiration for children's drawing and painting. What can be fun is to slightly vary the theme of "draw what it makes you think of" and using a taped collection of calm, smooth, frenzied and staccato rhythms, let the children—on a suitably long or high paper—interpret this in lines varying from the dainty and minute to the vigorous and huge.

Lines around us

Certainly I do not use our immediate environment nearly enough. Just a look through the classroom window shows the infinite variety of "line" material around us. Look at the venetians, strips of wood, window frames so readily available. What about all the possibilities of using string, wool, long strips of paper in art and number work? Now we have many mass-produced aids to help with the exploration of line: plastic straws with connectors enable the children to explore three dimensional linear structures—perhaps enabling them to produce attractive mobiles for the classroom. Drinking straws and straight pins are just as suitable for older children and less expensive, for I find my "bought" straws ever diminishing as several of my children are still at the stage when most things have to be explored by mouth. Cube shapes I find not only invaluable as a straight-forward mathematical aid but also as a linear space experiment and estimation aid. We are fortunate in having a large quantity available. The children can explore long lengths of corridor, the heights of rooms and furniture, and construct divisions for fields, zoos, houses and schools, and this helps them to become familiar with estimation and the need also for accuracy in constructing lines of a more controlled shape.

One day when my energy and courage are running high I would love to cover the hall, or an equally large area, with a huge piece of paper and let the class use this enormous expanse to explore such a space with marks of all kinds—perhaps next week . . .

"Just a look through the classroom window shows the infinite variety of 'line' material around us"

Children tracing simple patterns

Teaching modern art

Modern art is the skill of representing images in symbols. Conventional art may also be defined in the same terms but conventional art tries to represent the images more or less as they appear to the artist. Modern art may bend straight lines, put parts in juxtaposition or impose the artist's private feelings into the work.

In this sense, much of children's art in infant and junior school is modern art. Work is done without regard for the "rules" of art and observation. For instance, if a child is asked to draw a bungalow, the windows are often misplaced, the door does not reach the ground and, of course, it has an intrusive upstairs. The child has imposed his own thoughts and feelings about the bungalow and has drawn it based on a real dwelling but with alterations to suit his own interpretation. It is modern art.

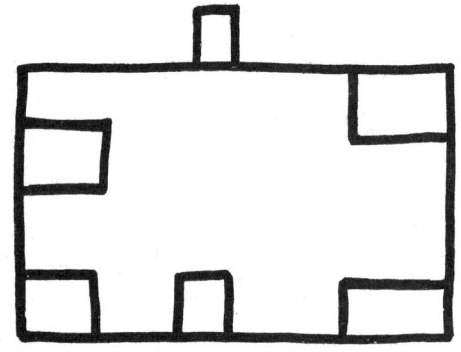

Indeed if one asked the child, he may say it has no upstairs but the top windows are the back windows and one is looking *through* the building in perspective.

To teach children to understand modern art and to make pictures with an insight into what they are doing, two important principles are necessary (1) breaking down (2) building up.

Breaking Down

As children are already familiar with the house shape this is a suitable place to begin. First they can cut out the basic rectangle from coloured sticky paper and stick it in various ways on to a larger sheet of paper or they can draw the rectangle using a template. The rectangle should not overlap at this stage: the object is to familiarise the child with the basic pattern. The rectangles can be big or small, vertical, horizontal or diagonal and in different colours. The child must be thoroughly acquainted with this stage and it should not be hurried on any account.

The next stage is to use window, door and chimney rectangles without the house shape. Again these should not overlap. Different colours can be used for each rectangle and the children can make either planned patterns or haphazard ones.

Now the window rectangles can be used followed by the door rectangles and the chimney rectangles until every part of the house has been dissected and used *separately*. Again these shapes should not overlap. They can be used in planned or unplanned patterns to give a pleasing product.

Window, door and chimney rectangles are separated. Different colours can be used for each rectangle and the children can make either planned patterns or haphazard ones

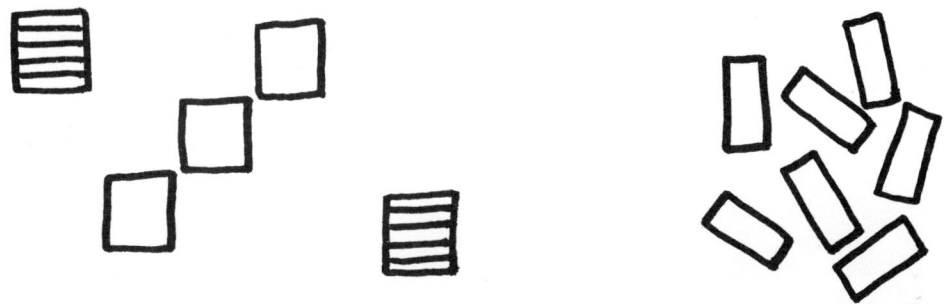

The shapes should not overlap. They can be used to form any variety of patterns. The process of breaking down is now complete

Finally all the shapes, including the basic house rectangle, can be brought together. The children must be encouraged to build up their pictures without putting the house back into its original shape

Building Up

The next stage is to use only the house rectangle using different colours again but this time to overlap it.

This gives depth as well as shape and colour and there is such a number of variations that the child should be encouraged to practise and experiment until he has made as many pictures as possible.

The window, door and chimney rectangles can now be used separately in the same way until the child is familiar with their possibilities also.

After this the window, door and chimney rectangles can be all used in one picture, using a different colour for each shape, overlapping and rearranging the shapes.

Finally all the shapes, including the basic house rectangle, can be brought together. The children should be encouraged to build up their pictures without putting the house back into its original shape. By this time they should understand how to break down and build up from component parts.

Once children are familiar with the techniques of breaking down and building up further work can be done with the house shapes. Pages about houses cut out from colour magazines can be embellished with house shapes in appropriate places. The back of the house can be drawn over the front of the house. The sides and back can fold out so that all four areas can be seen at once. A wall can be removed to show the inside.

After this the possibilities are limitless. Modern art is an important part of our culture. Adults may be baffled by it but children should be taught to understand it and the best way to understand it is to do it.

An example of modern art. Landscape study by Nicholas de Stael (The Tate Gallery, London)

From experiment to discovery through black and white

"When you set out, the truth you are looking for lies hidden at the bottom of things". Paul Klee

It was Moholy-Nagy who said artists must search for their roots. Paul Klee was able to recapitulate the history of graphics by taking the line back to its oldest ancestor the dot. Invariably the most successful experiments emerge from very simple beginnings—and concerning colour, black and white appear immediately to be very simple.

However stark black and white first appear to be, especially to pupils at the secondary school age—their admixtures, nuances, subtleties, confusions, vibrations and mélanges give adequate evidence for a field of research thick with exciting discoveries. Whatever you can make black and white do, the other colours can do just as, if not more, power-

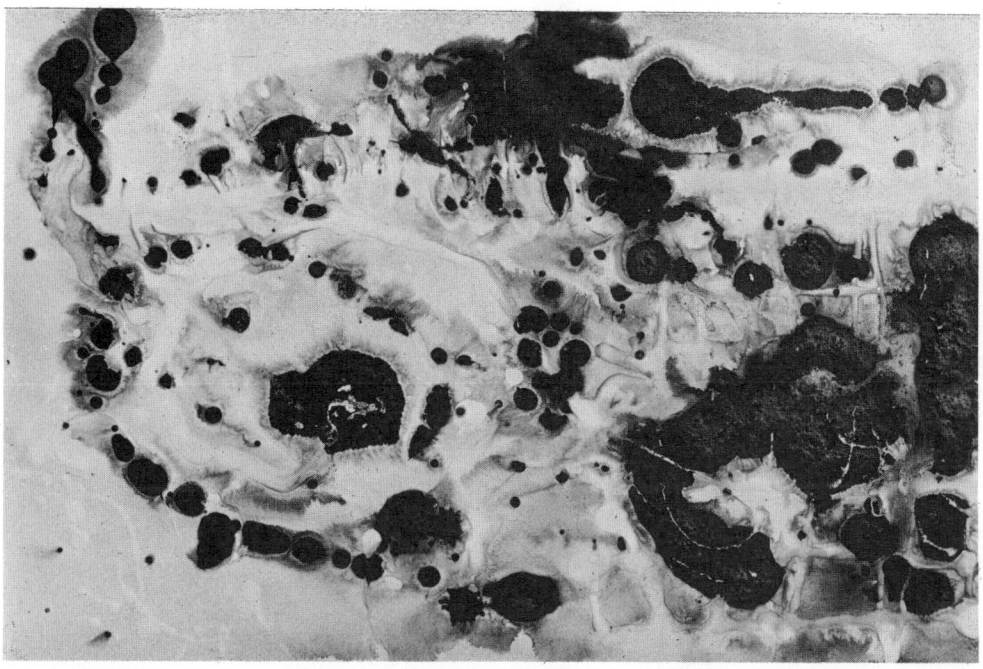

An "abstract" in black and white involving the powers of the two through interesting texture and spatial conflict

fully. A knowledge of the possibilities given by black and white alone provides a springboard to grappling with the primaries and secondaries.

Pupils already have accumulated a wealth of knowledge about black and white, through television, the older films at the cinema, black and white photographs. A quick discussion on black and white can result in a flowering of knowledge—black crows, black funerals, black cats, black midnight; and white baby clothes, white snow, white weddings, etc., the group can provide up to 50 examples of objects, occasions, or odds and ends that lend themselves either to one or the other. A more subtle continuation is the mixture of black and white into grey—with grey overalls, grey skies, grey ocean, grey linen, etc. One group led me to believe 100% that the black draughts always win over the white. Grey emerges as dull and monotonous. I wonder why school uniforms have a habit of being grey!

Having debated the difference in appearance of the two, the group should be invited to dabble with the colours in the raw and sample the textures, visual effects—the "feel" of them both.

1 A valuable introductory exercise at this stage is to divide up a sheet of white cartridge paper into six equal rectangles. The white column on the left and the black on the right. The first two at the top should be painted as watery as possible, extremely diluted, vague, insecure, blurry, oozing so that they even merge and swim together in a grey maze in the middle. The second two should be painted normally, just as you would paint a picture which had nothing to say apart from "this is black" and "this is white". The result should be clear, crisp, smart, lucid, definite, neat. The two colours will now appear at their greatest contrast, the black is at its blackest next to white, and *vice-versa*. Thirdly, apply the two as thick as

possible. This is best done with large amounts of powder-paint (or Acrylic) and just enough water to make the paint lumpy. The rectangles should protrude with exciting lumps, bumps, discords of texture, ugly, brutal, powerful, heavy. They emerge from the paper and tend to "fight" each other. This exercise will introduce the pupils to the three immediate possibilities of black and white, the diluted will retire and become timid; the normal will stay secure and clean; the thick impasto will become twisted and expressive. These are three "personalities" or "characters", each a valid relative of black and white.

2 This exercise can be made more sophisticated by introducing the element of scale, from three major differences to eight minor changes from the vaguely watery to the strident and lumpy.

3 At this stage it will become necessary to introduce grey—which itself will tend to take on the "characters" of the texture-differences of black and white. Experiments can be made with unusual equations, diluted white with a grotesquely thick black—or a medium black with a fairly thick white. The scale can be enlarged from 16 to 24 texture possibilities.

4 The experiments will now show three major important colour facts. (a) the differences between black and grey, grey and white, black and white (HUE); (b) the differences in quality of brightness—white pure and bright, black pure and dark, grey intermediary and mid-way (TONE); (c) the differences in saturation, of the amount of colour content over water or other media content—profound or limp, etc.—(CHROMA).

5 The next step will probably suggest itself depending on the success of the experiments and the willingness of the pupils to progress to greater discoveries. If the best results are shown, an immediate reaction will take into account expansion and contraction—the fact that the white rectangles appear to be bigger than the grey and black. There also emerges simultaneously a feeling of differences in weight, where black is heavy, cumbersome, bulky and dark it falls to the bottom and where white is bright, airy, and light, it tends to rise to the top. Grey is trapped between them. Try painting different levels in three horizontal bands; white-grey-black, grey-black-white, black-grey-white, white-black-grey, etc. and ask for comments on which appears to be "right". Invariably the white should be at the top, the grey sandwiched in the middle, and the black at the bottom.

At this stage the character of the three should be discussed—white tends to exaggerate and embrace. Black on the other hand is inward-looking, while grey is somehow trapped in between—wanting to be released.

6 From character to temperature. White might suggest itself as cold as snow, or as hot as white coals in a furnace. Black might become as heavy and warm as an African tribal dance, or as cold and bitter as jet. Eventually the lighter the colour, the warmer the temperature will be seen to be, and the darker the cooler.

7 The next step should invite problems on purity and comparative impurity—how much grey added to white numbs it? Prevents it from retaining the excitement of pure white? How much black added to grey makes it sinister and retiring? When does an impure white become effective? When it is mysterious, suggestive, devious, moody, calculating?

8 Finally within this context, paintings can be made in which black and white can be naturally hostile or be made to undulate together in harmony. They can be used in expressive, impressionist, surrealist and optical suggestion—they can be used as different intensities of shadow—they can emerge through the use of pencil (H hard, B black, F fine, etc.). The sources of white lead and lamp-black can be investigated, and their respective uses in prehistoric art.

Thinking about paint

Tim started school a year ago. He was four-and-a-half when he came, sturdy and vigorous, and there was certainly no doubting his presence. Noisy, popular, great fun but usually very exuberant and boisterous, he tried to demand an unfair share of my attention. With thirty-eight other very young children you can imagine my problems.

It was on his third day in school when he first painted. The noise level of the room dropped several decibels and I had discovered the activity which absorbed Tim deeply. He was not just occupied, he was concentrating with fervour on producing a very detailed linear painting of a large block of flats. Most of the other children were just experimenting with colour or perhaps producing a completely red picture of Mummy, but Tim was applying his paint in a masterly way—changing the angle of his brush to make thinner and thicker lines. The expression on his face and the way he stood altered his whole decorum.

So I had an ally in paint and it seemed likely that through this good quality enjoyment I could begin to build that bridge of mutual trust and understanding so necessary to the child/teacher rapport. If he was capable of this level of concentration I knew that the task, although not easy, was going to be interesting.

I think it is tempting when a demanding child finds such a great interest to over-exploit this area. Naturally it is quality of concentration I want to develop in these children and I realised that if I were to rely too heavily on

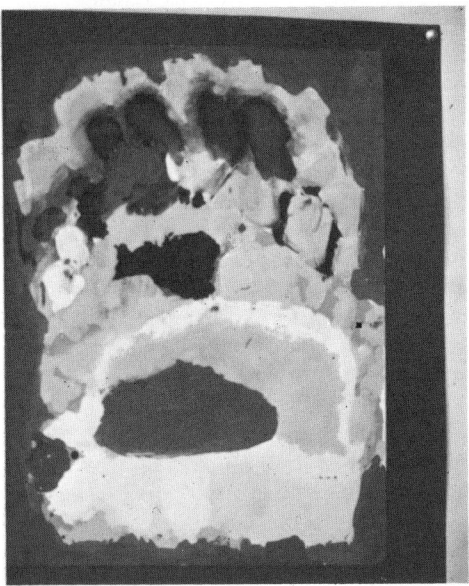

An early pattern by Tim

paint I would gradually weather away the foundations I wanted to build on. So as the weeks passed by I tried to preserve this quality of attitude in him towards painting. In those early days, though, paint was the main channel of communication. He began to explore the possibilities of paint. One did not need to suggest that he test what would happen if he used the wooden handle of the brush to add texture to thick areas of paint, he did it. Paint was dribbled, pushed, picked at, used sparingly and extravagantly. Of course, we had "off" days when the outside of the porcelain sink and the taps were painted, when he painted his hands and lower arms completely and for some unknown reason the pigment in this green paint was particularly strong. He went home looking like a Jumblie and what's more, despite some good scrubs, stayed like it for several days.

Since these early days much has been gained. Tim is usually keen to be helpful with anything in the painting line and will decorate "bits and pieces" boxes, produce delicate patterns by using thinnish spots of paint and blowing them through a straw and enormously aggressive patterns from powder paint mixed with detergent liquid—the latter gives the paint a very satisfying, thick and almost luminous texture.

The class watched a programme on television which showed an artist decorating huge panels for the sides of multi-storey car parks and other large buildings. This fascinated the children—particularly Tim and a group. They came back and found a large, prepared hardboard sheet and made a very satisfactory decorative panel by blobbing paint then tipping the board first longways and then sideways. It was the first bit of child-controlled co-operation which really worked. Tim is five-and-a-half now, a competent, confident boy. Still lively but much less disruptive to other people and their work. He has just been an enormous help when we have been producing finger paintings printed on to various sugar papers for book covers. His drawings and paintings are detailed and usually full of a great deal of thought. The other day he was painting a tractor and a farmer. I returned to have another look and saw a huge red splodge on the painting. I thought he had regressed for a moment: "That", he said, "is the spray from the crop sprayer. The farmer is just going home to bed. He is exhausted because he's been mending his combine harvester. He's in bed snoring now".

I think many children find painting thera-peutic and soothing but for a great number of children it can be so much more than this. It is something all children can do, those reluctant to get "dirty" are shown how well the overalls cover up everything and have it explained carefully that the paint will wash from hands easily. It is something to do by oneself—in producing a painting all kinds of levels of experience can be passed through. Those people who push adult standards and imagery on to children's work sadden me, for all too soon infant confidence disappears with the desire for accuracy.

Tim is beginning to show a keenness to read these days, particularly as I captioned an exciting series of his action man paintings. His interest in paint has formed a base for fostering helpful links with many subjects. The local carnival, which he remembered in detail, provided another opportunity for extending his interest in the visual. He has recently painted an autumn picture to illustrate one of our poems. An old subject, but one never to be discarded for all children seem to love scrunching through leaves. Of course, we still have a long way to go and I am pleased to have the opportunity of watching Tim's development in the next two years.

A dribble pattern by Tim

Working with paint

There was a time when art with young children was regarded as an activity which was unlike any other in the school curriculum. It was on the time table to be sure but one did not have to teach it. "Experts" who had watched children paint and model had proclaimed that it was wise to provide a range of materials, make the children aware of the colours and textures that were around them, create a workshop atmosphere then stand back and enjoy the results.

While this philosophy seemed to work for those who were fortunate enough to have a flair for art orientated activities, many teachers discovered, somewhat ruefully, that however creative the environment, however rich the room in paint, paper and brushes, a significantly large proportion of children seemed to expect the teacher to provide something in addition to this. For want of a better term I propose to call this something "direction".

Now had these views been expressed in a professional paper in the mid sixties there would have been a public outcry. Significantly, however, there has in recent years been a steady shift away from discovery for its own sake to discovery with a purpose—not only in Art but also in Maths and in the Physical Sciences. We, the mature adults, because of our own experience and knowledge appreciate that all things being equal, certain results can be expected when we cause certain given fundamentals to interact. Thus just as we can expect a ball thrown upwards to fall to earth, so we can

Paint can be applied with a brush, knife, rag, sponge or roller

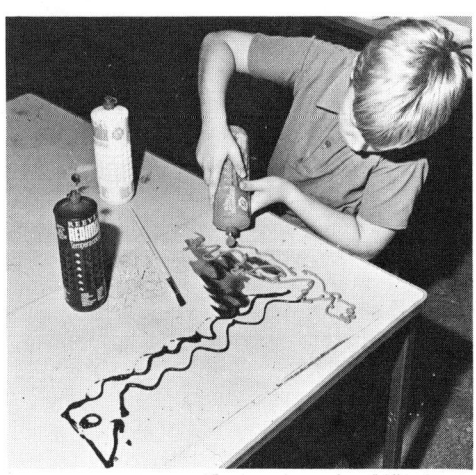

A design made by using the paint directly from the dispenser

expect paint squeezed on to paper from a plastic bottle to have quite a different texture, and effect upon the eye, to dry powder colour spattered on to wet paper.

Having said that direction is needed when children are learning the qualities and peculiarities of particular materials, I should add that the direction often comes from the sorts of materials the teacher provides rather than from the spoken word.

Let's examine for a moment what this implies . . . and where better to begin than with the material we all have to have before we begin to make a picture—the working surface, which for those of us who teach in Primary Schools will probably be paper. Is it enough to give children virgin sheets of sugar paper on which to work, sheets which week after week are of the same size, texture, quality and colour? Would not our role

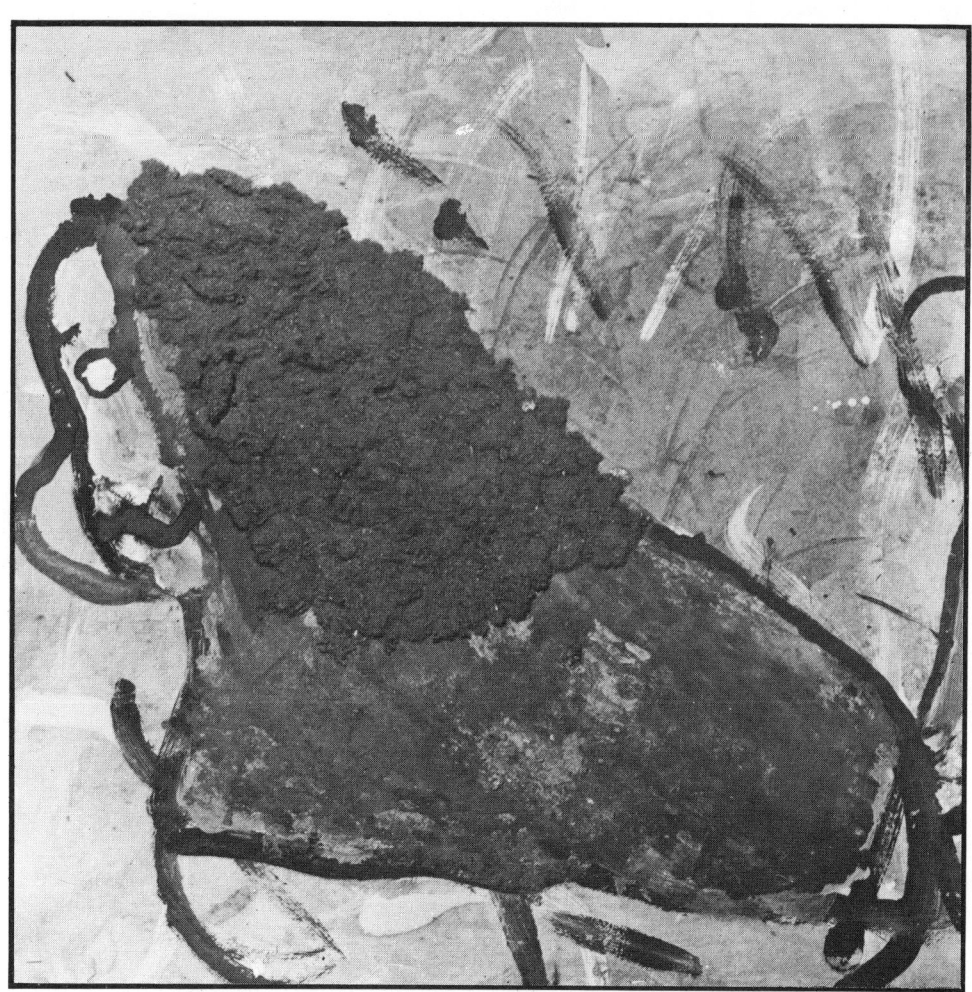

Collage 'The Lion'. Temperapolymer and carpet scraps

be far more positive if we allowed the children to choose the colour of the paper before each began to paint? The least sensitive child quickly appreciates that 'night' pictures are not easy to paint on white paper, or fire pictures on old gold. This gives the group dramatic insight into colour values and of the effect of one colour upon another. It should also lead to discussion . . . why do snow pictures worked on pale blue paper have a rather special quality? Is snow blue, white or grey? If the picture is dependent upon the use of 'hot' colours is it more effective to use papers which are 'hot' or 'cold' or neutral?

The shape of the paper will also to some extent determine the child's response. The rectangular paper we most often use has no magical quality. Surprising results often come when the children are faced with a thin strip, a square or a circle . . . for the edge of the paper imposes a certain discipline upon the lines drawn within it.

While considering this aspect of art work it is also as well to remember that as many children fail because they are asked to restrict their paintings to imperial size as who fail because imperial is far too large a sheet for them to manage! The eight year olds who painted 'The Building Site' were successful because they were given a piece of paper "which filled their table just as the cranes filled the sky" (as one of them put it). Then I could ask why we invariably suggest that children should work on dry paper? What would happen if they dampened the paper with a wet sponge before they began to paint? Does this help them obtain more interesting cloud effects, for example? What if the paper is dripping wet? Does working on dry, damp or wet paper have certain advantages for certain things?

It is possible to extend this enquiry to the papers the children are using, relating the experiences to the types of paint that are available. Thus for some water-based paints

Dry paint on wet paper produces strange results

newsprint is ideal; for others a far more substantial base is essential.

Another way in which we can influence the direction of children's art experiences is by putting the brush in its rightful place—*as but one method of applying colour.* Could we attempt to make some pictures without using a brush at all? How could we apply the colour? The possibilities are endless—small twigs, the fingers, match sticks, drinking straws, swabs of cotton wool, rags, rollers, knives, sponges, scraps of card and paper, small stones and pebbles. Each 'instrument' will give a line or pattern of its own—some sharp and hard, others soft and gently textured. For some children this form of picture making might appear very much akin to printing, but if the overall effect is pleasing (in that it enables the child to say those things that he wishes to say) the technique employed is of minor importance.

Then there is the brush itself. How many of us tend to order a brush because it is reasonably multipurpose—like a hog head No. 8. This particular brush is a bit too small for really large scale work and a little too big for small scale work—but it's an excellent compromise between the two extremes. Is this a good enough reason for restricting children to one sort of brush? I think it far better to have a range of brushes available so that each child is able to make a choice. We would not expect a lumber-jack to cut down a giant tree with a fret-saw. Should we expect a nine year old to paint a hardboard panel with a squirrel hair brush?

Let us assume, however, that there is a supply of paper in a range of colours and sizes and a variety of brushes. What water-based paints could we make available? The art material most common to our Primary Schools is powder colour. Although water is the usual wetting agent, experiment will reveal that many other liquids could also be used. Indeed by varying the wetting agent it is possible to alter the "dry" finish of the paint. Thus if we stir detergent into dry powder colour a thick smooth mixture is produced which is excellent for finger painting. Powder colour may also be mixed with gum. This mixture gives additional strength to all forms of papier mâché work, such as puppet heads, and dries with a semi-gloss finish. Other wetting agents which could be experimented with include paper varnish, egg white and linseed oil.

The egg-shell must be carefully handled throughout this process as it is used for a measure. If working with young children the teacher should make the mixture, although nine year olds and over should manage without undue difficulty.

Break a small hole in the top of the egg-shell and empty the whole egg, including yolk, in a water jar. Using the empty shell as a measure add the following:—

1 egg-shell full of linseed oil
3 egg-shells full of water.
Stir into a thick cream.

This medium is used as the wetting agent for dry powder colour (mix on a palette or in bun trays). Pictures may be painted on oil sketching paper or sized cardboard, using hog hair brushes or a palette knife. The paintings dry quickly and have a gentle gloss.

Brushes should be washed out in warm soapy water after use.

Whatever is used it is important to remind the children that to achieve an even mix the wetting agent is always added to the dry colour, *never the reverse*. In my experience children are more likely to be successful in handling paint if the colours are thickly mixed, to the consistency of single cream. Although I have found that it is more economic to premix colours, some dry colour should also be available so that the children can prepare their own range of tones should they so wish. Indeed, if the group are being encouraged to experiment by working on wet surfaces, dry colour becomes an absolute essential.

However well we train children to use powder colour it does have the disadvantage of being difficult to store because of its bulk and a little messy in use. If classroom conditions are cramped and storage space is at a premium, Temperablocks provide an ideal substitute. There is an excellent range of colours and the trays are stackable when not in use. The only drawback to these paints is that it is more difficult to get a thick wash of colour than with any other of the paints mentioned. However, once the blocks are really dampened, the amount of colour which a wet brush will pick up is quite surprising. Temperablocks also come into their own when small numbers of children are painting while the rest of the class follow some other activity, e.g. for colouring small pictures in individual study books, preparing charts to illustrate mathematical topics.

Sometimes it is necessary to produce thin, even washes of colour to tint the background of a picture worked in some other media.

A group of six year olds had been to some woods near the school.

It was Autumn. Using crayon they drew themselves, the trees and the interesting things they had seen. They cut out the drawings and mounted them on a large sheet of sugar paper. The background, however, looked flat and, after pasting, somewhat messy . . . so a wash of thin colour was applied over the whole picture with a decorator's brush. This wash was resisted by the crayon cut outs, giving a most attractive finish to the whole design.

There is yet another water-based paint. Here we have a thick liquid colour in a plastic dispenser which is economic in use since very small quantities can be distributed in water jars or paint trays. There is little need to list its possible applications for it may be applied with roller or brush on almost any surface from thin paper to wood or card. Interesting 'off beat' effects are obtainable however, by squeezing colour from the pack —a 'cake icing' technique which appeals to boys and girls alike. Of course the colours are intermixable and may be thinned with water. If a really heavy covering of paint is required, Temperapaste comes into its own. Temperapaste is rather like thick poster colour to handle. It is excellent for printing (with such things as leaves or vegetables), painting with knife, roller or brush and for colouring models made from card, wood, junk or papier mâché.

Temperapolymer is also water soluble. However, it has a number of unique characteristics which merit detailed consideration. A wide range of effects is possible. By using the paint direct from the tube heavy impasto layers can be built up. If clear, almost transparent washes are required, the colour is simply thinned with clear water. Temperapolymer, however, is more than just

Group picture 'The woods in Autumn'. Colour wash over crayon cut outs (6 year olds)

another paint. It is also an excellent adhesive which can be used on almost any grease-free surface (e.g. plastic, wood, card, paper, fabric) and with almost any material (metal scraps, foil, fibre, stone, shells, string, ceramic scraps, glass). This means that collage work is brought within the range of quite young children. After painting the background, the materials to be used in the composition are simply pushed into the colour whilst it is still wet. The process may be extended further for Temperapolymer also has excellent covering qualities. Thus, once the child has constructed a picture using the paint as an adhesive, detail can be added to the collage using Temperapolymer as a paint applied with a fine brush.

This type of activity does indicate how versatile Temperapolymer is, for almost any paper becomes a suitable working surface. Old newspapers are transformed into richly textured painting surfaces by applying Temperapolymer with a roller. When dry the print will have disappeared and the paper will resemble tough parchment. Fabric lengths, cardboard, acrylic, wood, plaster, board and hardboard can be treated in a similar way, the very unevenness of the colour application adding much to the children's work.

When working with Temperapolymer one rule must be observed, the brushes must be kept in water when not in use. When the painting session is over, wash the brush heads thoroughly in water to remove all traces of the colour (failure to do this will result in brush heads clogged with virtually immovable paint).

These ideas are meant to serve as starting points. *Unless we introduce new colours, a range of brushes and a variety of papers the children are never going to be able to discover for themselves how different paints behave on different surfaces.*

Once the children have begun to use paint and paper with discrimination these simple techniques will develop almost intuitively.

1. To make a smudge print apply the colour on a folded sheet of sugar paper

2. Smooth the fold

3. Open carefully to reveal the print

43

Using dry colours

Crayons

A touch of the Orient

The spiral in art

Decoration

'All scattered in the bottom
of the sea'

Using dry colours

As a child develops co-ordination and starts to walk and talk he will also start to draw, and it is important at this early stage that he should be given the right type of drawing materials so that he can play freely. We cannot expect this freedom of expression if we give him adult tools to handle like ball-point pens and pencils. In this context, big wax crayons, chalks and finger paints are ideal as they allow a free flow of ideas, without the need to master complicated techniques. As shown in Fig. 1 children will draw quickly and spontaneously and therefore need materials which produce an instant mark.

Naturally as the child grows older the images he draws change and his need for drawing is somewhat different. It is at this stage that a variety of art materials and activities can be introduced to give him new experiences and new ways of working. This will help him to develop his drawings from one stage to the next. As we can observe in a child's drawing, if a theme continually recurs, it is usually because this aspect of the subject has not changed in the child's experience, or he has been unable to resolve it.

Before dealing with the specific techniques and problems associated with drawing it is important to remember that drawings can be made for many different reasons, It is not only the artist that needs to make drawings and one can see in the classroom situation drawings being made as part of mathematical projects (Fig. 2), studies for history and geography and for environmental notebooks.

In many cases these drawings are far more successful than the drawings associated with art. This is, one feels, because these 'non-art' drawings have been made for a specific purpose and, therefore, have relevance, both as drawings and as part of the student's general classroom studies.

The activity of drawing must not be done in isolation, but always as part of other projects. In terms of art, drawings should therefore be made as preliminary work for paintings, three dimensional models, embroideries, etc. As these drawings give information they should be linked, wherever possible, with a collection of photographs to create personal files or notebooks (not sketch books). As in Fig. 3 drawings and photographs have been collected on the single theme 'textures'.

The majority of adult artists work from notes and drawings in this way and this point can be emphasised when introducing this process of working to the children. To be able to justify a way of working is of particular importance in the middle school, when children are beginning to question the reasons for learning.

A need for exploration

The materials associated with drawing are in nearly all cases reasonably priced and the mechanics of drawing very simple. Why is it then that these conventional drawing materials such as pencils, ball-point pens, felt pens, charcoal, chalks and pastels are usually used in such a limited way?

Fig. 1. Illustration of a clown in wax crayon and chalk. Young children need drawing materials which they can easily handle

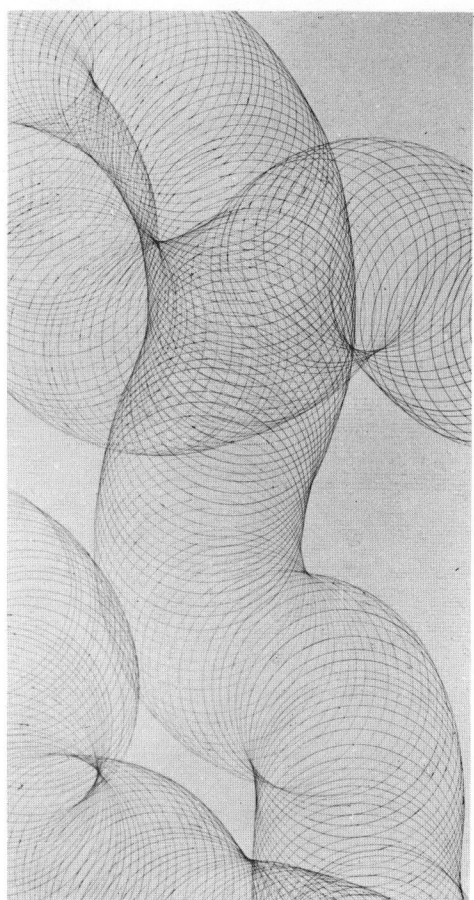

Fig. 2. Mathematical forms completed in a fine point ball-point pen

I feel that there are two main reasons for this:

1. That these materials are so familiar to the artist that there is a lack of any initial exploration when they are being handled.

2. Through a lack of knowledge the wrong material or combination of media is often used for a particular subject. For example, a ball-point pen might be used when the subject demands large areas of flat tone or a 4B pencil when great detail is required.

When teaching children to draw or, more correctly, when teaching them to look, I have found that it is most important to start each project with a period of experimentation, no matter what the media or the age of the pupils. This way of introducing drawing materials does not emphasise 'tricks of the trade', but is simply a way of encouraging children to see how many different types of marks, lines, textures, etc. can be obtained from a particular drawing tool, whether it be a piece of chalk or a stick of charcoal.

If one does not have this period of explora-

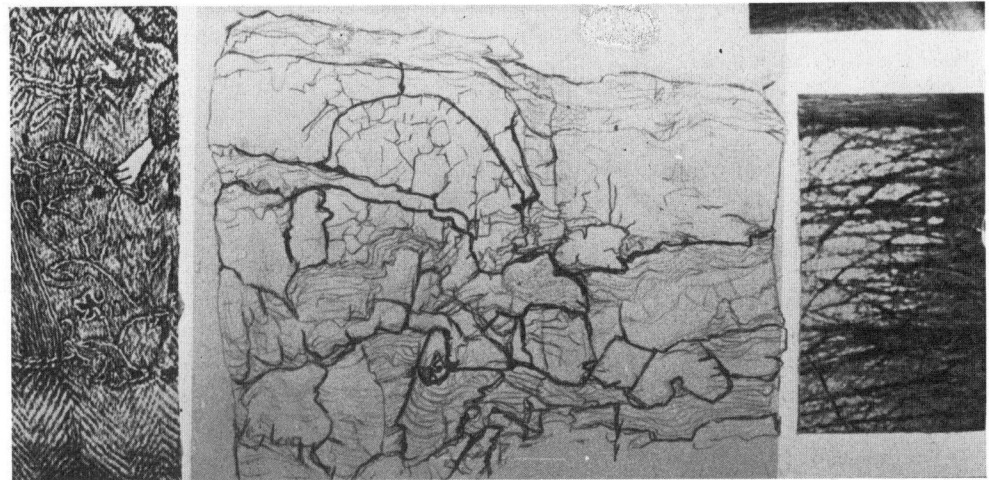

Fig. 3. Sheet of photographs and drawing on the theme of trees and bark. Colour supplements are particularly useful as source material

tion when the student can explore the media freely, before starting his drawing, he will tend to always draw in the same way and usually in the same media. To quote John Constable: 'Artists always draw what they know "how to draw"', and children are the same!

Mixed media

From my own work I can appreciate how difficult it is to produce an interesting drawing if only one drawing instrument is used. Alas, few of us can handle a black pencil like Van Gogh or a pen like Picasso. I, therefore, always encourage children to work in different media and in a combination of media, so that there is no one answer to a particular drawing problem. One hopes that in time the pupils will begin to appreciate the particular qualities of these various drawing media and, therefore, not always strive for photographic realism with one media, which may well be beyond their capabilities.

Listed below are some of the drawing processes which have been evolved out of these early experiments. These techniques

then become the language with which the artist communicates, and the art materials the tools of his trade. What he has to say is, of course, the most important thing and for this reason the illustrations have been chosen to show how the artists have tried to use the right material for their particular drawings, whether it is of an old woman sitting in a chair done in chalk on to coloured paper, Fig. 4, or an art nouveau design completed in oil pastel and ink, Fig. 5.

Pencils

Pencils are possibly the most widely used drawing media in schools and yet the one that causes the most frustration and failure. Examinations have in the past been much to blame for this, but, as emphasised above, the type of pencil chosen can influence to a very large degree the eventual failure or success of the drawing.

Pencils can be bought in a great variety of sizes, colours and degrees of hardness from 6B to 6H. As a general rule the pencils with the B prefix are used for drawing with the 6B being the softest and the H pencils for more

Fig. 6. Study of an old barn. The foreground has been resolved into very strong patterns and could easily be translated into a block print

Fig. 4. Line drawing in white chalk on terracotta pastel paper. This type of study can be developed into a successful painting

Fig. 5. Design in black ink and oil pastel. To emphasise the colour range the pastels have been blended together

49

detailed graphic work and maps and diagrams etc. If only two types are to be bought, 2B and HB pencils will give the widest variety of tone and line definition as well as holding their point, which is very important in schools.

For very strong black drawings a black beauty and a charcoal pencil should be included in this range. These darker pencils are especially useful when working out of doors to make drawings for paintings, Fig. 6.

Conté crayons and black wax crayons

These are also very exciting drawing materials. These dark drawing materials give a very strong line and can be used to very good effect on coloured pastel papers or sugar papers. This way of working gives the artist the added advantage of being able to emphasise shapes by using white chalk in conjunction with the darker areas of tone, Fig. 7.

Coloured pencils

In most cases these pencils are made up of a pigment colour plus kaolin which has been bonded together with a gum and then encased in wood. They are manufactured in some seventy different colours and are usually packaged in very attractive boxes. However, I do feel that they are not the most satisfactory drawing materials, as they tend to give a rather limited colour laydown which cannot be mixed successfully on the paper surface. Their advantage over some of the other colouring materials is that the resulting surface does not rub off and therefore one sees them as a useful material for notebooks and some detailed illustration work.

Exercises using pencils

Exercises using pencil rubbings can be linked successfully with pattern and print making and sheets of different kinds of surface rubbings can be collected. In these particular studies the student was asked to make rubbings of various surfaces using a soft 2B pencil. These surfaces then had to be drawn graphically and finally printed which, of course, destroyed the quality of the surface. By working in this way the pupils were encouraged to look at simple things in a new way and consequently build up a new vocabulary of marks made with a pencil. In turn these drawings could be used as starting points for woven surfaces or as the introduction of micro-enlargements and detailed seeing.

Pencil erasers

Although one would always try and emphasise the method of working that starts with faint marks and then gets stronger as the drawing progresses; this concept of drawing is rather adult and children will, at times, want to rub out their mistakes. This way of working is natural enough, especially if the artist wants to work precisely, and as long as the pupil does not rely on the rubber to destroy every line, I think that they should be available. Speaking personally, I only have a few good quality soft rubbers in use and, therefore, always try and encourage the artist to work into his drawing by overdrawing instead of always rubbing the image off the paper.

When using charcoal a most interesting drawing technique can be introduced where the rubber is used to draw into the charcoal surface to reveal the colour of the paper beneath. Bread can also be used in this way, Fig. 8.

Papers

All types of papers can, of course, be used for drawing, from cartridge to newsprint. However I do feel that it is false economy if children are always asked to draw on very cheap paper. I appreciate the economics involved but I would stress that it is almost impossible to produce a good drawing on very cheap paper; especially if one is encouraging them to work into their drawings in a variety of media. It is simply that the paper will become tired and deteriorate, therefore making the whole activity valueless.

Activities like printing and some types of painting might well be done on to newspaper and colour supplements, thus leaving the better paper for drawing. Local sources such as a newspaper works or printers might also sell end rolls of newsheet and thus help to augment the paper cupboard.

If I had to choose a limited range of paper for a year's work I would naturally try and give the most variety as possible, but without buying the most expensive or the cheapest qualities. For example I would order:

One type middle priced drawing paper, imperial and half imperial.

Sheets of paper in various colours including black.

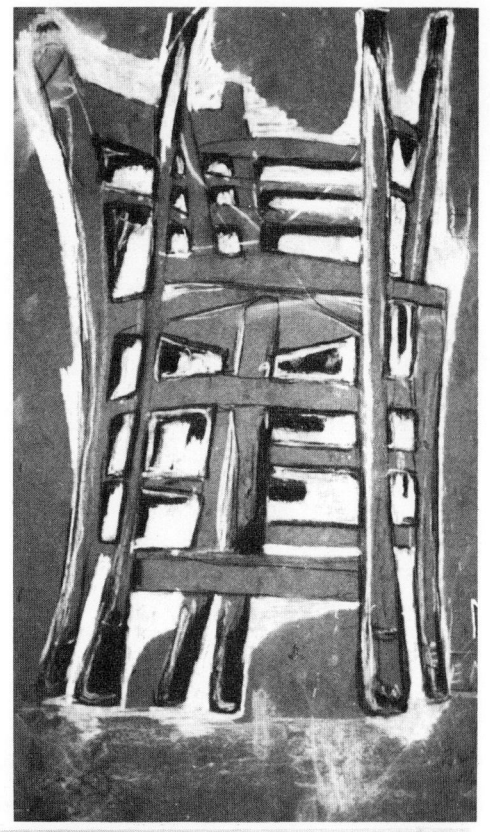

Fig. 7 (right). Realistic study of chairs. By working on a coloured ground the shapes have been emphasised with white chalk

Fig. 8 (below). Study of negative forms using charcoal on grey paper. A soft rubber has been used to draw into the areas of charcoal

Rolls of frieze paper—black, red and blue (for background).
Rolls of cheap lining paper (for mono printing).
Duplicating paper—ideal for making drawings which are then to be placed into loose leaf folders.
Also manila paper and thin card—if money allows.

Ball-point pens

Over the last ten years the use of ball-point pens has grown enormously, both as a substitute for pencils and in general writing in place of fountain pens. As an art material they can be of great use if considered creatively. For example biros can be bought in a variety of thicknesses and if these are used together one can build up a very interesting drawing full of linear perspective. Likewise, I would envisage drawings that incorporate the use of pencil, ball-point pen and felt pen with each material producing a different type of mark, Fig. 9. As a ball-point pen is an ideal material to produce great detail it can also be used in conjunction with paint or wax crayon to give emphasis over areas of colour, Fig. 10.

Felt pens

These are now available in all sizes and, depending on the type of 'nib', all prices.
The cheapest type has a soft felt nib and although initially they give a very instant and bright mark, they do dry up quickly if the cap

Fig. 9 (below). Life drawing in 2B pencil and ball-point pen. This study is particularly concerned with the inter-relationship of shapes, the ball-point pen being used to emphasise and clarify certain areas

Fig. 10 (right). A mixed media drawing. Here ball-point pen has been used to create the detail in the foreground with the other faces incised through layers of wax crayon

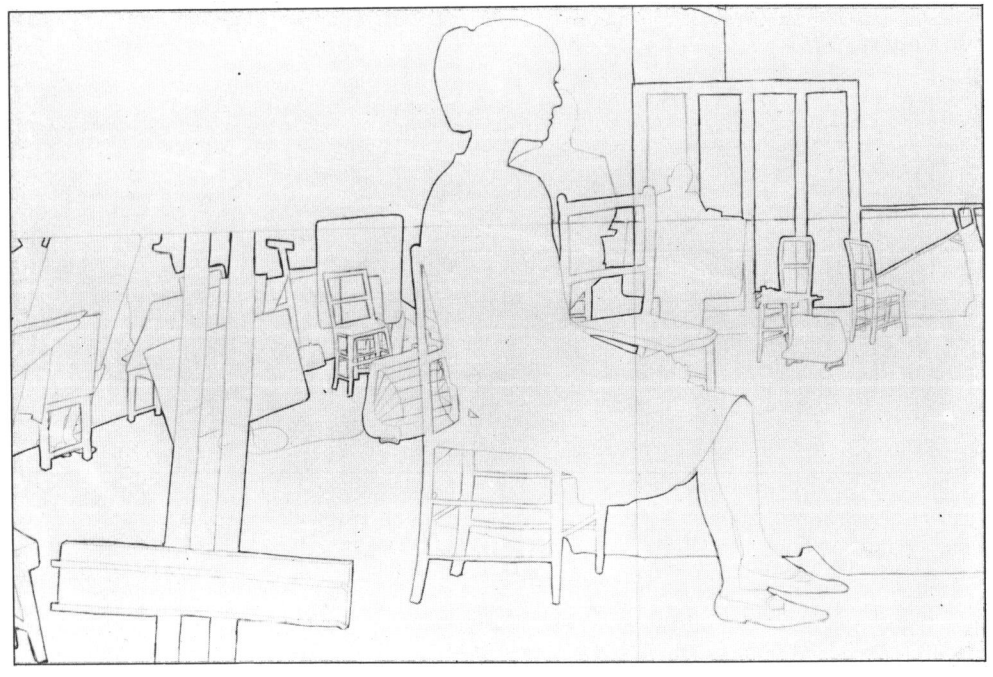

52

53

is left off for even a short period. This disadvantage makes them difficult to handle in the classroom, which is a pity, as the intensity of the mark makes them an ideal drawing material for decorative design work.

The more expensive felt pens have a harder tip which tends to last longer if they are carefully handled. This type of pen, especially in black, is a most useful drawing tool for outside drawings and for figure studies as seen in Fig. 11. Here felt pen was used to make a preliminary sketch before the more detailed pastel drawing was attempted.

Charcoal

As is commonly known, charcoal is made from burnt wood and can be bought in stick form or encased in wood. Older children, especially, enjoy working in charcoal which gives a dark, crumbly line. However, this does create certain problems as the drawn image can be easily smudged.

As mentioned when discussing the exploration of materials in general terms, it is these very characteristics which should be emphasised, so that the student learns to combine areas of rubbed or softened charcoal with areas that are more detailed. In this way he will be able to use the material to its maximum.

Fixing a charcoal drawing

In isolation or in combination with chalk the drawing will have to be fixed. This can be done by spraying, using a manufactured fixative in an aerosol can or by using a mouth spray diffuser and a bottle of fixative. If the latter method is used, care must be taken to ensure that the diffuser is carefully washed after use to keep the holes clear.

Fig. 11. Two studies of the same figure. First, the drawing on the left in felt pen to established the rhythms of the figure. Secondly, the study on the right using chalk pastels with the colour being emphasised

Another method of fixing a charcoal drawing is to dampen both sides of the paper before use, with a solution of gum arabic or good quality watercolour which has a gum base.

Polymer gloss mediums can also be used as a varnish to fix charcoal very successfully as well as the charcoal being drawn directly into a wet gesso ground.

For advanced work with older students a fixative can be made by mixing mastic, or shellac, or copal varnish with a dilute solution of alcohol.

All these methods outlined above tend to change, slightly, the appearance of the charcoal drawing and if the exact image is required white tissue paper can be laid over the drawing to protect it. For the same reason, charcoal drawings which are to be exhibited are usually mounted under non-reflective glass.

Charcoal has many similar drawing qualities as chalk and chalk pastels and this family of materials will be considered below.

Chalks

Chalk is used universally in schools and yet tends to be neglected in the art room especially at secondary level.

In the infant and nursery schools we see children drawing with chalk on to blackboards or drawing directly on to the playground with large sticks of chalk; but as children grow older chalk is often disregarded both by the teacher and the pupil as the line is not so permanent as one created with a crayon or pencil. This assessment of the use of chalk is, one feels, very superficial, as it is a most versatile colouring agent and

Fig. 12. Chalk and paint. In parts the chalk was applied directly on the wet paint. Detail was then drawn into the surface with chalk when the paper had dried

can be used in many different ways if the pupil is prepared to experiment.

Before dealing with the techniques related to chalk it is important to remember that there are two main types of chalk available to schools; dust free chalks for blackboard use and moulded chalks which are cheaper and are used for more general purposes. The dust free variety are extruded under pressure when manufactured and although they are excellent for blackboard use, their hard coating makes them a rather unsympathetic drawing material. For this reason moulded chalks which are much softer are recommended and the Britannia No. 2 range is particularly good as they give a very strong colour laydown.

Chalk rubbings

The very nature of this soft chalk makes it very suitable for rubbings and stencils. Coloured papers are particularly successful when used with coloured chalks and most detailed multiple friezes can be quickly created in this way. Textured papers such as sandpaper and wallpaper can all be added to the templates to give the chalk rubbing an interesting texture.

Chalk stencils

Stencils have become very non-educational in recent years and obviously the manufactured variety give very little to the child. However, if the children make their own stencils they can be used to create very exciting backgrounds for pictures and multiple group friezes.

The technique is very simple. If, for example, a townscape is required, the children would start by cutting out a stencil of rooftops. Both positive and negative pieces should be kept as both might be of use. Working on a coloured sugar paper they would then rub the side of the crayon over the card shape to make the stencil image. This could be repeated in a number of colours, overlapping one another. Using the same technique trees, people, cars etc. could all be added in contrasting colours to create the foreground.

As is obvious when using chalk or chalk pastels the resulting surface is not stable and needs to be fixed. This disadvantage can, however, be easily overcome by combining the chalk with other materials. In all the remaining processes related to chalk the adhesive qualities of the other materials is used to stabilise the bright chalk colours.

Chalk and tempera

When used in combination with powder colour or tempera, chalks produce some very interesting results.

Method. First cover the paper with a thick coating of paint, using light colours or white. Using the chalk as a stylus draw into the paint surface whilst it is still wet. The resulting picture will be very exciting as the chalk colours will have blurred into the paint, which in turn will have acted as a fixative, so that these pastel colours will not rub off. Fig. 12 uses a variation on this technique to complete the picture of the two cottages.

Chalk and starch

Method. Make a liquid, half starch, half water and apply to a manila-type sheet. Whilst it is still damp draw into the surface with the coloured chalks which will be fixed on to the surface by the starch solution. If more detail is required when the paper has dried, simply dip the end of the chalk into a starch solution and draw in the usual way.

Chalk and sugar

Method. As in the technique using starch, the drawing is made with chalk on to a paper which has been dipped, in this case, into a solution of sugar. Likewise the chalk can also be dipped directly into a solution of one part sugar to three parts water.

To reduce the chance of tearing the wet

paper when drawing, it should first be placed on to a bed of dry newspaper.

Chalk and powdered milk
Unlike the other processes which are basically graphic techniques and therefore appropriate only on paper, this method of working is particularly successful when used on cloth as the colours are emphasised and fixed relatively permanently into the fabric by the casein solution.

Method. Wet a piece of cotton or linen in a solution of diluted powdered milk and then create the design directly on to the cloth using coloured chalks. Before the cloth has completely dried set the iron to cotton and press the back of the drawing to fix it.

This method of working is particularly successful when used as a beginning for a collage embroidery as the design is established very quickly as a background for the design.

Chalk and polymer medium
As the pupils experiment, new ways of working will evolve and new media explored. As mentioned in the paragraph on charcoal, acrylic polymer mediums are of particular interest when used in conjunction with chalks. Many interesting methods of painting can be developed either by drawing with chalk directly into the polymer medium whilst it is still wet or by mixing ground coloured chalk into the acrylic before applying it on to the prepared ground. This last technique gives a very impasto effect when applied with a palette knife, whereas the chalk when drawn into a mixture of Liquitex modelling paste and polymer gloss medium is far more translucent.

Drawing pastels
In the drawing techniques discussed above drawing chalks or chalk pastels are recommended. However, there is still one type of chalk which has not been discussed, namely the true artists' pastel.

Pastels are in nearly all respects similar to coloured chalks, except that they are made in smaller sticks and come in a greater variety of colours.

Traditionally, drawing pastels were made from finely ground colour plus gum arabic and are associated in history with such artists as Degas and Chardin. In terms of the art room they do have a place, as even the basic colour range will give a good range of tonal effects and are ideal for life drawing and objective studies.

Method. The paper for this type of work should have a good tooth and be of a colour in sympathy with the subject. A limited range of eight to twelve coloured pastels should be sufficient for most types of work. In the initial work the pupils should be encouraged to mix the colour directly on to the paper using dark colours over light. As the work progresses light areas can be re-introduced for emphasis and to improve the shape of the figure or object. In this way the pupils will not be afraid of making mistakes and will be able to reconsider and improve the drawing as it develops. As shown in Fig. 13, light pastel can be effectively used to clarify the negative shapes in a complicated study.

Oil pastels
As the pupils' drawing techniques develop, oil pastels can be introduced as their particular characteristics are a natural link between drawing and painting.

As the name suggests oil pastels are oil based and consequently have many properties which distinguish them from wax crayons, on the one hand, and chalk pastels on the other.

I always feel that the most important characteristic of an oil pastel is its immediacy as it gives a very intense coloured mark. This

![Study using chalk pastels, white chalk and charcoal on a coloured paper]

Fig. 13 (above). Study using chalk pastels, white chalk and charcoal on a coloured paper

Fig. 14 (right). Oil pastels used for theatrical designs. The strong, almost fluorescent colours are ideal for this kind of work

makes them particularly useful for dramatic image making, as illustrated in the design for a theatrical mask, Fig. 14.

Oil pastels are available in some fifty different colours and it is, therefore, not essential to mix them together to produce the particular colours one requires. However as in all colour work a more personal range of colours can be obtained by blending a range of colours together. This is particularly easy with oil pastels as the surface is soft and can be rubbed using the fingers or a rag.

The resulting effect obtained from blending these colours together is very similar to an out-of-focus colour slide and this similarity can be used very successfully with students to show how areas of the foreground can be

Fig. 15. Oil pastel used in a realistic picture. Blending the background area creates an interesting atmospheric effect

brought into focus by the addition of stronger drawing or by a change in technique. The picture of the boats, Fig. 15, uses this method very successfully to obtain the right atmospheric effects.

Many of the techniques associated with wax crayons are equally applicable to oil pastels and the method of overlaying dark colour over light colours and then etching a design is an interesting way of producing areas of detail.

Oil pastels will adhere to most surfaces and all types of paper. The only art materials which are not compatible with oil pastels are the acrylic polymer family because of their chemical reaction with the oil-base.

Oil pastel used with turpentine
The oil content does allow oil pastels to be easily blended with turpentine and the resulting drawings are very similar to some types of oil paintings.

Method. The drawing is first completed in thick areas of colour. The turpentine is then painted over the surface and blends the colours together to create a completely new type of image, as in the picture of the church, Fig. 16. If the turps is applied too thickly it will tend to lift the colour and obviously this must be avoided.

Oil pastels used as a resist
Oil pastels can also be used in conjunction with water colours or tempera paint in a resist technique. This way of working is particularly effective if the artist wishes to unify his drawing or design.

Conclusion
In this article we have looked at some of the techniques associated with simple drawing materials, and although we have limited this

study to dry colour, the other drawing materials such as inks, gouache and wax crayons are, of course, just as important. Likewise, if we define painting as drawing with colour, then the whole range of paints becomes equally important as drawing media. All art materials that make a mark are drawing materials and one should try to avoid the situation in the classroom where one has two distinct activities, one drawing, the other painting.

As stressed in the introduction the activity of drawing must never be attempted in a void, but as an integral part of a wider art

Fig. 16 (right). Oil pastel overpainted with turpentine. This technique gives a very soft quality to the picture

Fig. 17 (below). Experimenting with a light box made of frosted glass. Shapes were hung between the glass and appeared distorted producing unusual shapes and patterns. Working with chalks and acrylics these images were translated into a design which could eventually be used for fabric

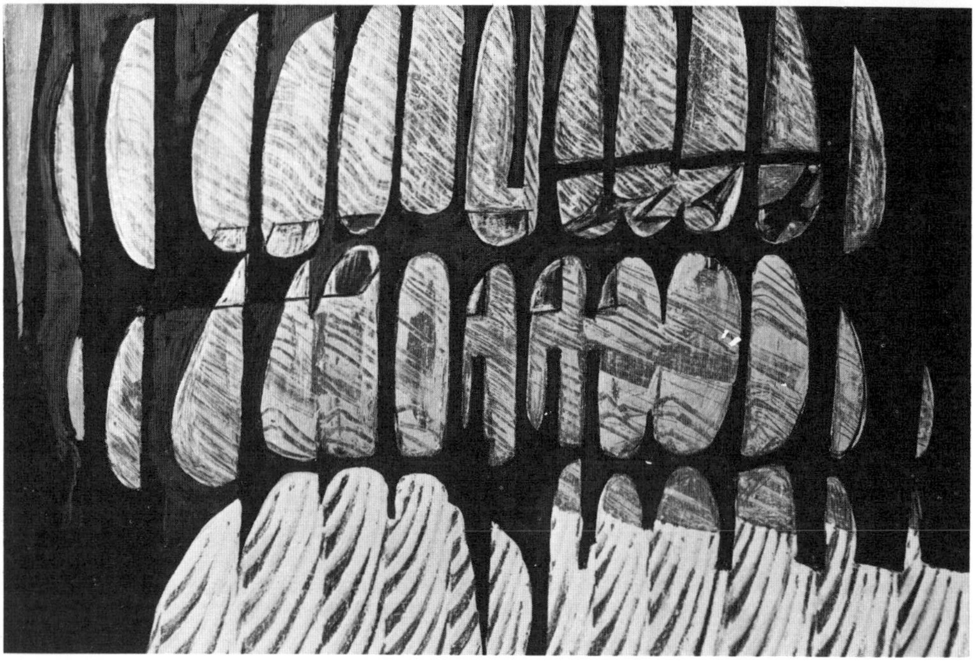

curriculum. It does not matter whether children draw in chalk and starch or oil pastel and turpentine, the important point is that the pupils know why they are working in a particular technique. In my own teaching, I always try and link this type of 'material research' with personally chosen themes. In this way the techniques have a unity of subject matter and the pupil can see a logical reason for trying to discover new ways of interpreting their own chosen theme. Fig. 17 shows a development in chalk and Liquitex on the theme of distortion through frosted glass, whereas the drawing of the organic form, Fig. 18, was completed as part of a project on trees and bark forms. Technical information on chalks—Binney & Smith Ltd., Bedford. Photographs by Arthur Veasey.

Fig. 18 (below). A realistic study of a piece of wood using charcoal and conté crayon

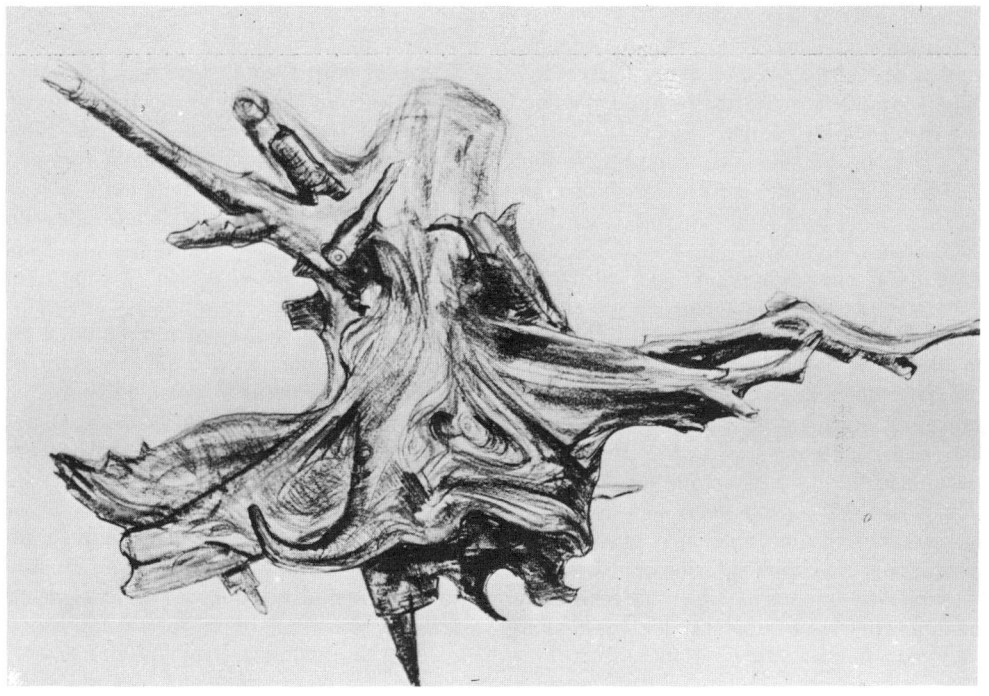

Crayons

The main aim of using any art material in the classroom is that the child learns to use that material to its best advantage.

Although a drawing in crayon alone can look very good if executed well, more lively work usually comes from the combination of using one material with another.

This way of working also encourages the accidental quality of mixing materials to take place. This, in time, helps the young artist to overcome the necessity to always try and produce a photographic image, which is usually the end product when using a pencil or a ballpoint pen.

In this article we look at how a number of different topics have been handled by children of all ages, using mainly wax crayons. The one constant factor is that the artists have used the right technique for their particular subject having been introduced to these techniques or "processes of working" when applicable, thus allowing each child to develop his work and also gain the maximum benefit from the use of the particular materials, or combination of materials.

This point was emphasised recently when I had the opportunity of seeing many thousands of crayon drawings submitted for a national competition. Almost without exception the most interesting work was done by children who had been encouraged to develop their drawings, beyond the "first phase" stage of just drawing in line.

After seeing these pictures and from my own experience of teaching, I have come to the following conclusions, concerning the use of wax crayons.

Drawing with Wax Crayons

When used by the very young, a wax crayon gives an instant mark. Because these crayons can be bought in a great variety of sizes and colours, they encourage a large and colourful approach which is often enriched by making the drawings on a rough texture like wallpaper or over a rough surface. Many of these drawings are interesting enough to keep in their own right, but a thin wash of dark ink, brusho, or thin paint will bring out the colours and also add a magical quality to the design (Illus. 1).

In complete contrast the small crayons now available in plastic containers are the ideal material for recording shapes and detail out of doors. Even with the very young pupil, delightful objective studies can be made, brought inside, cut out, and used as part of a frieze. Houses, skylines, trees, cars, people, all look more interesting if they have first been studied, no matter for how short a time.

As the children grow older, a wider range of surfaces can be introduced as backgrounds for their pictures. For example the paper can be crumpled up and then wet, before the ink, paint and finally crayon are added. The main aim at this age is to keep the pictures moving, by constantly creating a situation where new things are happening and new problems are to be solved. The children are encouraged to make a collection of many different textures. These are then assembled to make a picture and a rubbing is taken. This method is ideal if a number of units are required to make up part of a big picture. For example soldiers going into battle or crowds of people watching a football game can both be built up using this method. Wherever possible the children should be encouraged to look for new ways of working, new groups of colours and new combinations of materials.

This article explores some of the various combinations of materials and their effects using wax crayons as one part of the process but it is hoped that the children themselves will learn to extend their own vocabulary of surfaces and textures, and the relevance of the techniques.

Simple Resist

Children tend to press lightly with crayons when colouring large spaces and will often produce pictures with areas of empty paper. The resist technique encourages a firmer approach with the crayon and a chance to continue it with paint or ink in order to complete a picture, by quickly applying areas of colour. The basic technique is simple.

Make a picture or pattern pressing firmly with your crayons. Use ebony stain or powder mixed thinly (about one level tablespoonful with a little water—a third of an ordinary sized jam jar) and brush, or wash this right across the paper over the crayon, which will consequently resist the stain or paint and the colour will remain on the empty paper. Globules of it may remain on parts of the crayon, giving an interesting effect.

Above: A picture of a footballer drawn by a nine-year-old. The way the crayon has been applied shows the different surfaces

Illustration 1 (below)

Extension

Let the children experiment with consistency and choice of powder colour. Black is always very effective as a wash on bright oranges and yellows. Some exciting firework pictures can be produced in this way. If the colours are bright and thick then undiluted ebony stain will effectively resist the picture. Alternatively a silhouette picture made in black crayon looks most effective resisted with white or bright orange. Encourage a choice of crayons, resist colours, and background paper, according to the subject. Children often begin pictures with the most important characters, forgetting the difficulty or ignoring completely the importance of the background. Hence crayoned pictures often look incomplete. A crayoned snow scene with numerous figures, trees and houses is successfully unified and completed with a white wash of colour, again slight traces remaining on the crayon, giving added effect. So, the resist technique enables children to concentrate on the important figures in a picture, leaving the background until the end. Sometimes more than one resist colour can be used so that they merge together on the paper revealing soft tones and shades.

If the crayon is not thick enough it will not, of course, resist the stain or paint. One remedy for this is to hold the final picture under running water for a second or two allowing some of the paint to wash off. Gently move it about under the tap, perhaps letting the paint run across the paper. Put the picture on newspaper to dry.

White crayon or candle on white kitchen

A picture created by using rubbings from cardboard, corrugated card, net and wood shapes

paper, resisted with ebony stain or black paint, makes an interesting picture. Use a cheese grater to grate crayon onto a sheet of kitchen paper. Place another sheet on top and iron over this, melting or partly melting the crayon. The resulting pattern can be resisted. Crayon held briefly over a candle flame and dropped onto the paper can make thick layers of colour which can be resisted in stain or paint. This is an interesting technique for a subject like a fantastic bird or animal, or just a crayoned pattern called explosion of colour.

Rubbings

The simple technique of placing a coin under paper and watching the design appear as it is rubbed with a pencil is something all children find fascinating. A natural exten- sion of this is to let them take kitchen paper and crayon and take rubbings of as many interesting textured surfaces as possible. Black or dark blue, I think, is the colour to use at first for the most pleasing results. The paper should be held firmly on the surface to be rubbed and the side of the crayon used in firm sweeping motions so that the patterns emerge evenly. This is only a beginning. Encourage the children to fill the whole sheet of paper leaving no empty spaces or, alternatively, to cut out and use their rubbings to make a picture of their own.

Extension

Find interesting objects for the children to rub, such as leaves, corrugated card, pieces of wood, bark or materials. As well as this, pictures can be made from card, mounted

A rubbing from a piece of wood was the starting point of this picture

on strong paper or a large sheet of card. This raised picture is ideal for rubbing. Rubbings of, for example, a busy street scene can be made from card. A single car, house and pedestrians is all that is necessary. These can be rubbed a number of times by moving the paper after each rubbing. Similarly abstract designs can be made.

Coloured sticky paper on textured wallpaper is useful for effective rubbings. String or wool can be stuck on or just held firmly on some card with kitchen or cartridge paper placed over the top for the rubbing.

Brass rubbings are becoming very popular and children enjoy doing this, although permission must be obtained from the vicar of the church concerned as a fee is often now required. Wax crayons—(preferably black) are very effective for this with detail paper. If this is not used in your school then buy some lining paper from the wallpaper shop. It is cheap and easily obtained. The children should be encouraged to look around their playground for interesting surfaces.

These techniques can be combined with the "resist" technique. Take a rubbing which is considerably thickly waxed and use a stain or thin paint to wash across it.

Colour Combs

This is simple technique but the results are effective.

The paper must be covered with a variety of coloured crayons. Break them in half and cut several notches along the side, quite close together. Hold the crayon firmly and draw it across the paper in sweeping motions so that a trail of lines is left. Repeat this in a variety of colours, using twists and turns. If the crayon is heavily applied the picture can be resisted with ebony stain or paint. Use this technique on drawings—for example—waves on a ship picture, twirling clouds, the design on a clown's costume or just used to make a coloured background ready for a

A finely drawn design using the colour cutting technique

Industrial landscape in crayon sgraffito, cut paper and ink

paint picture—in this instance the paint should be either mixed with a little polycell glue or washing up liquid so that it adheres to the wax. An effective way is to make a black silhouette picture on this colourful crayoned background.

Colour Cutting in Crayon, in Soap and Powder Colour

Sgraffito is the term used for cutting into wax crayon. This requires perseverance and stamina! The initial stage is to completely colour a small sheet of card with wax colour—"Taking a line for a walk" is a useful beginning as the resulting stages can be coloured in. The next step involves the stamina and strength. The complete pattern must be waxed over with a black crayon. This thick waxy surface can now be scratched into with a variety of tools, scissors, sharp pencils, nails, knife, lino cutting tools or stick. The colour underneath will gradually be revealed. Encourage the children to vary the "scratching" technique, sometimes scraping a large area of wax away, sometimes making detailed line designs. Faces make ideal subjects for this technique.

Extension

Use a thick mixture of powder colour and liquid detergent to brush across the initial coloured wax design. This can either be worked on quickly when wet with fingers or comb card, or left to dry and the same scratching technique used as previously described. Younger children find it easier and quickly satisfying to use the wet mixture and fingers. They enjoy experimenting with different patterns by brushing out the design and trying a different one.

TEXTURES

Crayon and Oil

This is one of many ways of changing the surface quality of a wax crayon drawing and is ideal for decorative projects where a translucent image like a stained glass window is required. Using cotton wool or a brush, rub the back of the drawing with olive oil or machine oil. Obviously a design with fairly large areas of crayon will be most successful, as the light will pass through the crayon when attached to the window.

Another range of experiments using oil, is to apply a small amount of linseed oil to a

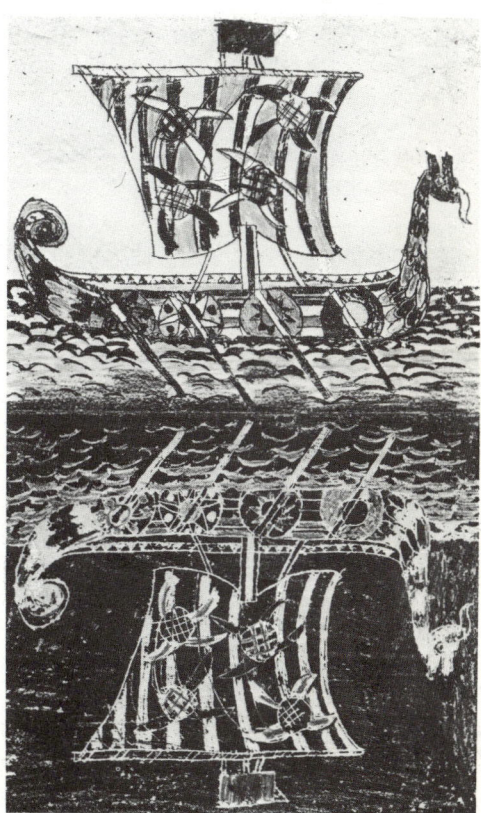

Illustration 2. Multiple patterns can either be left as a larger picture or cut out and re-assembled

wax crayon drawing. This has the effect of slightly softening the wax and allows the colours to be blended.

Crayon and Chalk

In the previous methods large areas of crayon were important. In this way of working detailed linear subjects can be chosen.

As shown in the illustration of the ship (Illus. 2), a mirror reflection has been produced. This is achieved by first laying down a covering of chalk onto one half of the paper. Then a layer of wax crayon over the chalk. Here a limited range of colours usually produces the best results. Fold over the top paper and then make the design by drawing on to the back of the top sheet using a biro. When the two halves of the design are revealed a positive and a negative picture will have been produced.

This way of working is ideal where a double image is required, i.e. ships, houses reflected in water, swans, etc. Another way of using these positive and negative images is to cut them out separately and then use them as units in a larger picture. The positive shapes in the front and the negative shapes behind give a very good impression of tonal perspective.

Crayon batik

This is another way of developing a crayon drawing and extends the previous methods discussed earlier. This will help the children to see a progression in their picture making. First the design is made in thick crayon covering the whole of the paper with colour. When the design is complete the paper is screwed up into a tight ball and dipped into water. The first exercise is to crack or craze the crayon layer. Then the water allows the

A batik design

paper to be smoothed out flat. When this has been done, then dark ink or powder colour is brushed over the picture. As one can see the paint goes into the cracks, completely changing the texture and surface appearance of the drawing (Illus. 3).

True batik uses wax and dye onto cloth and indeed melted wax crayon can be used in this process, in a similar way.

Sacking or spare pieces of hessian are useful for working on in crayon. Try using blotting paper to obtain a print from the crayon

First soften the tip in the candle flame and then print the crayon

design. This technique is ideal for battle scenes or crowd scenes.

The design is made by melting coloured wax on to white cotton or hessian. The cloth is then screwed up to crack and craze the surface area of the wax. Then the whole design is dipped into a cold water dye. When the cloth is dry it is then ironed from the back on to newspaper making the colours fast and also removing the wax. If a piece of white paper is placed under the cloth before ironing the wax colours will be transferred on to the paper. The reverse is also true if a melted crayon design on to paper is used face down on to cloth.

In this type of work enrichment using embroidery techniques, beads, buttons, raffia and other collage materials can be used to develop these designs even further. A brief study of the history of Batik is also of value at this stage.

Melted Crayon

Wax crayons have a very low melting point and this fact can be used in a most interesting range of activities.

For painting with melted crayon, a rigid background is recommended, because the crayon tends to flake when supplied to a non-rigid surface like paper. A bun tin to hold the separate colours, suspended over a small candle by two bricks, is the only equipment required plus some old hog hair brushes.

When the crayon has melted, the wax colour can be dribbled on to the surface, like the start for the witches (Illus. 4), or applied in thick vigorous brush strokes. This way of painting is very good for children as it encourages them to be direct and work quickly. If this way of working is to be used by very young children, the crayons need only be softened in the flame of the candle and then dribbled or printed on to the picture. Again thin ink brushed over these pictures will bring out the colour.

As an extension of these encaustic techniques with older pupils and even college students, a recipe of melted wax crayon, beeswax, turps and damar varnish gives the melted wax greater versatility as it remains fluid longer and is more adhesive. With older students projects using melted crayon on to glass, between sheets of acrylic and applied on to polystyrene are most exciting. The last method was found to burn into the surface of the material, at varying depths, depending on what colour was used. For example gold and silver crayons added a metallic surface with little erosion to the polystyrene.

In the sculptural field, melted crayon poured into clay moulds or on to kitchen foil will produce some very interesting forms which could be used as starting points for coloured abstract sculpture or bas reliefs.

Mixed Media

As emphasised earlier, the important part of making a picture is that the surface can be developed as the work progresses.

Teachers have often said that wax crayons have limitations when used by older children. This need not be so. Illustration 5 shows a very detailed picture of a demolition site using predominantly wax crayons and resulting in some interesting textures.

As mentioned before very thick crayon, overlaid with thick paint, allows the artist to incise great detail if required, and also allows areas to be blocked in, or isolated in strong relief. In both cases preliminary drawings have been made and then the shapes transposed into very professional pieces of work.

Single colour sgraffito using black crayon over white crayon can result in the most intricate and detailed drawings.

It is important to remember that examples such as these do not just happen by chance. The teacher must create a situation in the classroom which allows the children to be creative. As stressed before these techniques should be introduced where applicable, not as numbered lessons. Also the classroom should be arranged in such a way, that the children have an opportunity to try out these techniques, such as melting crayons and applying them in a variety of ways. What we must avoid is the situation where the child is asked only to draw in one material or in one technique.

An illustration drawn by an older child on the theme of demolition

A touch of the Orient

The all-embracing nature of art provides the ready means of introducing children to the countries and peoples of the world. We can proceed from the known to the unknown; say, from the local town's coat-of-arms to the dragons and other symbols on the Imperial robes of ancient China; from the school badge to the mon of the Japanese families; from the lucky horseshoe to the mandala.

The designs set out here are unusual and intricate. They have been drawn as a designer might draw them, step by step.

Children enjoy using geometrical instruments and patterns like this afford the opportunity of showing them how to use these instruments in ways other than the proving of theorems.

Conversely, it gives the teacher in the Junior school the means of introducing basic geometry and the handling of the instruments.

All these motifs look extraordinarily effective when used as a repeat pattern, or as a large single unit. The colours can be of the children's own choice.

Chinese Motifs

These decorative symbols seen on Chinese articles date back a long time in Chinese history. Their significance is to wish the receiver of the article the good fortune symbolized by the motif.

There is a great number of these good fortune symbols. These shown here are those which occur most frequently:

1. Yang Yin—The Dual Principle. The circle is divided into two equal parts, the light representing heaven, and the dark earth. Many other forms of duality are often represented by this type of motif.
2. Shen Mien—The symbol of Heavenly Perfection.
3. Lu—Riches.
4. Hsi—Double joy, e.g. married happiness.
5. Fang Sheng—One of the eight precious things.

Japanese Motifs

Anyone may use a crest of his own in Japan. It can be worn on the kimono or outer garment. When the material for the kimono is dyed, a stencil of the mon or crest is pasted on it and appears white on the finished garment:

1. Ho—A sail
2. Sakura—Cherry blossom
3. Hidachi—The sun
4. Janomi—Snake eyes
5. Kuyo—Heavenly bodies

The Embassy of Japan has an excellent film which is free on loan and is entitled 'Living Arts of Japan'. It is in colour, runs for about thirty minutes and is suitable for children of all ages. Books can be borrowed from the library on Japanese art.

Pattern making by dyeing

There are innumerable ways of making patterns and it is sometimes useful to look towards traditional crafts from any part of

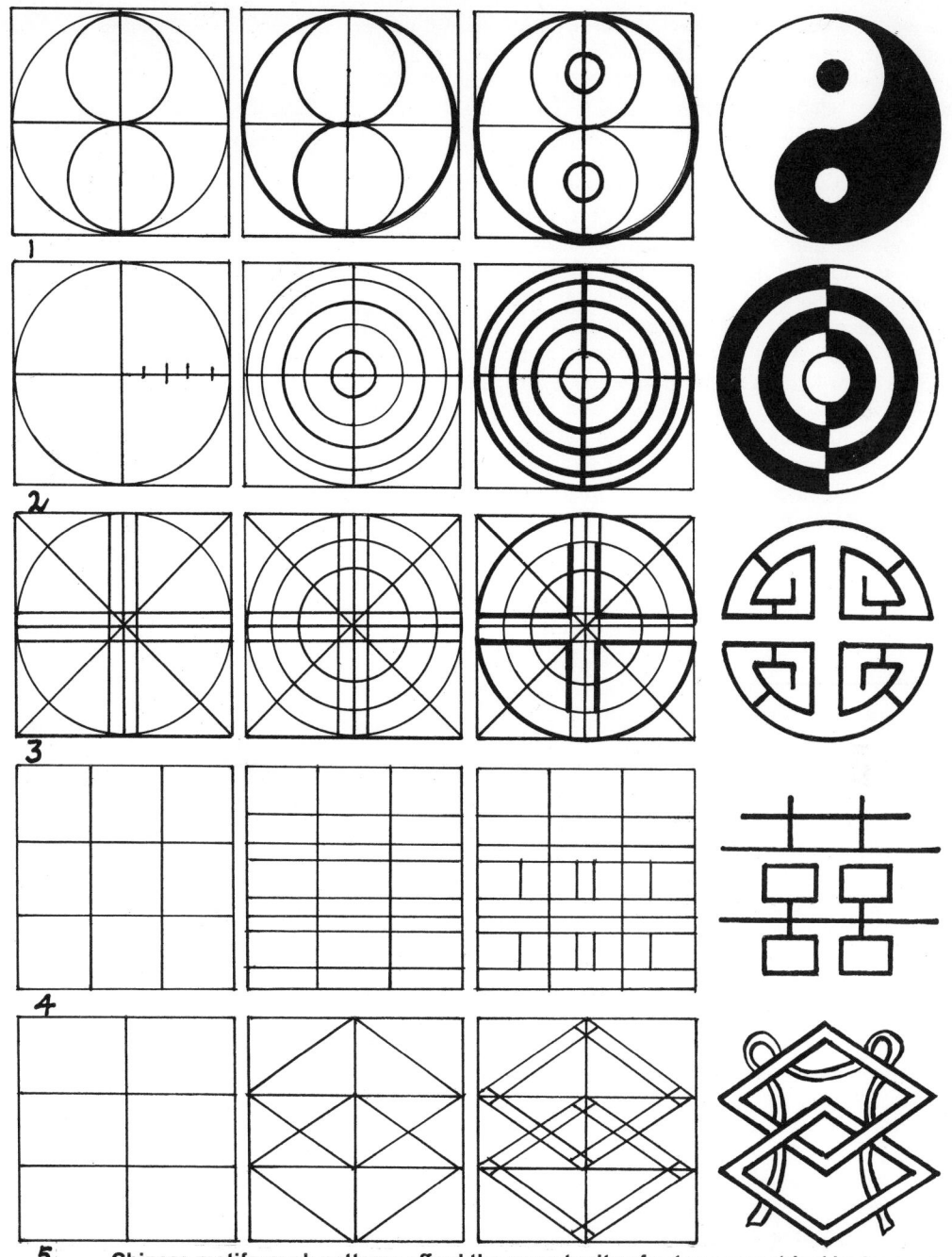

5 Chinese motifs: such patterns afford the opportunity of using geometrical instruments

the world to get ideas of how to begin. The Japanese are masters of papermaking and paper dyeing and books have been written about their elegant parcel wrappings. Two ways in which they prepare the paper to achieve simple and effective patterns are easy to master and offer scope for individual expression in the choice of colour, the way it is applied and the stimulating of further ideas for folding and application of dye. Japanese paper dyed in these ways can be bought in sheets. The simpler method of folding is to take a sheet of white paper, newsprint or kitchen paper seems ideal for its absorbency, and fold it in half and half again and so on until one has a long narrow strip in an enclosed fold. Open it out and begin folding it again, using the previous folds as a guide, but this time folding fanwise forwards and backwards. Crease the edges crisply. This can be dyed in different ways. One colour might be used and each edge dipped in, leaving a white line down the middle of the strip, hold the strip tightly together while dipping. Let it dry before unfolding. The ends, instead of the edges, could be dipped in the dye, it will be noticed that the dye will creep up the folds. The dye could be applied with a brush to the edges of the folds instead of dipping. Two or more colours could be used. The strip might be dipped in one colour at each edge, or dipped using two colours, putting one side in each colour and then spots of a different colour applied with a brush to the damp edges. How many different patterns can be achieved just by this method of dipping and spotting might be a task undertaken with the greatest satisfaction by some children. There is no right or wrong method of dyeing paper in this way. Almost any way of folding and putting on the dye produces patterns.

The second Japanese method of folding takes us a step further than the first. Having achieved the strip of paper folded as a fan the whole is then creased into a pile of

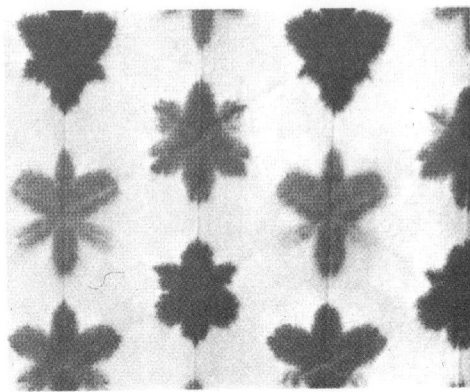

Japanese paper folded and dyed

Newsprint folded and dyed in two Brusho colours. Illustrations from 'Dyeing and Printing' by B. Ash and A. Dyson, published by Batsford

triangles. It is difficult to do this satisfactorily if the strip is narrower than about two inches, though this would be possible with thin strong paper, greaseproof, tissue, etc. Take the fan folded strip and bend the corner over on itself in a diagonal fold, then back again to the straight edge and continue to make diagonal and straight folds along the strip until the whole appears to be a pile of folded triangles. Hold this together tightly, with the fingers or a clothes peg or two and dip the corners only in the dye. Use the same colour for each corner, or the same

1

2

72°

3

4

5

Japanese motifs: these patterns look equally effective when used as a repeat pattern

colour for two corners and another colour for the third, or three different colours one for each corner. Fold another and try dipping all the corners in the same colour and then spotting the tips with a brush dipped in another colour. A little experimenting with folding the paper in other ways will soon show the possibilities of putting regular and irregular patterns on to a piece by merely dipping in the dye.

A plentiful supply of paper is needed if the investigation of pattern is to be taken as far as possible. Newsprint is cheap and while not very suitable for painting it is ideal for dyeing. But try other kinds of paper as well. Get the children collecting sheets of clean wrapping paper, large paper bags, and big used envelopes. Old posters from news-agents are being thrown out continually and one can often find a source of paper offcuts. Consider damping the paper when it is folded before dyeing it. Is the result different from the dry dyeing? What happens if it is folded, dyed and then put under the tap or dipped in water? Do different papers react in the same way or different ways?

Brusho dye is excellent for this work. It is in powder form and can be mixed with a little water as needed or a pint at a time. The colours mix together well and it will be found that with some colours on some papers the pigments separate forming different shades or even different colours. If the work develops experimentally from such a beginning children could collect natural materials such as blackberries, elderberries, onion skins, fading flower heads to soak in water or boil up to produce dye. The chemically minded might then see what happens when they dye a piece of paper in blackberry juice and spot it with common soda solution or vinegar.

The spiral in art

The spiral is one of the very early forms of decoration. It originated, as far as is known, during the transition from the hunter to agricultural communities, which took place in Western Asia between 10,000 and 4,000 B.C.

Some authorities think that it derives from the snake as a symbol of the soil; it carried with it the idea of life and the constant renewal of life.

On a walk across a Cornish moor on a hot summer day, it is not unusual to surprise an adder coiled up on a sun-drenched rock. Startled, the coil springs to life and disappears quickly into the heather. Sloughs on the grass evoke the idea of rebirth.

When, in Anatolia, man first discovered how to make clay pots, the spiral design came as an apt form of decoration.

The motif spread westwards into Europe and

A clever use of the spiral to form a pattern. Prehistoric temple at Tarxien, Malta

eastwards to Siberia. From China and Japan it journeyed among the archipelagos of Oceania. Entering America by way of the Bering Straits, it became part of Eskimo art and continued in many variations through North and South America.

The incidence of this motif in widely spread parts of the world forms one of the clues whereby the anthropologist arrives at his theories of origins.

Some spiral decorations, such as that found on Chinese bronze ornaments of the Han dynasty, and that on pottery of pre-Columbian America of 1,500 years later require great skill and sense of form in the artist-craftsman. There are however simple spiral forms which children will find interesting to draw and use as decorative patterns. Experiment should first be made with the drawing of spirals freehand. Its correlation with geometry is shown in the accompanying diagram.

Fortunately, at this distance in time, we can regard this and similar motifs purely as a decoration significant in the evolution of art. If, for one expert, it was inspired by the

Attic Black-Figured Amphor 540-530 B.C. **showing the spiral as additional decoration** (photo: Trustees of the British Museum)

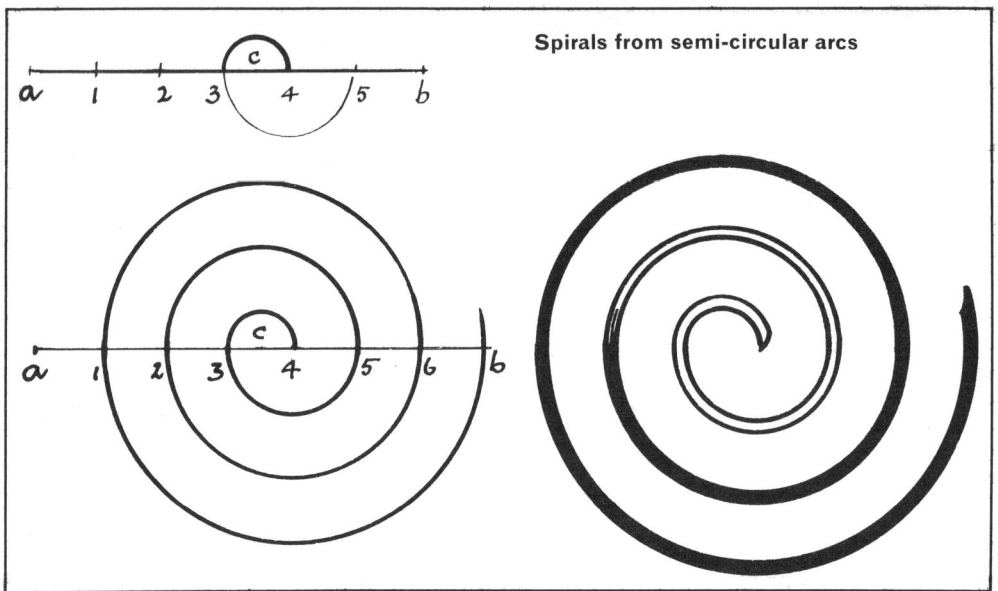

Spirals from semi-circular arcs

horns of the ram, or another sees it as representing the sacred tree of life, we can charitably lend an ear, while keeping our eye on the form.

Spirals from semi-circular arcs
Draw a line **ab** and divide it into twice the number of convolutions required: here six parts for three convolutions.
Divide the middle part equally, and mark it **c**: 3 and 4 with **c** as the centre.
With the points of the compasses at **c** and the radius **c**3 draw the semi-circle from 3 to 4.
With the point of the compasses at 4 and the radius 43 draw the semi-circle 35: shown by the thin line. The compasses now return to **c** with the radius **c**5 and so on, alternating with the point of the compasses at **c** and 4 to form the spiral.
Thickness can be added afterwards by altering the radius of the compasses.

Bronze wine vessel in the shape of an owl with a complex spiral motif. Chinese, Shang-Yin Dynasty (photo: Trustees of the British Museum)

Bronze ritual food vessel (Kuei) eleventh century B.C. showing spiral patterning (photo: Trustees of the British Museum)

Decoration

The art of decoration is the use of ornament to enhance a bare surface. Since the very earliest times man has done this. He has not been content with merely producing something useful for his everyday needs, he has had to add some ornament to it. We find prehistoric tools and weapons with the beginning of pattern upon them and it is as though from the very outset man has sought not only to feed his body but also to please his mind.

The making of a pattern satisfies an urge deep within human nature. Even an elementary motif of zigzag lines shows a mind at work endeavouring to bring order and beauty where none existed before. It is this endeavour which has ennobled man's handiwork through the ages.

When a boy in the country cuts a straight hazel stick and whittles a pattern in the wood, he may have no purpose other than the pleasure in the use of a sharp knife. But he may take a pride in what he is doing; and he may also be carving a pattern which will mark the stick as his.

The earliest decorative motif of which we have any record dates back to something like 20,000 years ago. It consists of lines scratched on horn. We may wonder why it was made; perhaps it came about in a manner similar to a boy's whittling on a stick.

But the lines could have been magic signs drawn to give the owner protection and to confer power on what may have been a weapon.

Early patterns on earthenware vessels such as water jars and storage pots were almost certainly designed to set them aside as very special vessels to be used only for tribal rites and not for everyday use.

This is guessing, but archaeologists who make these guesses believe them to be reasonable ones based partly on what is observed of the practices of primitive peoples living today.

But there can be no doubt that the figuring of this early ornament was the beginning of art, the first step on the road to a Michaelangelo masterpiece.

Decorative motives play a large part in the art and architecture of the early civilizations. By 2000 B.C. there was already an advanced form of ornamental art in Egypt. This sprang from Egyptian mythology and was full of meaning for the people concerned. For example the lotus was painted in a number of different ways to decorate walls and ceilings and it was used in architecture in the form of capitals on graceful columns. In Egypt the lotus was the symbol of Nefertem, the god who was the rising sun; he arose out of a lotus flower every morning and sank back into it at night, when the flower closed its petals.

From Egypt the lotus, as a decorative motif, spread into Assyria and India, and later into Japan. It was taken over by the Greeks, and the Romans had it from them. And it is still going strong, as are many other early motifs. Decorative motifs from plants were very popular in early times. The rosette might be

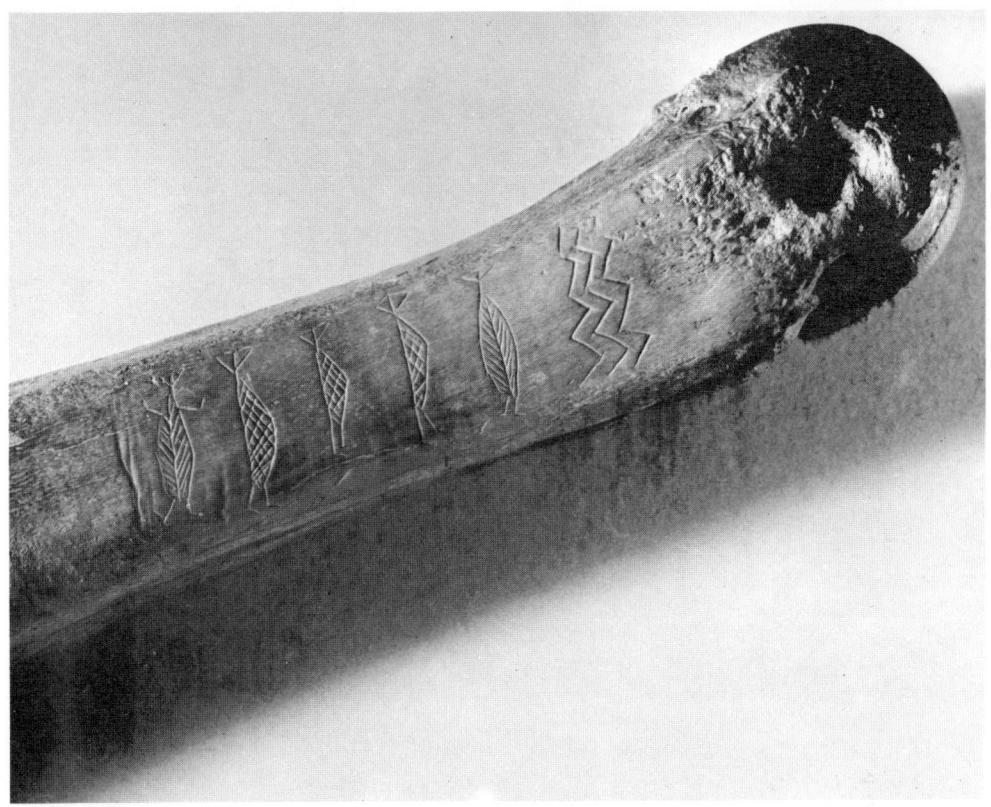

Auroch's bone from Ryemarksgaard, approx. 6000 B.C. (Courtesy of the Danish National Museum)

any kind of flower with its petals radiating from its centre to form a circle. It is one of the best-known of Assyrian ornaments; the Assyrian artists arranged them into band patterns and these patterns are seen on their architecture.

Much later the rosette became a favourite with the people of northern Europe, who used them to decorate metalwork.

The rosette, as well as representing a flower, might also be a symbol of the sun and its rays and in some very early ornament it is used as such.

Between 2000 and 1000 B.C. Chinese artists began to make decorative objects from bronze. They twisted animal shapes into ornament in the form of an S. Later this animal style is adopted by the Scythians, who entered southern Russia in about the eighth century B.C. The Scythian artists develop this style into intricate interlacing figures which came over the centuries into Europe to influence Celtic and Scandinavian artists.

Early Christian symbols, principally the cross, the lily and the Chi-Rho or Chrismon (P over an X) were much used in Byzantine art, and from Byzantium they came into Western Europe during the Middle Ages to be used as motifs on church furniture and vestments.

From Rome and Byzantium there come also

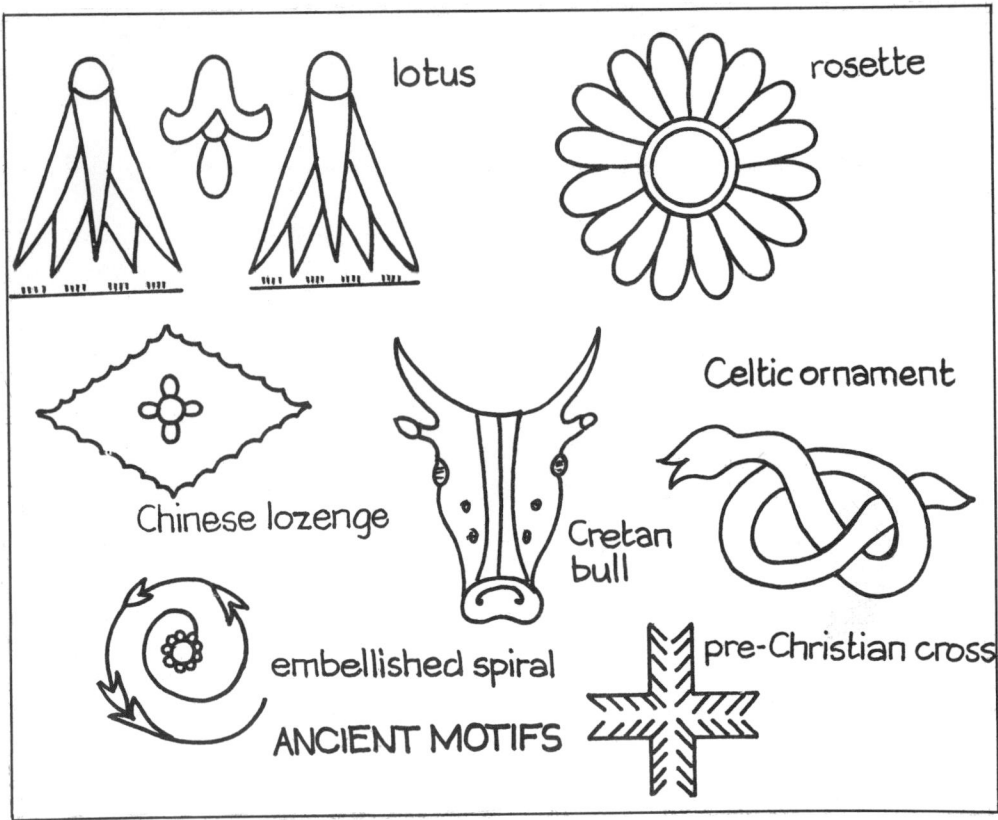

lotus

rosette

Celtic ornament

Chinese lozenge

Cretan bull

embellished spiral

pre-Christian cross

ANCIENT MOTIFS

foliated scrolls and spirals which decorate much Renaissance and Neo-Classical work. To follow the spread and development of motifs in another direction we look to China and across the Pacific to the Americas.

Early Chinese art reveals a fascinating wonderland of decorative motifs. It is thought that early trade took the basic elements of decoration into China. From these elements the Chinese artists created a variety of intricate motifs; the zigzag becomes a series of lozenge patterns, which enhance silks, jade and other materials; the spiral develops into stylised clouds and mountains which continued throughout the centuries to play a part in Chinese art.

The Chinese animal motifs already men-

tioned eventually find their way, most probably via Japan, into the Pacific islands and the special way these motifs are treated there make them a part of the art of Oceania. In the Americas culture arose more slowly. Man is thought to have entered America by way of the Bering Strait at least 15,000 years ago. It took until about 1000 B.C., so far as we know at present, for fishing and agricultural villages to become firmly established in South America. The well-known civilizations of the Incas, Mayas and Aztecs all reached their peaks and declined with our own Christian era.

Many of the decorative motifs of these civilizations bear a striking resemblance to the motifs of the Ancient World; for example

Cypriote jar, circa 2500 B.C. (Victoria and Albert Museum)

Clay jug from Aegina, first half of seventh century B.C. (photo: Trustees of the British Museum)

to the familiar zigzags and spirals, rosettes and animal forms.

But in this we need not see a direct connection with the Ancient World, although it is intriguing to speculate on how there might have been some world-wide communication in early times.

It would seem that all civilizations pass through certain similar stages of development, and an explanation for people far apart possessing similar works of art may be simply that human beings tend to think along similar lines.

All this should encourage the non-specialist teacher in the junior school.

It can and does happen that the teacher comes up against a blank wall, ideas fail.

When this occurs, a consideration of origins will often act as a stimulus. This is true of any subject, but most of all of art. In this very brief look at decorative motifs of the past we may well become aware of how under various forms they continue into the present. Among other things, it could lead us down many fruitful byways of history and geography.

It should stimulate our ideas about pattern work in the junior school. At the very least, it should show us the reason for and the justification of the children's pattern work, which they take to like a duck to water. We shall see it as a natural stage in the development of their human personality leading on to higher things.

'All scattered in the bottom of the sea'

A Shell is a common enough natural object which we all just take for granted, and yet it has structural form, surface textures, colours and patterns which can be excellent stimuli for creative interpretation in all manner of ways. In fact ideas for pattern making can be developed which either retain direct connections with the original shell—as, for example, in analytical drawing or painting done from observation—or which lead to abstract renderings of a purer form in paint, collage, embroidery, print or other aspects. Perhaps a good way to begin is to hold a selected shell in your hands. This will give you an opportunity to examine it with care, while feeling its bumps and crenellations and looking at it with microscopic precision. This can lead to a deeper consideration of its unique individuality—its shape, original habitat under the sea or on the shore, its size, its weight—and such an approach will certainly foster a questioning attitude with links in mathematics and the natural sciences. Will your shell spin or rock if placed on an horizontal surface? Does its rolling motion suggest ideas for a moving sculpture in fibre-glass or paper and wire? Does it inspire pattern making in printed textiles through the medium of potato or lino printing? If a shallow scallop shell is covered in ink and rocked gently on a piece of paper will interesting images be formed which call out to be developed further in line, texture and colour?

A shell's shape may be translated into a line depicting its perimeter in profile. This immediately reduces its form to a simple, flat motif suitable for use as a pattern unit and it is possible to make designs in string-collage or with cut paper shapes. Its three-dimensional character may be recorded by a line varying in thickness and tone so as to impart sensitivity to the image as well as adding information about actual changes in its structural form.

Feeling the shell will tell us much about its texture; indeed, close inspection of its surface will reveal textured and coloured qualities suggesting patterns to be interpreted in a mixture of media—rough crayon work over smooth ink; tissue paper pasted

Dog Whelks can be found in a variety of colours

over thick poster colour; plaster, scrim and wire; powder colour, glue and sand.

A shell may have very interesting surface qualities with colours varying from a deep chestnut brown through to yellow ochre or off-white, and clearly definable in the shapes these occupy. Shapes such as these may be made to radiate from the centre point— the shell's oldest part—and may suggest the use of a point and radiating lines as a start to producing patterns. Textured ridges, caused by periodic growth pauses, may demand a linear treatment.

Some shells have an inherent spiral structure which is complemented by a network of radial colours and there is a superb harmony between structure, colour and texture which can be of great help to the young designer. It might be a good thing to ignore size, for many shells are quite tiny. Patterns can be produced on a very large scale and some might even finish up as mural paintings. Think of large buildings and relate the shell-forms to architecture or landscape so that large group paintings or collage pictures result.

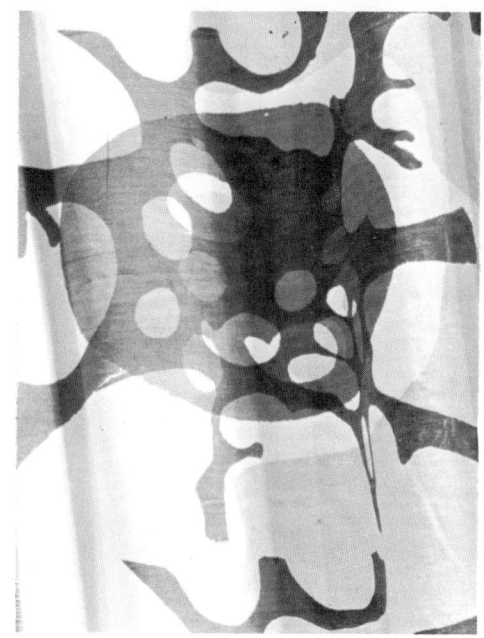

Fabric designs based on shell patterns

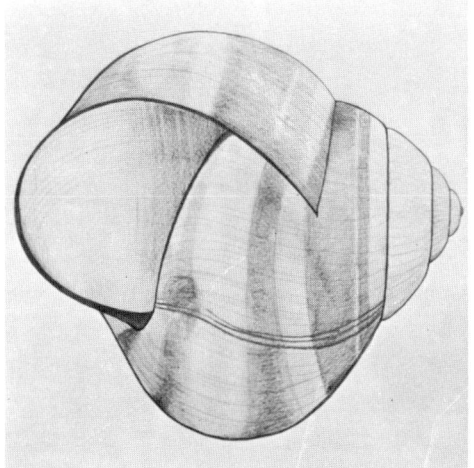

Ideas for pattern making can be developed from a careful drawing of the shell

Cut-paper collage showing pattern developments

Modelling in clay

More clay ideas

Printing with clay

Slab pots

Larger models

Using sand

Modelling with clay

Of all plastic modelling materials, clay is the cheapest, the most versatile, the most easy to use, and probably the most satisfying. Its one disadvantage for teachers, so it is said, is its messiness. But used properly, clay should be no more messy than paint or plaster of Paris or papier mâché. It really depends on how it is used.

Clay can be found, in one form or another, almost anywhere. Dig deep enough, and you will inevitably find it under your own school playground. You might even be fortunate enough to have a source of clay from a nearby building site, clay pit, brick-making yard, or just the local stream. If you do, the clay obtained from these sources will usually be quite adequate for simple modelling in the classroom.

More often, clay is obtained from a pottery supplier. For general use, purchase a quantity of one of the cheaper modelling clays, brown or white. They are basically both the same. Ignore the expensive stoneware or porcelain clays. But do insist on 'plastic' clay. This is usually packed in plastic bags in quantities of $\frac{1}{2}$cwt, and is ready to use. Powdered clay, which is also available and which must be mixed with water to the correct consistency, is hardly cheaper, yet creates unnecessary work for the teacher. When the clay arrives, store it carefully. To keep it soft and plastic, ensure that it is always stored in an airtight container. The plastic bag, in which it arrives, is quite adequate for this. But never leave the bag open. Keep the ends fastened with a strong elastic band or strip of wire. Failing that, keep the clay in a dustbin; preferably a plastic one. Always replace the lid after use, and keep a wet sack inside to cover the clay. Kept in such conditions, the clay will remain soft for months and months, if not years.

The minute that clay is exposed to air, particularly in a warm classroom, and manipulated with warm hands, it begins to dry. Inevitably, therefore, we find ourselves left with quantities of clay, too hard for modelling. What is to be done. Firstly, at the end of each lesson, collect together all the pieces of hard clay; put them into a bin or bucket, and cover with water. In about twenty-four hours, the hard pieces will break down into a slurry or slip—a thick, creamy mess. Allow the clay to settle, and pour off the excess water. The slurry which is left, should then be spread out on to an old sack, and left to dry in the open air. On a warm day this will take about four to eight hours, depending on the quantity and consistency. You should now be left with good, soft, plastic clay. Knead it all together, as you would with dough, and replace it in the plastic clay container. It is now ready to use again. If, as sometimes happens, particularly during the holidays, your entire clay store gets too hard, the same reconditioning process applies. Simply break down the hard mass into small pieces; soak in water; dry out on sacks, and knead the clay back into shape.

The same also applies to clay models which have been made and allowed to dry out

Fig. 1. Start by modelling simple shapes, cubes, balls, pyramids, etc.

completely. Painted or not, they can still be watered down and used again. Models which have been varnished should not be used.

Equipment

The equipment needed for clay modelling in the classroom is minimal.

Firstly, some kind of covering for the work area. Newspapers will do, or a large sheet of plastic, with a modelling board of plywood or hardboard for each child.

Secondly, a selection of tools and brushes.

The tools can be made by the children themselves from pieces of wood. Thin sticks of wood, sandpapered down, are quite adequate. But do collect any old lollipop sticks, old brush handles, toothbrushes, lengths of metal or plastic. Rolling pins will be useful, or lengths of broomstick handle.

Thirdly, a selection of odds and ends for pattern making and decorating. Shells, pebbles, old combs, nails, pieces of metal, corks, and so on.

Fourthly, a selection of rags, cloths and sponges.

Methods of working

First steps in modelling should be directed

Fig. 2. Experiments with texture can start by simply pressing objects into the clay

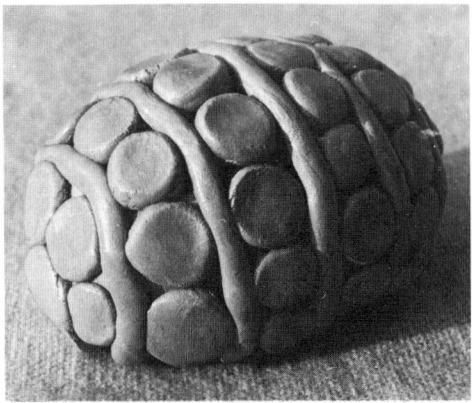

Fig. 3. Building up the surface with small pieces of clay

Fig. 4. A smooth shape can rely on a painted design for interest

Fig. 5. Scratching through a layer of paint to create the design

towards 'getting the feel' of the clay, growing accustomed to its limitations and becoming aware of its possibilities. We might begin by making simple shapes by patting, rolling and pressing, Fig. 1.

Some of the shapes can be made smooth; others can be decorated. Smoothing can be done with the fingers, or with a damp piece of rag or sponge, when the clay is 'cheese-hard' (literally when the clay is the consissistency of hard cheese); or by rubbing down with sandpaper or wire wool, when the clay is completely dry.

Decorating can be done in a variety of ways.
1. By impressing tools and objects into the soft clay. Almost anything can be used. The scope for impressed decoration is limitless. Fingers, sticks, pencils, brushes, coins, old combs, pieces of metal and plastic, pebbles, shells, etc. Interesting designs can be made by rolling the soft clay in some coarsely textured material; sugar, sand, seeds, rice,

tapioca, and so on. Or by pressing the clay into meshes and open-weave fabrics. Or even by wrapping the soft clay shape with cotton, string or wool, and then removing it. To facilitate these experiments, start a collection of various materials, make them readily available, and encourage their use, Fig. 2.

2. By applying pieces of clay to the surface of the shape. This should be done whilst the clay is still fairly soft, and the added pieces should be pressed on firmly. If not, they will begin to fall off as the clay dries out. Fig. 3 shows a simple shape decorated with coils and round pellets. But there are many other methods.

3. By painting the dry shape, this is only possible for models which are not to be fired later. Any colouring medium could be used; powder paints, poster colours, pencils, crayons, felt pens and so on, Fig. 4.

4. By sgraffito, scratching through the surface of a layer of paint to reveal the colour of the clay beneath. Fig. 5 shows a simple clay shape modelled in a pale-coloured clay, and painted with a layer of dark blue paint. The sgraffito design was scratched out with the end of a pair of scissors.

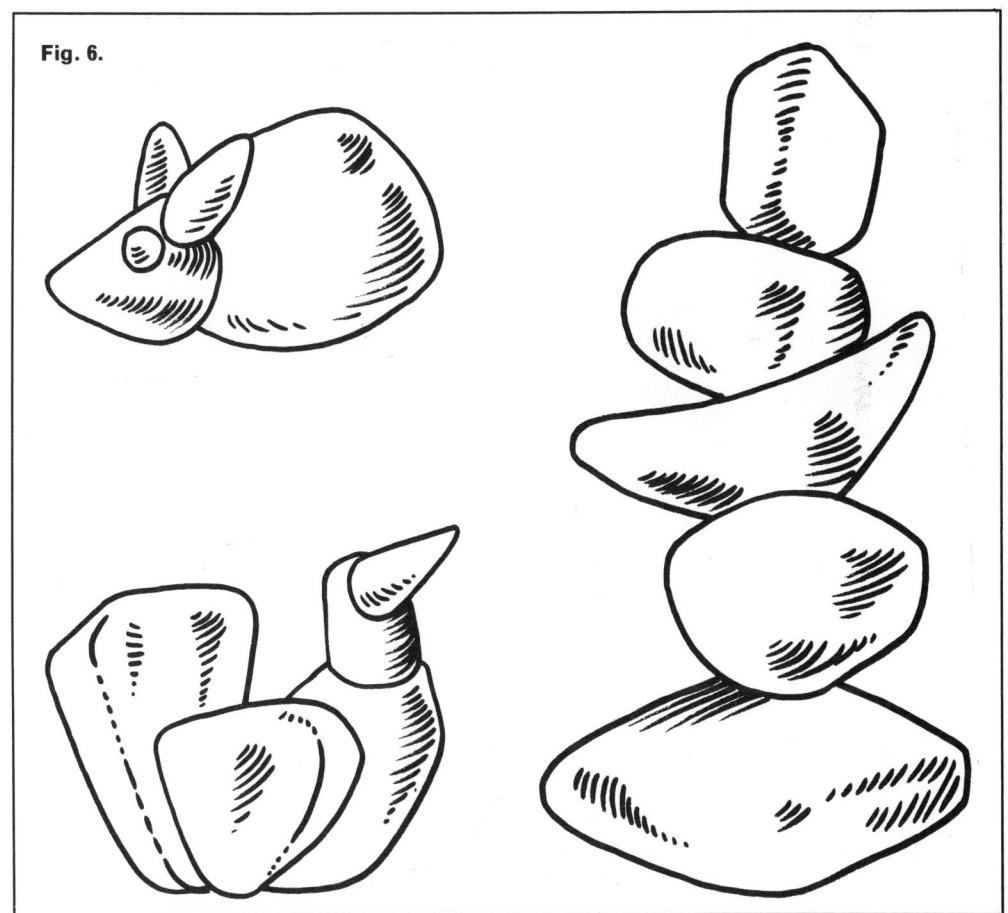

Fig. 6.

Later on, we could begin to create more complicated models by joining together a number of simple shapes, Fig. 6. The surfaces to be joined together should first be roughened with a modelling tool or a piece of stick; painted with a thick layer of 'slip' (a creamy mixture of water and clay), and pressed firmly together.

These initial experiments with shaping, smoothing, decorating and fastening are a vital part of one's understanding of the nature of clay; and they provide a basis for all future work. The successful making of almost all clay models depends on one's understanding of these basic processes. Figs. 7 and 8 show two simple abstract models by junior school children, made simply by pressing and rolling the clay with the fingers. Fig. 9 is developed from a simple basic shape, with the addition of separate pieces for feet, beak and head. Figs. 10 and 11 are built up from a large number of thick and thin coils and simple shapes.

Pinch or thumb pot models
A pinch pot, or a thumb pot, is made by taking a ball of clay about the size of an apple, pushing one's finger or thumb into the centre to make a small hole, and gradually widening the hole to make a simple bowl shape as in Fig. 12. The wall of the pot should be kept fairly thick.

Two of such shapes, roughly the same size, can be joined together to make a clay sphere.

Fig. 10 (right). Building up a model using thick coils

Fig. 7.

Fig. 8.

Fig. 9.

95

To fasten them together, the lip of each pot should be roughened with a modelling tool, painted with a thick layer of slip, pressed firmly together and the join carefully smoothed over. This clay sphere can now be used in a variety of ways as the basis for a model animal, fish or bird, by adding on further strips, coils, etc., Fig. 13.

Alternatively, we could make a whole series of pinch pots of varying size, to be joined together to make an abstract model, as in Fig. 14.

Slab models

For these we must roll out the clay into a thickish slab, in much the same way that we

Fig. 11 (below). A more elaborate model built up from a single coil

Fig. 14 (right). An abstract model built up from pinch pots

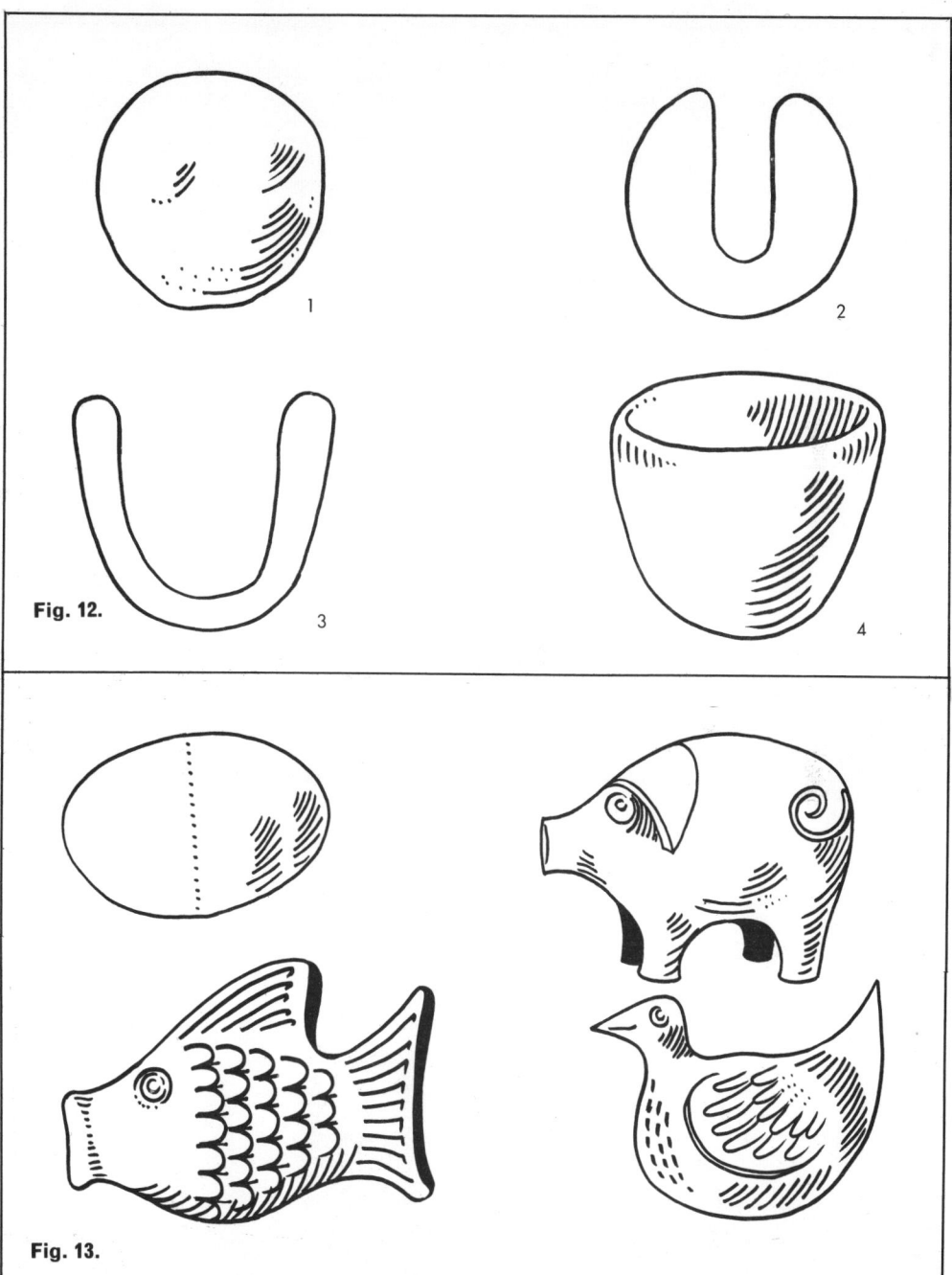

Fig. 12.

1

2

3

4

Fig. 13.

would roll out a piece of pastry. The important thing to remember is never to roll out the clay on a smooth or varnished surface for, like dough, it will stick. Always roll out the clay on a piece of paper, cloth or hessian. Obviously a rolling pin is best for rolling out, but a piece of broomstick handle, an empty milk bottle, or a thick cardboard tube, will do equally well. The thickness of the clay depends on the size of the model to be made. For most 'average' size models, about 1cm should be adequate. The sheet of clay can now be used, as one might use a sheet of card or paper in the making of a paper sculpture, by cutting out the desired shapes with a knife, and using them to create cylinders, cones, etc., Fig. 15.

Hollowed-out models

The hollowing-out of large clay models is done for three reasons. Firstly, to lessen the risk of accidents during firing. Secondly, to make the model lighter in weight and thirdly,

to limit the amount of clay being used. When large numbers of clay models are being made the latter reason is of some importance, unless one's stock of clay is inexhaustible.

Solid-based models, a figure group for instance, like Fig. 16, can be hollowed out quite simply from the base, by using a spoon or knife, whilst the clay is still soft.

Other models, (a free-standing animal, for instance), should first be cut in half; each half being hollowed out separately, before both pieces are re-fastened together, Fig. 17.

Clay carving

The carving of clay in its 'cheese-hard' state is a useful way of using up those odd pieces

Fig. 15 (left). Assembling clay slabs on a base

Fig. 16 (below). A figure group turned over to show how the base has been hollowed out

of clay which have become too hard for ordinary modelling. No special techniques are required, and almost any tools may be used for carving. Old kitchen knives, pieces of metal or plastic, spoons, etc. As a way of using clay, it introduces quite a new dimension, and is capable of a variety of different treatments.

Firing and finishing

The most satisfactory method of giving strength and permanence to any kind of clay model is by firing it in a kiln. But it is by no means the only method. Indeed, for much of the work which is carried out in schools, firing is not essential.

One of the advantages of non-firing, is that models can be decorated with a variety of paints, varnishes, and other materials, which are readily available. Firstly, dry clay models can be decorated with any kind of water-based or oil-based paints. Powder colours, water colour, oil and poster paints, household emulsions, lacquers, and so on. Crayons, chalks, pencils, felt pens, can also be used. All of these would be applied in the same way that one would apply them to paper.

Secondly, the clay models can be decorated with other materials. Feathers, seeds, threads, etc., can be pressed into the models whilst soft; or glued on to the models when hard.

Finally, both to strengthen the model, and to give it a hard, glossy finish, the model can be painted with varnish or P.V.A. adhesive. Any kind of varnish is suitable. The P.V.A. adhesive, usually available as a thick, white, treacly substance, should be diluted with water to the consistency of thin cream.

Although models treated in this way lack some of the real permanence achieved by firing, they are quite strong enough for normal use.

Fig. 17.

More clay ideas

Clay modelling has a rather sad history in many of our schools. A sad history and a not too exciting present. It is even non-existent in some. The reasons are real enough, ranging from the brittle and unsatisfactory nature of the materials available to the inevitable mess and the complaining care-takers and cleaners.

It is all very sad and all the more so because of the obvious delight exhibited by the children when engaged in this activity.

Yet it is the purpose of what follows to show that not all the materials presently available are nearly so difficult and not necessarily so messy, and if you agree that modelling is one of the basic and essential experiences in a child's development—an experience not obtainable in many homes—then you must at least investigate the matter further. Send for some leaflets, read the blurb, and then order a small quantity of one or the other. Try them out for yourself and by yourself. Try some of the suggestions that follow this, they are made with specific materials in mind. Indeed many of the ideas will not necessarily work with ordinary clay. At least one of the recommended sub-stitutes is very little more expensive than clay so that price need not be a handicap. Above all else, realise that a new start can be made. These new materials are a whole lot cleaner in use, much less brittle, usually hygienic, and mostly good to model with.

This chapter, it must be pointed out, is solely about modelling and has nothing to do with pottery. Yet most of us were taught

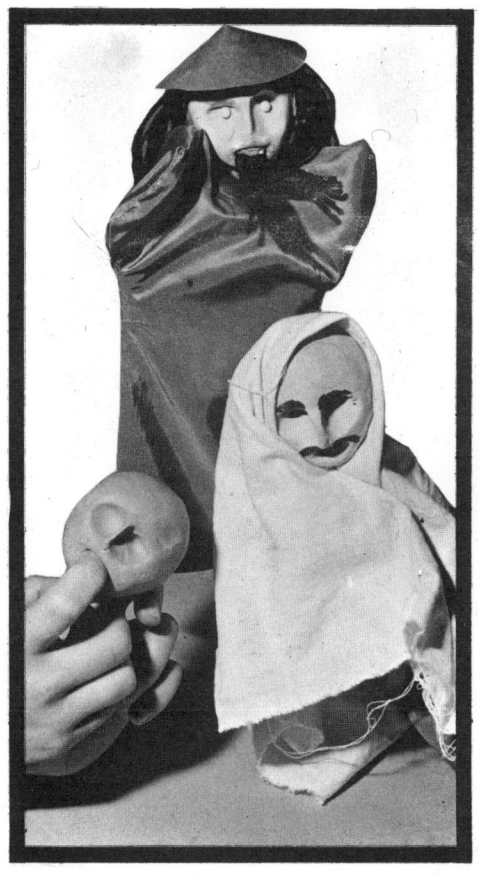

There is no such thing as a childish subject. A simple puppet head can extend any intelligent modeller and it is best to make a start with something really simple.

our modelling as a by-product of a pottery course. A complete re-think of many aspects of the craft is necessary. For instance, you are not, in pottery, permitted to glue clay to clay. There would be no point in that it would fall apart in the kiln. But in modelling this is quite in order. If a leg proves to be inadequately joined you glue it back again. If a prematurely finished piece needs a few extra clay shapes to make it work then make them and glue them on. The piece may be dry and the additional shapes wet, but that is all right, they will stay. It is often difficult to keep clay models damp over a period but this need not be such a nuisance if you know that you can add to it at a later date. Take advantage of the extra strength of the new materials and incidentally make good use of the new strength glues as well. Combine the use of clay with card, string, wire, seeds and all the rest of them, but use a good quick-acting glue too.

Decorative pieces

A note. The word 'clay' will often be used where the term 'modelling material' might be more correct, but this is for obvious simplicity.

This is a typical example of the new thinking where the modelling material is used as a decoration on a cardboard tube or a box. Previously it was never really possible to glue clay to other surfaces in that the adhesion was too temporary. However, the greater strength of the "moderns" will take this in their stride.

A small pellet of clay, not much larger than a marble, is all that is necessary for each shape. Beat down on it with the edge of the hand 'karate' style until it is flat and thin. Do all this on a piece of paper as wet clay has a tendency to stick to non-absorbent surfaces. There is no special need to trim

Examples of decorations that can be used

the edges to obtain a neat disc, but if it is rolled edgeways between the finger and thumb like a wheel on the desk, the shape will improve.

The marks that will be made into the surface of this disc should be pressed. The implement can be anything that is at hand, pencil, piece of stick, a key, anything, and the tooling should be the characteristic of that tool. In other words it should not be used to draw with. Drawing on clay is seldom satisfactory—producing a ragged, rather scratchy quality, unattractive to see and to feel.

Thin shapes such as these will dry and stiffen very quickly, although you can always make use of the radiator or sunshine to speed it up.

For the colouration of these materials you may use any of the colours that you have in the cupboard, all will serve well enough, but if it is powder, then for the decoration of small models it would be as well to see that it is pre-mixed into a liquid colour. A liquid colour served up in small quantities for use with a squirrel or sable brush. Number 'eights' are about right; neat and clean. This is not work for a large hog's hair brush after a vigorous mix of powder in water.

Paint the shapes and once the colour is dry cover it with a gloss finish. Place a blob of adhesive right in the middle of the back and stick them to the tube. The largest pieces first, filling in the vacant spaces with the ever decreasing sizes. This is the exciting stage, but the whole thing is very easy to organise, very neat, and the result is pleasing.

Texture and Relief

The effect that texture has on a surface is of so much significance in a given setting that time should be spent in modelling lessons discussing this as a detached subject. Then

Decorated pieces of clay have been used to embellish a cardboard box

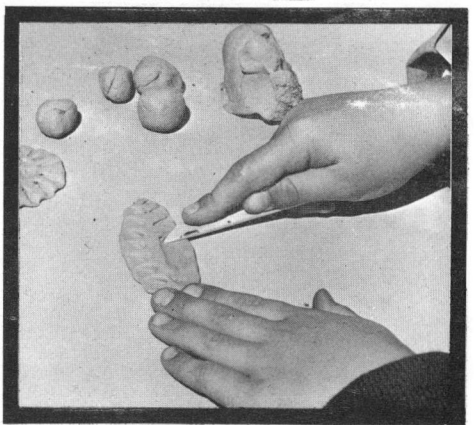

Decorative impressions being made into the "clay"

follow this up by putting textures into a context and you will begin to introduce the children to a greater realisation of the importance of textural qualities in the world about them. You probably do this already in many other ways; crayon rubbings for example. Here we shall attempt to do the same sort of thing but in clay.

Thump, or roll out in the approved manner, a piece of clay into a pancake and then with any instrument that is at hand press into or score the surface until it is covered with marks. Alternatively, press the slab against

Different textured surfaces being formed

a surface that has already a texture of its own. Tree bark, basket work, rough brick, anything that shows an interesting quality noting the effect that these have when reversed. Save the best of all these pieces until you have built up a selection of widely differing surfaces. A tag stating how each was obtained will serve as a future reminder. These pieces can be cut to shape, coloured and glossed—a gloss finish heightens the effect—and then glued to a cardboard box.

Now make use of the technique. Plan a simple picture to be made on thick card involving one or two large forms such as leaves, a fish, a boat, large flower head, one or two pieces of fruit, something very simple and big. Now roll out pieces of clay and cut them to occupy parts of the picture. Referring to the new 'library' of textures for ideas, each piece is given a quality that enhances its role in the picture. Allow them to dry, colour them and glue them into place.

Printing with clay

Taking a break from clay used as a modelling material, here it is suggested for use as a printing block. As such the implications are wide and far reaching. The technique is offered as an easier alternative to potato printing and with many more exciting possibilities.

You start by taking a ball of clay, something smaller than a tennis ball and rather on the firm side. Now thump this down on to the table and you then have the equivalent to half a potato. Press some marks into the flat surface and then tap it lightly on to the table to regain the flatness. It is now ready for printing.

Acquire some plastic meat dishes and in the bottom of each place a piece of thick cloth or, better still, a thin layer of foam sponge. Pour on some liquid colour of some sort, enough to wet the whole area. Press the block against the pad and print on to the paper, material or whatever.

It is as easy as that, but therein lies the danger for the unwary. If you organise your art as a formal lesson this process is all so easy and quickly done that the school paper will be in immediate peril. These are new techniques that you are introducing, so start each session printing on newspaper; a sheet in front of each child which is divided into four practice areas. Each is for a progressive and careful work out and a discussion with you before making a start on the final piece. After each area has been printed the block is wiped more or less clean

A clay ball ready for printing

Fascinating prints taken from clay impressions of screws, nails, nuts and bolts and a spanner

with a sponge and then the clay rolled into a ball for a fresh start to be made; and insist that they work clean.

This is the basic idea. Here is a way of developing it.

The children start with a repeat pattern of a formal shape. This is an obvious introduction as it is so similar to the potato printing with which they are all familiar. Follow this by a random arrangement of these formal shapes in two or three colours. Now a complete break with the familiar. Tear off a piece of clay from the lump, and without shaping it press it down on to the flat and then start to print with the unaltered splodge as a repeat pattern. They will note that any splodge printed in neat rows can form into a very precise pattern. If they see into this shape the likeness of a crab, a flower, or a Red Indian, and develop it as such we are now beginning to make room for an imaginative element in the work. Next, and very much more difficult, the random placing of these random shapes, and then the final stage, yet the one that offers the greatest scope for the widest range of interpretation, picture making. For this the printing blocks may be accurately fashioned or just torn-off shapes, just as the user decides. A roughly torn piece can be used at varying angles to leave a wide range of marks. The piece of clay becomes as a brush making the marks that build up the picture.

Lots of scrap paper may be needed for this type of work experimenting to find the shape they want, but in time they may be just as happy with a piece of clay as with a brush.

Other techniques are suggested here but mostly they will become obvious as the children become more familiar with the method and they will delight in discovering many others for themselves. It is perhaps worth adding that a particularly successful block may be retained indefinitely if it is allowed to harden.

Example of clay prints using numbers

Clay print of fish

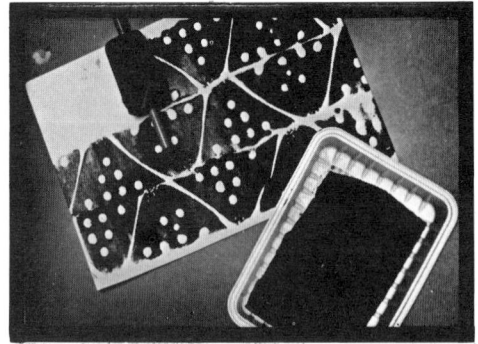

Prints taken from impressions made into a clay roller

Slab pots

Two points to be made here on technique. Both are quite basic and appear obvious, but neither is as easy as it seems.

A great deal of modelling and even more of pottery involves the use of clay slabs that require some ability in rolling out the clay using a rolling pin, pastry fashion. Ideally, this operation should be done on a thick, dry piece of cloth, but very often a piece of paper has to serve.

Here again a thick piece will be better than thin. If you attempt to roll out the clay straight on to the bench it will stick, particularly if the surface is a non-absorbent plastic. Even the rolling pin should be of wood and be dry for use. If you intend to expand the clay modelling activities of the class then three or four extra pins and a few strong pieces of canvas will prove useful.

As soon as you start to roll out clay it spreads but at the same time takes a grip of the cloth and so is able to resist further spreading. Pick it up to release it and carry on rolling. As you roll, continue to pick up the clay at regular intervals and if you doubt the necessity for all this then try it without picking up and see the difference.

By the method of construction shown here, you stand a former—a lump of wood, a brick, cardboard box—in the middle of the rolled out clay and then cut away the unwanted as indicated in the diagram. Close the sides up around the former damping the edges and pinching the joints together as you go. It would be a wise precaution to cover the former with newspaper to facilitate easy extraction and replacement. Take out the former to improve the inside of the joints and then replace it to permit some robust working on the outside. Beat it with a ruler for a start. Cut along the top to make it level or add the odd coil or two to increase the height and possibly thicken the rim.

Always extract the former for drying or you may never get it out without major surgery. The surface of slab pots cry out for decora-

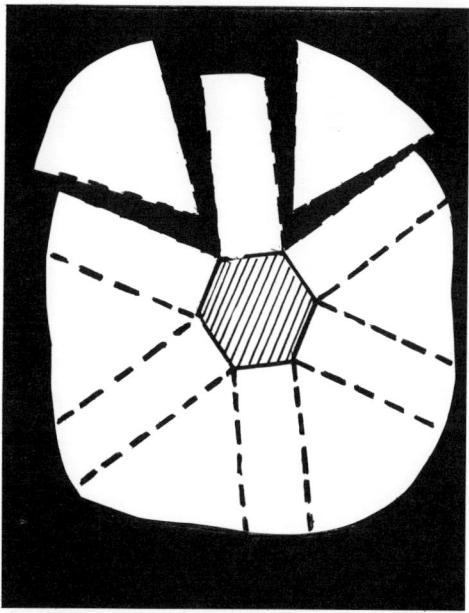

Diagram showing initial stage of construction.

tion. The fish on the side of the pot shown here is a clay print, integrating the techniques if you like. Had the pot been round, printing would still have been possible by bending the soft clay block.

The surfaces of the other two boxes shown are textured and then coloured with a trace of gold dust added to the colour, and then coated with a satin finish. Not everybody's cup of tea, but I like it.

Long boxes with lids are attractive but not quite so easily made. The box itself may not be difficult but the lid can be. Some sort of locating band has to be fitted so that the lid does not slide off the box. If the fit is too sloppy, the misplaced lid looks ugly, and worse, if it is too tight it will not close at all. All this has to be made with a clay that will shrink and a box that may distort. It might be a better idea to make the lid out of balsa. Another range of work and one that is quite detached from pot making is the construction of abstract shapes. There is no room here for a discussion on the merits of this approach, sufficient to say that there are no great problems in the making, and it seems to me that the results are often interesting and well worth while.

Abstract shapes

Examples of slab-sided pots

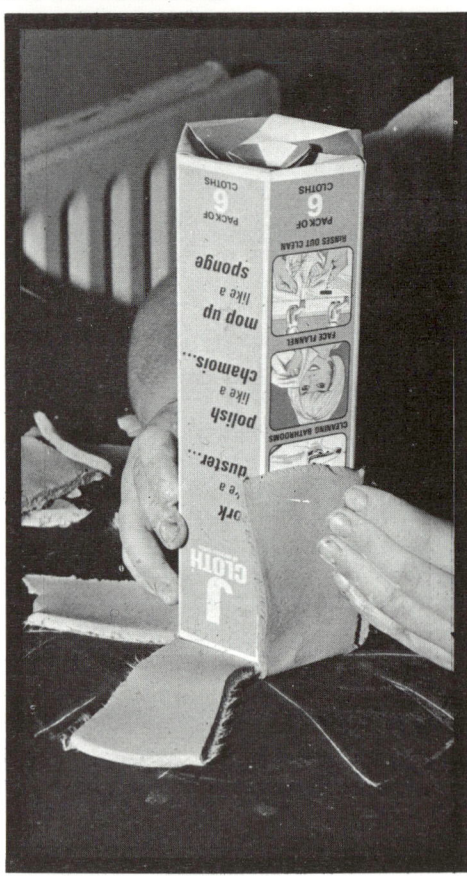

The "slabs" of clay being closed up around the sides of the former

Larger models

Models that are made from large masses of clay are not only heavy but also rather expensive in the context of the school allowance. To overcome this it is often possible to engulf large masses of paper with a thin layer of clay and thereby, and without expending too much time, produce a sturdy and relatively light ball ready to be developed into the required form.

For something the size of a grapefruit you will require one large double sheet from the daily paper. A child might need a little help in compressing this much paper, although a slight damping will make it easier and reduce the tendency to spring open. Pull the clay off a piece at a time and mould it into a thin pat about the size of the palm. This is then applied to the paper ball, one pat at a time, joining each edge to edge as you go. With all joints reasonably secure beat the ball gently with a ruler, compacting the clay and the paper within. Should a hole develop smear a piece of clay over it and carry on beating. Such a ball should float.

This will provide the basis for innumerable models such as fat pigs or contented cats, chickens or fish. Start by exploring the many possibilities without drastically altering the shape at all. The surface can be incised, textured or patterned with pellets of clay, even "taking a line for a walk" and then filling in the areas with different textures and colours.

To develop the ball into a model the extra clay would be added by the normal method

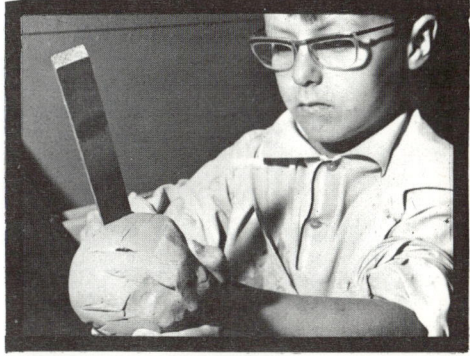

Thin pieces of clay being moulded around a paper ball

of damping and smearing in place. This is conventional modelling with the usual problems. This aspect of modelling should always be made light of in the sense that the object of the exercise is to produce a shape that is both exciting and interesting but not necessarily anatomically correct.

Using sand

Throughout the nineteenth century, the seashore provided a wealth of inspiration for the amateur naturalist and artist. From collections of dried seaweeds, to shell-covered trinket boxes; not to mention the "sand pictures" by the ladies of Alum Bay in the Isle of Wight.

An English king actually employed a certain Benjamin Zobel as Head Table Decker in sand decorations. These decorations, designed in coloured sands, adorned the dining tables of the Royal residences. Perhaps Zobel's exasperation at having his masterpieces swept away after the port and walnuts, induced him to make his creations more lasting by glueing them to board, and exhibiting them in frames, some of which can still be seen in Luton Art Gallery.

Whilst Zobel's art is now forgotten, we can still use sand as a creative medium in school. Firstly by using it as a mould material; secondly by using it as an additive to paint, glue and plaster of Paris.

Casting in Sand

The technique of casting in sand is extremely simple. We need a bed of sand, at least one to two inches deep, into which marks are made by scoring or pressing in, with all manner of objects, tools, etc. The completed design is covered with liquid plaster of Paris, and allowed to set. Within ten minutes or so, the hardened plaster can be pulled away, giving us the finished cast. Large, or intricate casts should be left longer, up to twenty-four hours before removing.

The Sand

Any kind of sand will do; ordinary builders' sand is ideal. Damp sand will hold its shape better; and a drop of disinfectant is advisable.

The Plaster

Preferably, superfine dental plaster which is pure white and dries quickly. Builders' plaster which is coarse in texture, takes longer to dry.

The Mould

A cardboard box with a layer of sand is quite satisfactory. Large casts, which will require a deep layer of sand can be made in deep trays, or taken direct from any bed of sand; a sand-pit is ideal. A stiff cardboard surround will keep the plaster in place.

The Cast

Casts over one foot square should be strengthened by incorporating wire-netting or scrim in the wet plaster; casts which are to be hung on a wall should have a wire hook embedded in the plaster before it sets. The completed cast, naturally enough, will show the graininess of the sand from which it is taken, wherein lies much of its charm. Other interesting effects can be obtained by adding powder paint to the plaster before casting, or by treating the finished cast with paint, varnishes, polish, shoe polish, for instance, wood stains, and bronzing powders.

Sand as an Additive

A variety of textural and bas-relief effects can be obtained by the addition of sand to paint or adhesive, or both. In essence, we are painting with a sand/paint mixture, but

The addition of sand to plaster of Paris produces a rich, grainy texture

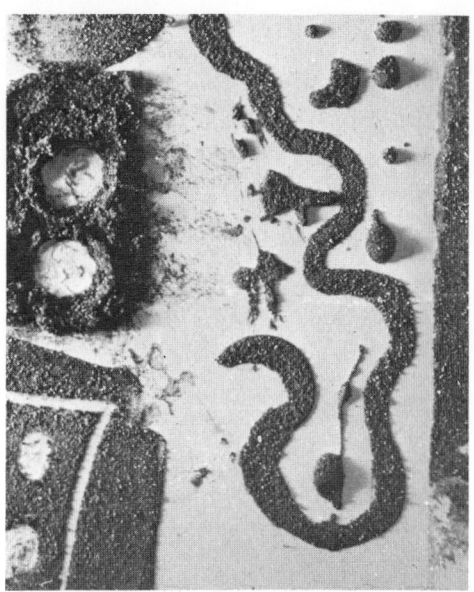

Painting with sand, using a mixture of powder paint, sand and PVA medium

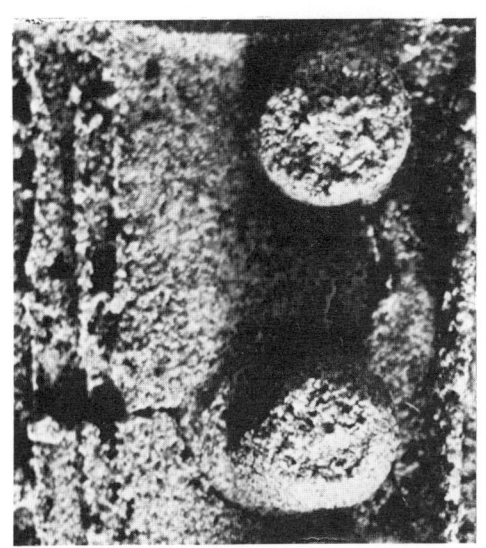

Detail from a large sand-cast mural

since the mixture is fairly heavy, we need a strong support to paint on. A thick cartridge paper will do, but card or hardboard is best and a palette knife to apply it.

If tempera or powder paint is used, an adhesive should also be added to bind the sand together, any P.V.A. adhesive can be used. If polymer or oil paints are being added use a sand and adhesive medium, which, if required, can be painted with ordinary paint after drying.

Other effects can be obtained by "painting" directly with glue, and sanding the design before it dries.

Finally, sand can be used as an additive to plaster of Paris, when casting blocks for carving. Not only do we make the plaster "go further", but we achieve a carving medium which is easier to carve than ordinary plaster on its own and which is richer in surface texture.

Print making

How a print is made

Thinking ink

Printmaking

Making prints is one of the most exciting combinations of an art and a craft, and while it is exacting, demanding accuracy and precision, it is also extremely easy once we understand the few basic principles of printmaking.

We are dealing with hand methods of printmaking so we need only concern ourselves with one such principle, and this is that everything we print will appear in the reverse image of the original, so we must, whenever necessary, make allowances for this. If we take a print from a leaf there is no problem because a leaf looks like a leaf whether in reverse or not. When we are printing from a block which includes lettering, however, we will have to make sure that the letters are cut in reverse first, so that they print the right way round. The same must apply to anything which we do not want to print in reverse.

These hand methods of printing using basic, and often very unconventional materials, will provide hours of enjoyment. It does not matter what the source of the printed image was originally intended for, or whether it is a man-made material or a natural form. There are only a few things which will not make a print, in fact, almost anything prints.

What do we need

We can make simple prints with only a few basic pieces of equipment, but of course the wider the range of the equipment then the more varied the type of prints we can make.

The following will be found most useful.

Inking slab. This has to take quite a bit of pressure so if glass is to be used it must not be too thin and, in addition, it should be well padded underneath with a piece of felt or a wad of newspaper. Alternatively, the slab can be a sheet of perspex, metal, marble or even formica, as long as the surface is smooth and free from scratches.

Rollers. These are generally made of hard rubber and come in a variety of widths, the handiest sizes being two inch, four inch and six inch. Those soft foam rubber rollers used for decorating the house are also extremely useful for inking, being pliable enough to sink into the relief of the block and give a clearer image of the block.

Inks. I think that oil-based inks are better because, being tackier, they have a finer 'pick-up' quality, but a good water-based ink can be obtained in very economically priced tubes and with a good range of colours.

Paper. Any paper can be used to take a print and usually the thinner it is the better. If a thick cartridge paper is to be used it should be lightly dampened first with a moist sponge to soften the hard surface, allowing it to pick up a complete image from the block.

Palette knife. Used for spreading the ink on the slab and, later, for scraping it off after printing is finished.

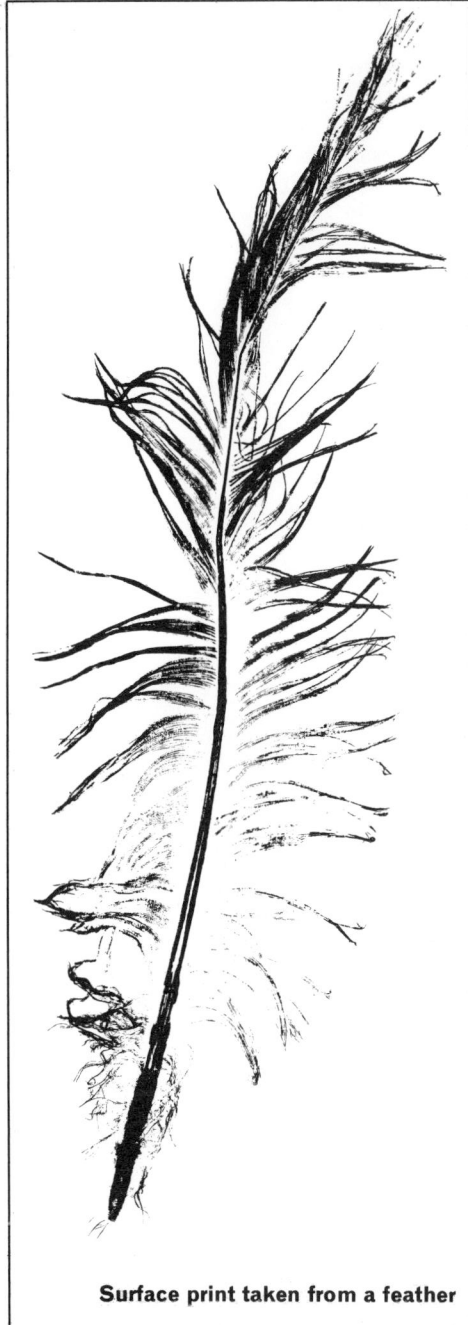

Surface print taken from a feather

Cutters. Knives, lino cutters, hacksaw blades, nails, screws, hammers and anything of this nature which can be used to cut or make impressions in the surface of the block. The shaped handles of lino cutters provide a better grip for small hands so they are the most suitable.

Adhesive. A strong quick-setting adhesive is necessary for sticking bits of collage to the surface of the block. It must, of course, withstand cleaning with water or turpentine.

Rags. These soon get clotted up and so a good supply is necessary. Newspaper is also used up at the same rate so it is also needed in good supply.

Turpentine. This must be used with oil-based inks, both as a thinner and for cleaning up. It can also be used to make patterns in the inked slab which can then be lifted in the form of monoprints.

Drying line. Prints have to dry where they will not stick together and where nothing will be inadvertently placed on top of them. A drying line is the best way of doing it and a length of thin rope or cord will do the job nicely. Stretch it across the printing area from wall to wall just above head height. A few dozen clothes pegs or paper clips should be enough to hold up the prints from one printing session until they are dry.

Bearing in mind that too many cooks spoil the broth it is not advisable to have too many children working in the printing area at any one time, but, at the same time, the printing area has to be big enough to accommodate about three people without them impeding one another.

Methods of printing
There are many methods of printing and just as many implements for applying the neces-

sary amount of pressure and, be it ever so humble, the human hand is as good as many of them and it should be tried first.

The spoon. Either a large dessert spoon or, better still, a wooden salad spoon which can be lightly oiled on the back so that it does not stick and catch the back of the print paper. When using this method, having inked the block and placed the print paper on top, hold it firmly with one hand so that it cannot slip and smudge, then rub with the spoon working outwards from the centre towards each edge. Lift one of the corners to see if the print is ready before moving your hand and then, only when you are satisfied, lift the paper clear of the block. When you hang the print up to dry make sure it does not touch the next print because they are liable to stick together as the ink dries.

The roller. This is very similar to the spoon method. The block is inked and the print paper placed in position on top. Again one hand is needed to keep the paper steady enough to avoid making a smudgy double imaged print. The roller is then used to apply pressure to the paper working away from the centre. Make certain that the paper is perfectly flat and level on the block or it might get creased by the roller.

The book press. A pile of books, provided they are heavy enough and you have unlimited time, can be used to make a print but a book press is better. Simply ink the block and place it in the press, add the print paper and a cover sheet to keep the back of the print and the press clean. Make sure that the press is level over the block before closing it and then apply the pressure to make the print.

Finally if you have an old washing wringer which has adjustable rollers this can easily be adapted to provide an excellent printing press. It must have rubber rollers, wooden ones are too hard and might crack a lino block, and because we are able to adjust the space between the rollers we can use any thickness of block within reason. The only extra piece of equipment we need to make the transformation complete is a sheet of rigid metal to carry the block and printpaper through the rollers without bending them. Inks and rags, which are inclined to become messy can be stored in the drum of the wringing machine out of harm's way.

Surface printing

With the realisation that almost anything will print, we can delay cutting into the print block for the moment and consider other, simpler sources of making a print. Direct surface printing is great fun and the search for the right object to print from can be almost as exciting as making the print. A collection of fallen leaves can make an interesting introduction. As soon as they are collected the leaves should be stored flat in an airtight container and for this a plastic bag is ideal. Leaves soon dry out and become too brittle to be of any use for printing. They must be dry but still pliable enough to withstand the pressure of the roller without flaking and falling apart I do emphasise that they must be dry, as must any surface we may print from, so that a water based ink can adhere itself sufficiently to the surface all over and pick up a full image. Any areas of moisture will dilute the ink and cause smudgy blotches on the finished print. A sheet of blotting paper pressed over the leaves just before they are to be inked will ensure that they are suitable for printing.

Chestnut, sycamore, fern leaves and others which are large enough can be inked and printed as monoprints having enough textural interest of their own, or they can be printed in a light colour as a background for smaller leaves, and other small objects, to be printed over in a darker colour.

Surface prints taken from natural materials

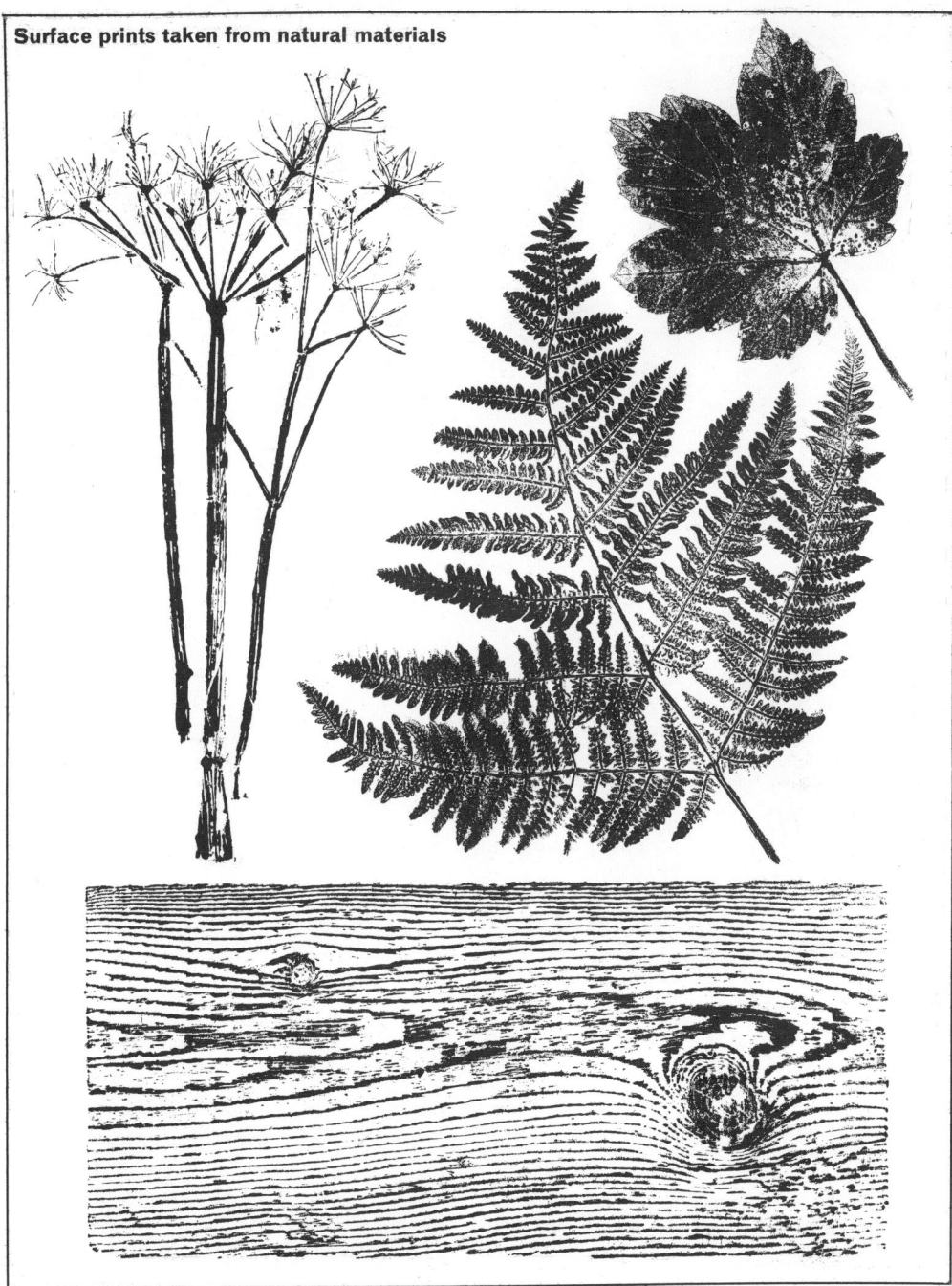

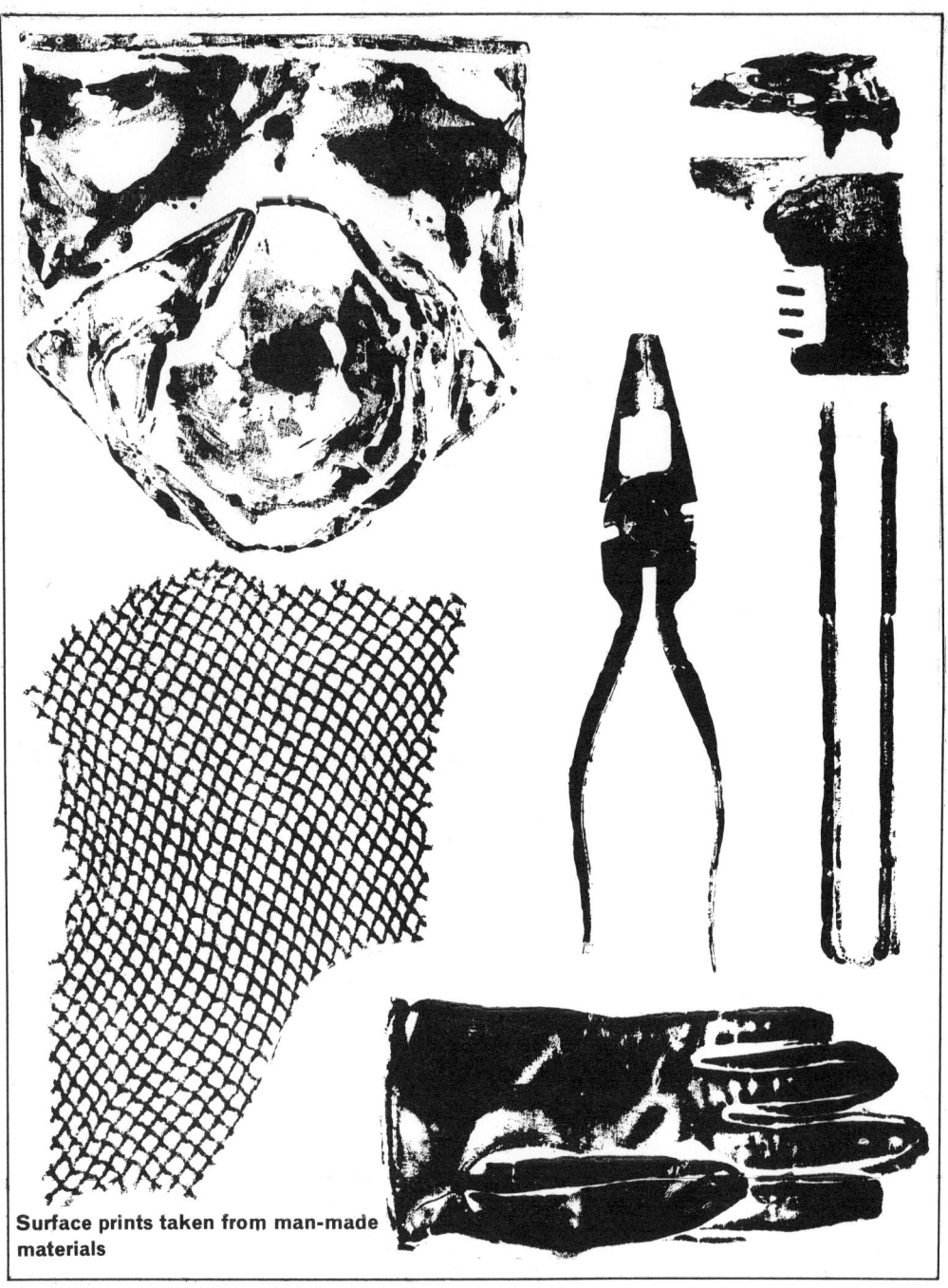

Surface prints taken from man-made
materials

A selection of leaves, large and small, glued to a sheet of stiff card so that they overlap each other will make an interesting pattern and if a rapid setting adhesive is used they will not dry up before you are ready to print. While dealing with natural materials that are to be found outside we can include tree barks, twig formations and the various, very pleasant, textured surfaces of wood grain. This type of object will give a good image if it is clean and dry. Before rolling up the wood, first rub it over gently with a piece of fine grade sandpaper so that any loose particles which might get mixed into the ink are removed. Try always to roll along the grain and not across it as the ink tends to drag on the raised edges and leave a blurred image. For this type of printing even pressure is required and a hand roller is best.

Still dealing with natural materials we should include those to be found indoors. Some vegetables like cabbage and lettuce can be peeled and printed in the same way as the leaves, or sliced into sections, dipped in the ink, and printed direct on to the paper with the pressure of one's hand. Others, such as potatoes and carrots, can be cut into pictorial or abstract shapes and used as miniature printing blocks. This is probably one of the oldest methods of printing in schools and, because of this, it might be disregarded as too old-fashioned, but really it is quite surprising what can be achieved with such a humble piece of equipment.

Man-made materials also provide a good source for direct surface printing. Netting and various types of cloth give good textural prints and, for greater interest, a piece of cloth can be folded into imaginative shapes before being rolled up and printed. A search around the school or home will reveal hundreds of suitable objects once you have developed your eye for looking at surfaces. Tools from the garage, pieces of wire, old cans which have been hammered flat, off-cuts from the metalwork room, sandpaper, kitchen foil, plastic bags, doll's clothes, try any of these then look for others, as long as they are clean and dry.

Of all the man-made materials, paper is the most versatile, and it should not be overlooked. Shapes cut from magazines, particularly action shapes; figures, animals, cars, etc, can be cut out, inked and pressed directly on to the print sheet to give coloured silhouettes. Using different shapes, or even the one shape printed a number of times and in different colours, very effective action prints can be made. What they lack in texture they can make up for in colour and movement.

Relief printing

We come now to what I consider to be one of the most interesting parts of printmaking. This is building up the surface of the print block to make relief prints. The method itself is quite basic.

First arrange a number of selected objects on the block, which can be a sheet of stiff cardboard or a smooth piece of wood, and glue them firmly. This will form the image and the main interest stems from what we use and how we arrange it on the block.

One advantage this method has for beginners is that small children can handle a pair of scissors easier and much safer than a sharp knife or lino cutter.

Let us begin with paper which is, as I have already said, the most versatile of materials. We can first draw a picture, a house, a group of figures, a ship, or, if the child is reluctant to draw but eager to make a print, we can cut a picture page from a magazine and glue it flat to a piece of card. Certain parts of the picture, perhaps those nearest the viewer or those which are most interesting, can be built up by gluing layers of cartridge paper over them. This will, when printed, give a definite edge to each particular part making

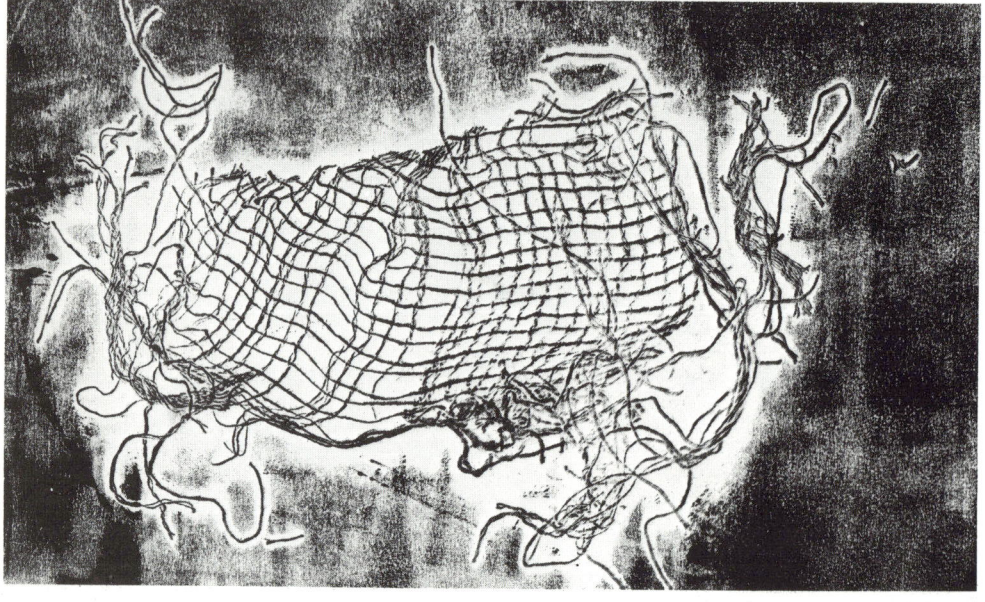

Above. Printing a paper shape several times   Below. Surface print from a piece of net

120

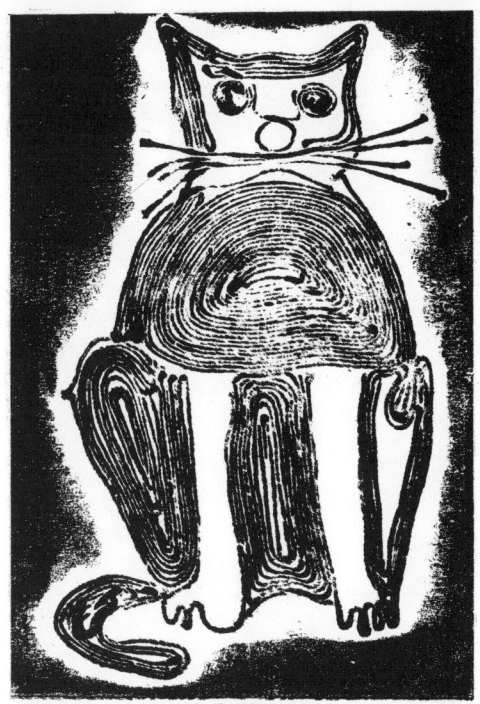

A string print in the shape of a cat

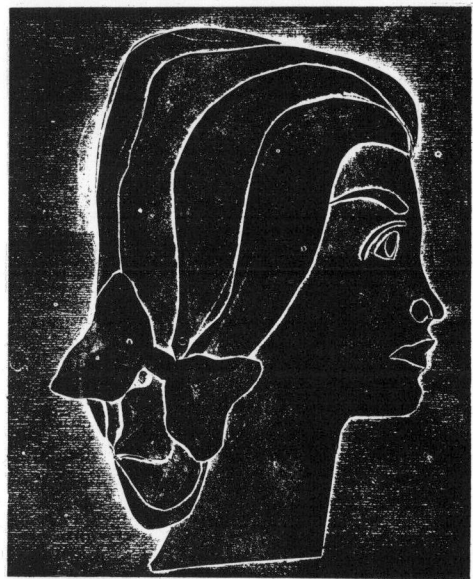

Design built up with several pieces of card

it stand proud of the rest and giving an impression of depth. If the block is rolled up in one colour and printed on a complimentary background, the result is most effective. There are a number of variations possible using paper to build up the printing surface. Interesting linear patterns can be created from gummed paper tape, which naturally suggests that there are possibilities also with sticky tape.

Extended paper patterns which may have resulted from previous art lessons will provide interesting ready-made printing blocks for two-colour prints. A set of letters, either those from a child's name or simply taken from a magazine, can be arranged (in reverse) into very effective patterns if they are overlapped and interwoven and then glued to a block. The method can be developed using card which, being thicker, gives a higher relief image. It can also be scored to obtain a certain amount of texture. Other materials will give added and equally interesting variations, such as string which can be glued into patterns on the block. Collage materials such as hessian and other fabrics can be included for their texture value.

Having seen what we can do when we build up the printing surface, now let us consider what will result when we cut away from the block. Plasticine and modelling clay, provided it is in a good, pliable, but not too sticky condition, will give us a good introduction. If the clay is rolled flat it can be cut into shapes, scored to form patterns or impressed with everyday objects. As a block making material it is ideal because when printing has finished it can be wiped clean and reformed to make a new block.

Balsa wood has a similar appeal because, being soft, it can be easily scored and punched with different objects and in addition it produces a soft grainy background. Hardboard too should be considered. It can be gouged, scored, cut and stamped and indeed it is cheap enough to use for practice.

Linoleum is the traditional material and it really is lovely stuff to work with. It does not have to be the best lino as long as it is not too thin and brittle, in fact, the thicker it is the better for then we can cut deep without digging into the hessian backing cloth. If the lino is too stiff and hard it can be softened by placing it on a warm radiator a few minutes.

A rule which must be observed at all times during cutting is that the hand which holds the lino block must always rest well behind the cutting blade. This is easily overlooked so it is worth overstressing. Possibly the best introduction to lino printing is the cutaway method. We begin by cutting away those parts of the lino block which are to remain white, and then we roll up the block in the first colour and print about half a dozen sheets. This gives us a colour print with a white motif. We cut away more of the block where we want the first colour to show and we print the same sheets again in a second colour.

This process goes on until we have a multi-colour print from the one block, which by the end of the exercise, will have very little lino left on it.

The simplest method of registration will do for this type of printmaking, we can carefully rest the lino block on top of the print using the corners to ensure that it registers accurately. The block can then be pressed from the back, or the two can be turned over, making sure that they do not slip, and the print can be pressed with a roller.

Finally, always remember to hang your prints up to dry as soon as you have examined them and satisfied yourself that it is a good print.

A simple, one colour lino print

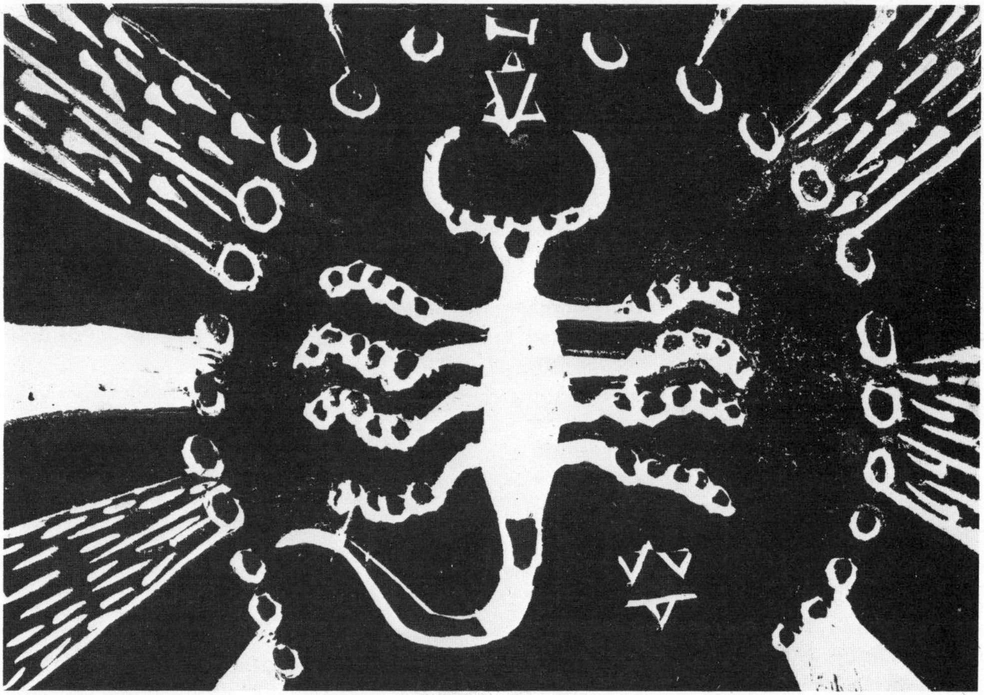

Above: A more complex, three colour print

Below: A surface print of a string vest combined with a lino printed fish

How a print is made

Today, printmaking ranks with painting, sculpture and drawing as one of the principal means by which artists express themselves. The word "print", however, is vague and to most people it means thousands of copies of a particular subject. The fact that a "print" can be both a multiple and an original (i.e. singular) work of art, seems to upset the dictionary definition. Basically there are two kinds of prints. Firstly, there are reproductions, and secondly original prints which are also referred to as graphics.

Let us first deal with reproductions, as most homes have at least one and they are mass produced and sell in their millions. While a reproduction might quite accurately portray an image, the artist has in no way contributed to the process of making the print: that is, he has not designed the plates. Thus while the image may be pretty it has no value beyond its purchase price.

On the other hand, original prints are of much greater interest and the last five years have seen a tremendous boom in the sale of graphics. Collecting can be great fun as occasionally one might purchase a cheap etching and find that the artist has in a period of a few years become quite famous, which means the print is sometimes worth 1000% more than the purchase price. This side of collecting, although quite important is not what we are going to deal with in this article. What is more important is how prints are made.

Today, etching, lithography and screen-printing form the main bulk of original prints available. Lino-cuts and wood-cuts, though a few years ago very popular, seem not to be so today.

Firstly, let me explain a few of the terms used

Etching by Brian Elliott

in connection with graphics. The first one is "Edition": this means the total number of prints made from one design. The size of the edition is usually 75 with always approximately five prints traditionally going to the artist, the publisher or gallery. Sometimes these Artist's Proofs fetch more than the list prices, though this is only of interest to collectors. The number of the print and the length of the edition are pencilled in the left-hand corner, e.g. 40/75. This has nothing to do with the quality or value. Editions are published by the artist or under the artist's supervision but with financial backing by museums, art dealers, printing firms or societies. Often a publisher's imprint will appear on the side of the print.

Many prints are actually taken by professional printers. This has no importance in itself. The main criterion that determines originality is the degree to which the artist has created the design for the print or done the actual work on the plate himself. The task of printing is a hard one. Each print must be done separately and if the artist does his own printing—which most contemporary artists do—he usually uses a hand press. Naturally, if each colour on a

"Portuguese Men of War". Aquatint by B. dos Santos

print has to be printed separately and each print carefully inked, the task is a long and time consuming one.

Signing a print is a relatively modern custom (as is numbering) and has nothing to do with the originality of the print. It does establish that the artist claims that print for his own work. Many prints are signed "in the plate", which is not the same thing.

Lithography is the most common printing method used, and has the most in common with drawing. The artist selects greasy crayon or greasy printers' ink and draws the design wanted directly on a zinc or stone plate. The stone is moistened with water which is unable to cover the greasy design, and greasy ink is rolled over the plate. The ink adheres only to the drawn area because of the natural antipathy of water and oil. Paper pressed on to stone will pick up only the image of that part of it which is inked. Each colour must be put on the stone in turn to be printed separately. This technique was discovered in about 1800, accidentally, by a German named Alois Senefelder when he tried to write out his laundry list with a piece of greasy chalk. The advantages of lithographic printing are simplicity and boldness of design, a good range of colour and tone separation, and a wide variety of subject matter.

Etchings belong to what is called the intaglio process, in which the image is incised on to a copper plate. Instead of cutting directly on to the plate, the artist covers the plate with acid resistant ground and then draws on the plate with special sharp tools to remove the ground where the design is to be. The plate is then immersed in an acid bath, which bites into the plate where the protective covering has been removed. By leaving different areas exposed to the acid for varying lengths of time, the quality of the line bitten can be controlled. The finished plate is then printed as an engraved plate would be.

Screenprint by Dereck Greaves

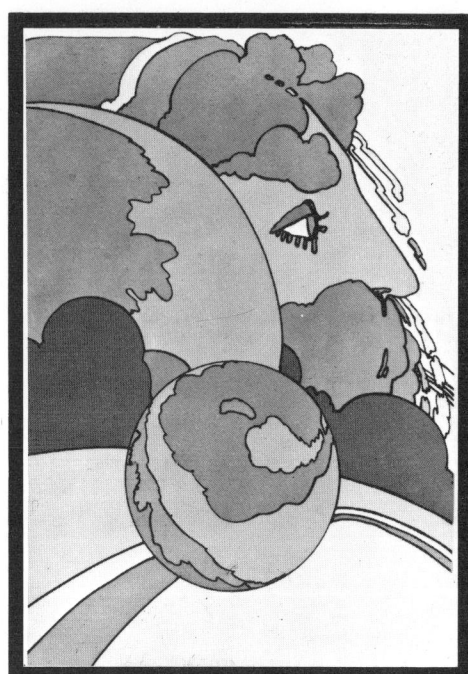

Detail of lithograph by Peter Max

Aquatints go one step further. Whole areas rather than lines are exposed to the acid. The plate is treated with granulated resin and then immersed so that the acid can bite at uncovered areas. Aquatinting is an

126

Colour etching by Norman Ackroyd

associate technique of engraving and etching. Imagery is of tone rather than line, and there is great variation between white and black. In engraving, lines are incised direct on the plate without the use of acid; it is the oldest and most simple of the intaglio processes.

Screenprinting involves the use of stencils supported on a fine mesh stretched over a frame. Each ink colour is squeezed on to the printing surface, other colour areas having being masked off. Screenprints can be both inventive and colourful, and it is therefore an ideal graphic medium for painters.

Although quite rare with contemporary artists, the woodcut first involved the use of a plank, cut parallel to the tree-trunk on which the artist drew a design, and then cut away the part of the wood not covered by the design. Linoleum is often used today to give a similar result, though its soft, crumbly texture does not allow for fine lines.

The cost of a limited print depends on the status of the artist and the length of the edition. The size and complexity is not always a deciding factor, nor is work by established names necessarily as expensive as you might assume. Don't have too many preconceptions when you set out to buy prints; you could be pleasantly surprised.

Thinking ink

Equipment used for colour printing
Rolling-up slabs are used for rolling up the printing ink so as to distribute it evenly over the surface of the roller and subsequently over the surface of the lino block. Plate glass placed over a sheet of white paper (in order to judge colour values correctly), is very suitable. However, any hard, non-porous material may be used such as plastic laminate.

Rollers are made in different sizes and vary in quality and construction. The smallest and cheapest are made of a wooden core covered over with rubber and mounted in a simple metal frame. Gelatine and plastic covered rollers are more expensive to buy. They are softer and more sensitive than the rubber version. Rubber or plastic rollers are suitable for both oil and water-based inks. Gelatine rollers are only suitable for oil-based inks; when cleaning, a soft rag and white spirit should be used, *never* hot water. The rubber rollers will take pretty rough handling, the others, although a better investment for good quality printmaking, need to be treated with greater care.

Palette knives are used for mixing and spreading the ink on the slab. A useful size is six inches or thereabouts. Old kitchen knives will do, although they lack the flexibility of the proper tool. More than one will save a lot of time when preparing several colour slabs at one session. Emphasise the necessity for a clean knife entering a tin of colour.

'Cathedral' by first year boy

Inks. The oil-based variety vary in degrees of transparency. They can be combined with painters' oils. They come in tubes or in tins, if bought in larger quantities. Colour is kept best in the tubes but is more economical in the tins; the same applies to the water-based. They do not mix with oil but can be used as an under-printing. The clearing up of water-based ink is simpler for the less able child or the very young. The disadvantage is that it evaporates very quickly and the slab will need cleaning and replenishing frequently even though it appears to be still well-charged. The advantage is that the prints dry quickly and a fairly rapid succession of printing can be achieved. This advantage applies more to the multi-block rather than the single-block procedure. White spirit (Turps substitute) is used for thinning oil colours and can be obtained from a hardware store.

The single-block method of printing is an excellent way of extending ones knowledge of the effects of printing and of over-printing one colour upon another.

Only too often lino-cutting is presented as a one-colour job. If the reason for this is one of economics and the lino is in short supply the single-block method will give a much richer result (providing of course that a choice of inks, water-based or oil-based, is available) without making inroads on the art-room stocks.

The single-block method entails the use of one piece of lino which is progressively cut away to create a series of colour blocks. The block is gradually cut away between the printing stages until only very small areas remain for printing the final colour.

Preparatory Work

At first it is advisable to plan the design with two or three colours, although it is possible to use a quantity. Practise with a few until some experience has been gained provides a grounding for more ambitious schemes.

Head in yellow, light and dark greens by fifth year pupil

An inked up lino block on registration board

Positioning the paper on the block

The use of the class's own topic or sketch books for design ideas is good but for those who have nothing suitable, geometric and abstract forms will do. Bearing in mind the size of lino available (as large as economics will allow), select the colour areas and reproduce these in water-colours. inks or tissue paper collage, in other words, transparent media which will, while building up the design, achieve something of the effect of the overprinting to come. You will need to take into account the fact that with the exception of the first colour all subsequent colours will be the effect of overprinting and not be 'pure'.

Transfer of Design

The tracing now should show the actual area of lino to be cut and the areas of selected colour. To transfer the design on to the lino, trace down the areas by using carbon paper (second-hand from the office will do), and a hardish pencil H or 2H; alternatively rub into

Three colour print by 1st year pupil

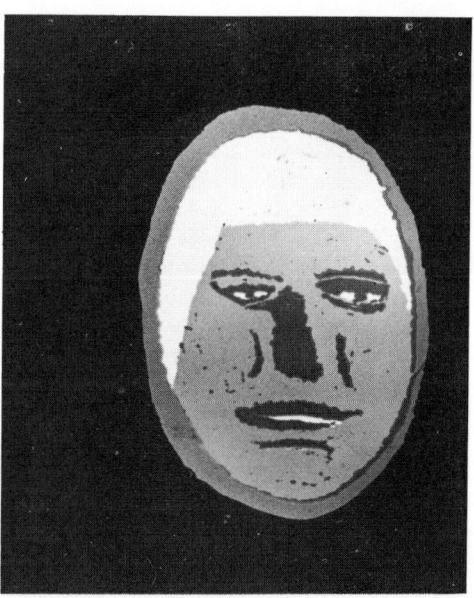

Four colour print by 6th year pupil

Racing car print by 5th year pupil

will be best as a starter. If you are using three colours, ink up the stage one block successively in the three colours, keeping these proofs and doing the same at each stage thereby giving a good variety of prints and demonstrating the effects of overprinting. Mark on each proof the order of colour so that these can provide you with information later on when you wish to achieve certain effects. Experiment too with opaque and transparent inks. Oil-based inks can be made even more translucent with a reducing 'thinner' medium.

The next stage requires a form of registration (unlike the one-print lino-cut design) and it is

the back of the tracing some blackboard chalk, flicking the front of the paper to remove excess dust. A light colour is best if you are using plain brown lino, but if you are using old bits of flooring and there is a strong pattern on it, it is better to use white paint, first mixing in a little detergent to counteract the layers of wax polish which will be rendering the surface greasy.

If the print is not to include any white areas at all the first 'cut' will be to trim the piece to the exact size. Any 'white' areas will be cut away from this (so-called 'white' because you may be using tinted paper). However, it may be that you require a flat first colour, un-cut. This colour will act as a ground for all successive colours, therefore experiment is advised at this stage in the choice and weight of colour tint. The usual rule of working from light through medium to dark does not necessarily apply here as it can be very effective to print light on dark. Until there has been considerable practice and experiment it is not easy to anticipate results. Happy accidents do occur but greater control will come eventually.

The choice of subject matter will influence the colour scheme but ink up your block in a variety of colours not just the one you think

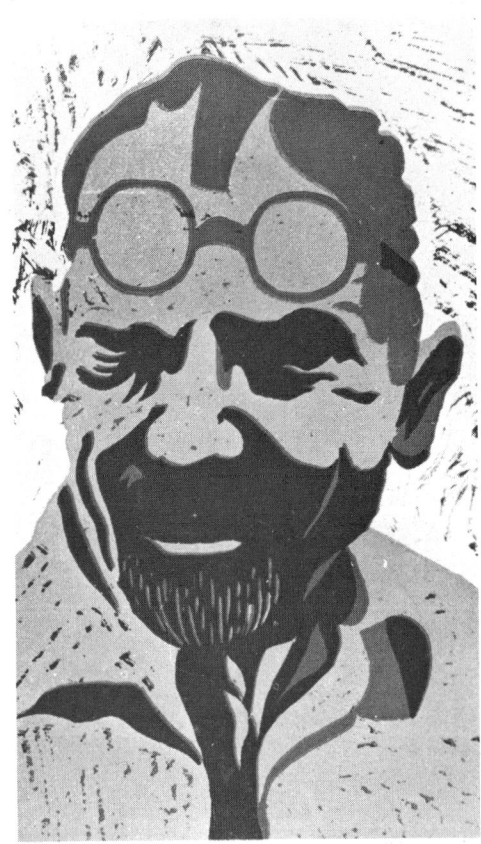

'Man with glasses'. Print in yellow, red and orange (6th year pupil)

vital to get this working efficiently.

A registration board can be made quite simply. The size should be in excess of the linocut. Then two strips of wood, the same thickness as the lino being used, should be fixed along two edges of the board at a right-angle forming an 'L' shape. These strips should be approximately 1 in. wide.

To make sure that you always feed the linocut into the registration frame the same way, make an identification mark on one corner of the reverse side. The paper can be fed into the angle of the L, making sure that it is fed in the correct way each printing. This must be kept unaltered throughout all the printing process. This rule applies to all methods of printing from the proofing press to the back of a spoon.

If a pinch press is used or a book-binder's press, it is important to ensure that every raised part of the block receives equal pressure. It is necessary to use packing (newsprint or rubber blanket) layered on top of the block when the block is positioned on the registration board.

To test if the ink has been correctly rolled and that the pressure is sufficient to lift the ink off on to the paper, peel back a single corner. Trial and error will soon make perfect both inking and printing.

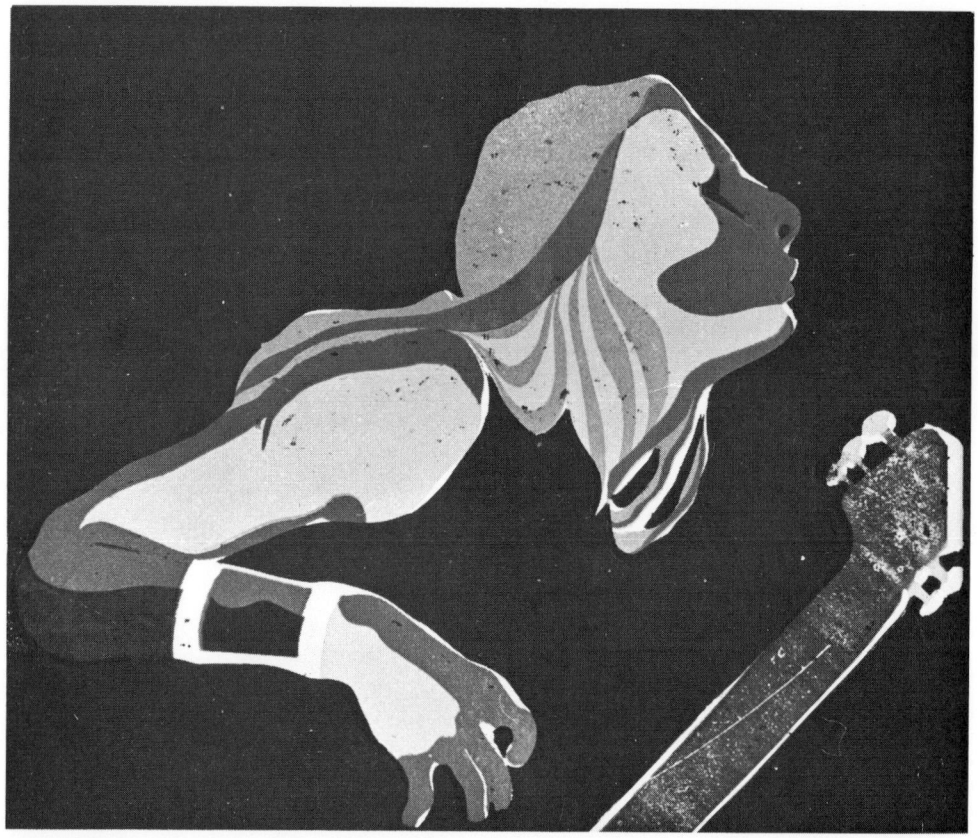

'Guitar Player' in six colours (6th year pupil)

Model-making with cardboard

Model-making with cardboard

Cardboard is simply thick paper. Some cardboard in fact, is very thick indeed—thick enough to be used in the building of real houses. The thinner sorts, however, can easily be cut and folded very much like paper. You can do the same sort of things with it as you might do with strong paper.

But model-making is not quite the same as paper folding or 'origami'. The origami expert learns to make all sorts of fascinating designs *just* by folding a single sheet of paper. The model-maker, on the other hand, normally uses several pieces of card and cuts them and sticks them together in different ways.

Nor is model-making quite the same as paper 'sculpture', though it has much in common with it. The sculptor in paper certainly cuts his material and sticks the pieces together, but he usually tries to keep his work very clean and fresh and simple, so that his designs show off the crispness and beauty of the paper itself. Good paper sculpture is not particularly easy, which is perhaps why we do not seem to see so much of it about these days.

Cardboard models can be very easy, provided you do not try to make them too complicated at first. There is no reason why you should not cut the material into almost any flat shape you like, or stick as many pieces together as you please. You can even use ready-made components like matchboxes, and if the model gets a little grimy whilst in the process of being built, it can always be painted or covered with paper.

The final result might not look like cardboard at all, it might resemble stone or brick or timber. Simple models, made of thin card, though they may not be very permanent, can be very effective. They can be made to look much more solid than they are, though they need to be handled carefully. They are also very good practice and can be built quickly. Thicker cardboard, which would need to be cut with a knife rather than scissors, can be used for more robust structures which will last indefinitely. They can be coated with emulsion paint or varnish. Generally speaking, for small models, cardboard is a *stronger* material than wood. For this reason it is much used by professional architectural model-makers for miniature housing projects and town planning schemes.

Different sorts of cardboard
The thinnest card (like the sort that postcards are made of) is usually called pasteboard or manilla. It is extremely useful stuff and can be obtained in large sheets (usually 63cm × 50cm) in various colours. The 4-sheet thickness is about right for easy cutting with scissors, and can be made into quite rigid small-scale models. It also folds easily.

A stiffer material is often referred to as pulpboard or greyboard or mounting board. There is also a very useful material, used for commercial packaging, known as bending board. Pulpboards of all sorts (sometimes coloured) come in various thicknesses. Some can still be cut with scissors, but most require a knife. This cardboard is fairly soft and it forms the basis of most permanent models. It cannot be cleanly folded unless first scored with a knife.

Another stout board is strawboard. Normally used for book covers, it is harder and more rigid than pulpboard. Although it is usually a mistake to try folding or detailed cutting, panels of this material can nevertheless be used to give strength to a model, especially simple wall shapes which can be joined edge to edge or with sticky tape.

An even stronger board is millboard. It is so tough you may need a small saw to cut it. Its main use is as a base board.

Cartons and packing cases are a good source of supply for corrugated cardboard—an important model-making material which it is almost impossible to buy in small

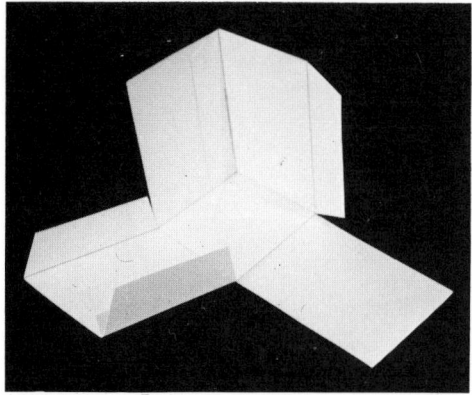

A simple rectangular box constructed from one piece of card

A parapet added, cut from thick corrugated card. The turret is a six-sided box with roof added

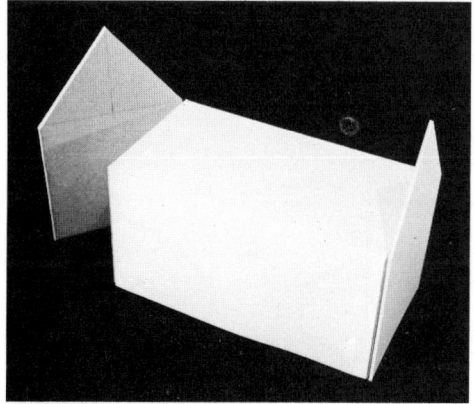

One way of making a simple house. The main box is made from thin card and the two end walls are cut from thick card

Stick the walls to the box and add a roof made from a single piece of corrugated cardboard, folded in half

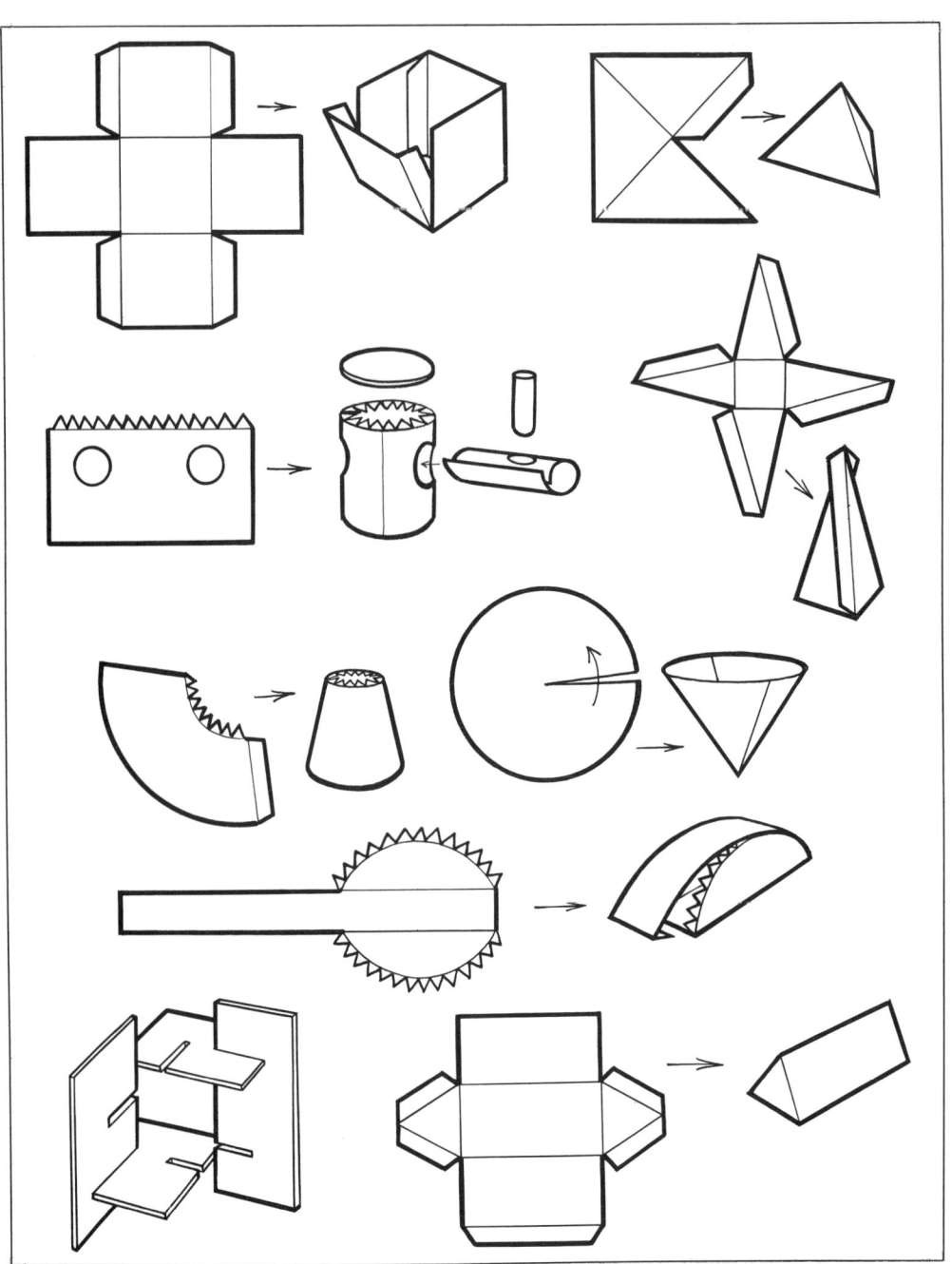

Some basic geometrical shapes

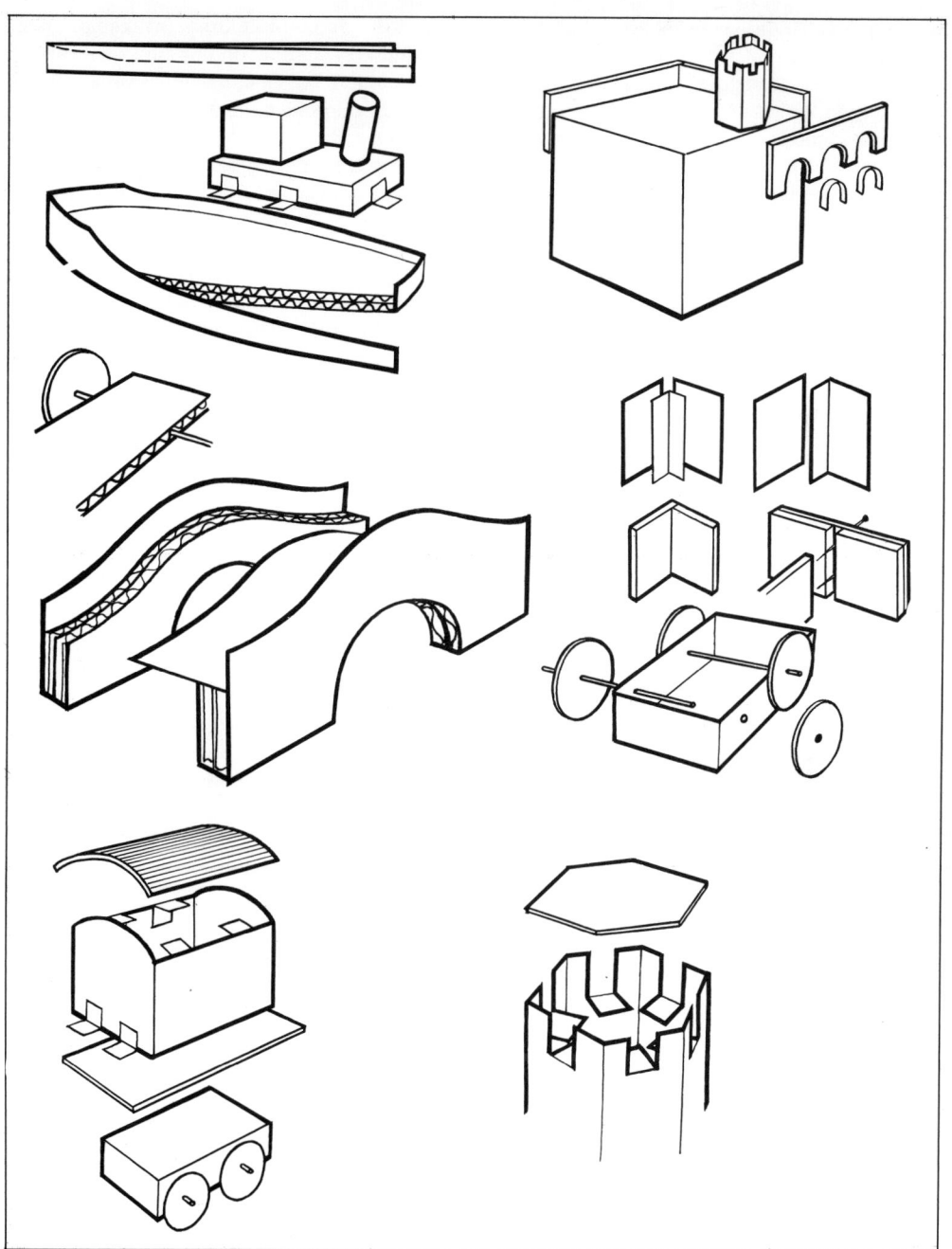

Simple models involving basic techniques

quantities. Corrugated cardboard is light and strong. It is not difficult to cut, although the edges tend to be ragged unless cut with a knife. When the model-maker wants to build up a considerable thickness, he can often do this best by sticking slabs together in the form of a corrugated cardboard sandwich. The corrugations or ridges in the material mean that it will only fold comfortably in one direction, but they give the cardboard great rigidity. The corrugations offer other advantages, because wires or sticks can easily be pushed through them for axles and fence posts and so on.

There are very many ready-made components which the model-maker will find useful. Apart from all sorts of cartons, postal tubes are also worth collecting, and the centres from rolls of sticky tape, drinking 'straws', pill boxes, cream tubs, cardboard plates, etc.

Other materials

In addition to the cardboard itself, some paper will be useful. You will probably need some stiff cartridge paper for building small details, and some tissue paper if you should decide to paste a final surface covering over the finished model. (If you do this, be careful to make the walls of stout material, because thin card will warp when the tissue shrinks on drying.) You can also buy paper ready-printed to resemble brick or stonework. Wallpaper samples are sometimes useful in this respect.

Crayons can be used for colouring. For painting, it is quite a good plan to have a small tin of ordinary household emulsion paint in some pale neutral colour and several jars of poster colour to mix with it. A clear spirit varnish or paper varnish can be used, but Copal varnish tends to turn unpainted cardboard brown.

Adhesives

A tube of strong, quick-setting glue is normally all that is required. There are various different makes available. Also available in larger economy packs are various kinds of P.V.A. adhesive which are very good general-purpose adhesives. For sticking very heavy cardboard an impact adhesive may be advisable. Modern glues are usually supplied in some convenient container with a spreader attachment. Otherwise a scrap of cardboard will serve to apply the glue.

For sticking paper over larger areas use a cellulose paste (used for wall papering) and spread it with a fairly stiff brush which can easily be rinsed in water afterwards.

Gumstrip paper and sticky tape are also useful for sticking models together.

Tools

The following list of implements is broadly in order of importance, the most essential first:

Scissors (preferably pointed, about 12cm long); pencil (2H) and sharpener; ruler; knife (preferably with replaceable blades); a metal straight-edge (e.g. a bevelled-edge safety steel ruler); a few basic drawing instruments such as a pair of compasses, a set-square, and a protractor; a cutting board (an offcut of hardboard would serve); a pair of card-cutting shears; a card-cutter or guillotine (an expensive item, but well worthwhile if preparing cardboard pieces in quantity for school use); paint brushes (one fine and pointed—No. 4 and one larger and flat—No. 12); paste brush; varnish brush (also some solvent, for cleaning).

Making the models

Cardboard model-making may be roughly divided into four basic operations:

1. Marking out
2. Cutting out
3. Fixing together
4. Colouring and finishing

**Above: The components for a lighthouse.
Note the triangular tabs round the top of
the main shaft and the gumstrip hinges at
the top of the cylinder for sticking**

Below. The finished lighthouse

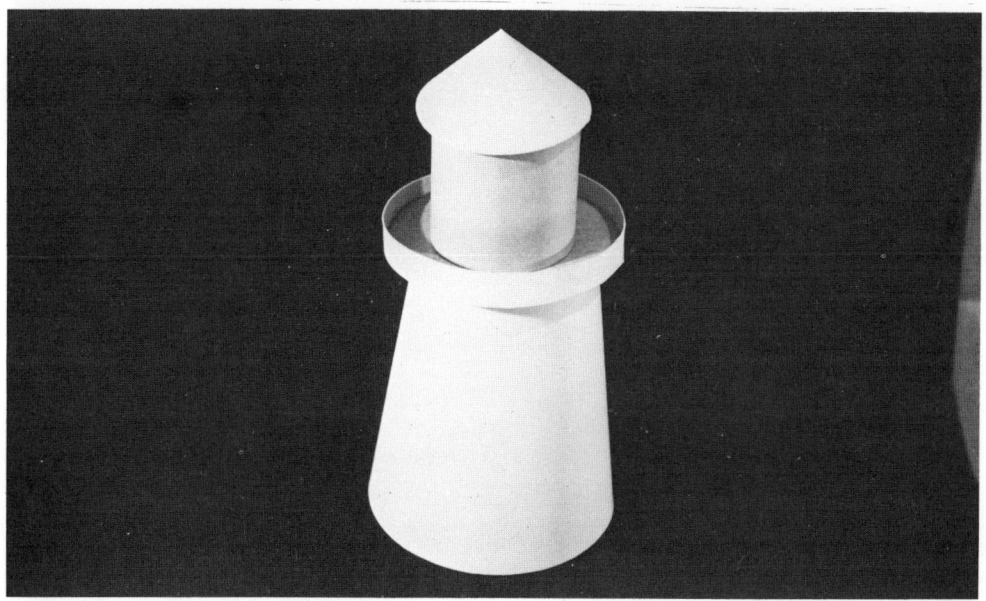

Marking out

If the model is going to consist of several pieces, decide which is the main piece, and make that first. Then the measurements for the remaining parts can be designed to fit. Try to imagine the shape as a flat pattern. It may help if you first take several factory-made cartons of different shapes and sizes, and carefully dismantle them to see what shape the cardboard was before it was assembled.

If thin card is being used it will be better if you can arrange the whole shape as a single piece which will then need only to be folded into shape. The folding lines should be firmly drawn with a sharp pencil. The card will then fold in the right place automatically. Remember to include in the original layout any extra 'tabs' for sticking. At this stage, it is important to get the measurements just right. It is no fun later on trying to fix parts which do not really fit.

Cutting out

Thin card can be cut with scissors, but do not attempt to turn round sharp angles if the back of the scissors is likely to damage the edge of the card. It is far better to approach tight angles from different directions so that the unwanted part falls away cleanly.

Thick cardboard needs to be cut with a sharp knife used against a metal straight-edge with a cutting board underneath. Hold the straight-edge very firmly (keeping fingers well out of reach of the knife blade), and keep the knife upright, running over the same cut several times if necessary.

When thick cardboard is to be folded it will need to be scored first with a sharp knife along the folding lines. Proceed just as though you were going to cut the cardboard, but be careful not to let the blade go more than about half way through. The cardboard will fold *away* from the scoring so that the

A simple ship combining a cylinder and rectangular boxes based on a hull of two layers of thick corrugated cardboard with a thin wall around

A bridge. The main structure is made from thick card with thinner walls and road added

A simple waggon. The wheels are fixed to axles made from wire, cane or sticks pushed through the lower box

A free grid system of interlocking rectangles. The pieces are simply slotted together without glue. The slots must be as wide as the thickness of the card

Several rectangular boxes make a good starting point for experimenting with group arrangements. Groupings like this are the beginnings of tower blocks and town centres

cut is 'opened out' slightly. Be sure to score on the right side.

Fixing together

Do not attempt to fix anything until the pieces have been folded roughly into shape. Thin card models will probably have tabs for sticking; it is then just a matter of applying glue and pressing them down in the right place. Remember that a ruler will often reach where fingers can't, and if you press too hard on an unsupported thin box you are liable to make a dent in it.

If you have forgotten the tabs you can usually add some by means of little 'hinges' of gumstrip. Corners of boxes or buildings can be joined from top to bottom with similar strips of gummed paper. Sellotape can be used in the same way, but its tackiness is sometimes a nuisance and it is not so easy to paint.

Gumstrip is often the best way of fixing pieces of thick cardboard together. Modern adhesives, however, are so good they will hold quite heavy pieces just by their edges. This method, known as butt jointing, results in a neat joint. If the cardboard is thick enough the joint can be further strengthened with ordinary dressmakers' pins pushed through one piece and into the edge of the other.

It is possible to join cardboard without any glue at all. This is done by cutting slots and simply pushing one piece of cardboard into another. The slots have to be exactly as wide as the thickness of the cardboard. By this means, models can be made which can be taken apart and re-assembled in different ways.

Colouring and finishing

If you are going to use crayons, it is far better to colour the model while it is still in flat pieces; then you can press as hard as you like without fear of denting the surface. Wax crayons are ideal for making textured effects.

Brickwork for example, can be achieved by applying two layers, red over yellow, and then scraping the pointing lines through with an old pen nib. Felt-tipped markers are also good for quick detail, but may be awkward to control on a model which has already been set up.

Once the model is built, of course, it is easier to see what's what, and at that stage, paint is probably the best form of colouring. Almost any sort of paint can be used. Emulsion paint gives a reasonably hard finish and dries quickly.

A covering of tissue paper (possibly tinted) will help to disguise any small faults in the construction, but this is only practicable when the underlying model is made of stout material.

Varnishing is a useful way of strengthening lighter models.

Scale

A vital factor in the design of any cardboard model is its size. The thinner grades of card, though easier to work, are not especially rigid. They will not span large distances and are not self-supporting for big models. One must think in terms of centimetres or inches rather than metres or feet. There are plenty of heavier grades of cardboard which can be used on a more ambitious scale if you have the right tools and enough strength in the fingers.

To get the best of both worlds, one approach would be to use a large substantial carton as a base, and then build on to it with more manageable material.

What to build

Model-making is usually thought of as a means of conveying information rather than a purely creative form of self-expression. Models may be historical, or scientific, or architectural; they may give tangible form to an original idea, but models are nearly always *of something else.*

An arrangement of cylinders with the addition of flat platforms. Arranged in groups the possibilities of such groups become apparent

Interlocking cylinders made from thin card. The largest cylinder is made first with circular holes through which the smaller cylinders are inserted

Cylinders can be set up in 'families' like tower blocks, in conjunction with flat platforms at intervals, or they can be fitted into one another to make structures which often look more complicated than they are. To make a cylinder, roll thin card around some convenient object such as a bottle or a broom handle, stick the card and then remove the object. Try making identical circular holes on opposite 'sides' of a cylinder, by drawing round a coin, and then form a smaller cylinder to fit through the holes, allowing the smaller roll to uncurl until it fits properly, before sticking it. Repeat the process with the small cylinder, and so on. To make a closed end for a cylinder, make the cylinder first, and then draw round it to make a circle of the right size. Whenever you can, make one shape by drawing round another. This is usually a good way of making sure they will fit.

Cones are made from circles. Make a single cut from any point on the circumference in to the middle and overlap the cut edges.

The more they overlap, the steeper will be the 'pitch' of the cone. Try making cones of varying pitch and joining them together. Similar experiments can be made with pyramids which are formed from triangles. Most models of actual objects are made up from basic shapes like those just mentioned. Even so, it is not a bad idea to start by inventing *shapes* and making three-dimensional patterns. You may well find that the results turn out like machines, or bridges, or cathedrals, or housing schemes. (Modern architecture has come a long way since the time when houses were always square boxes with pointed roofs.)

Rectangular boxes are perhaps the most obvious of simple shapes. Make several of varying proportions and experiment with different arrangements. The spaces between them are just as important as the shapes of the boxes themselves.

Try the same sort of thing using lots of flat slabs all slotted together. Now the space seems to go right through the structures.

145

Above: Cones of various size and pitch cut from circles of thin card

Below: An assemblage of cones. The smaller ones are attached with a little glue round the rim

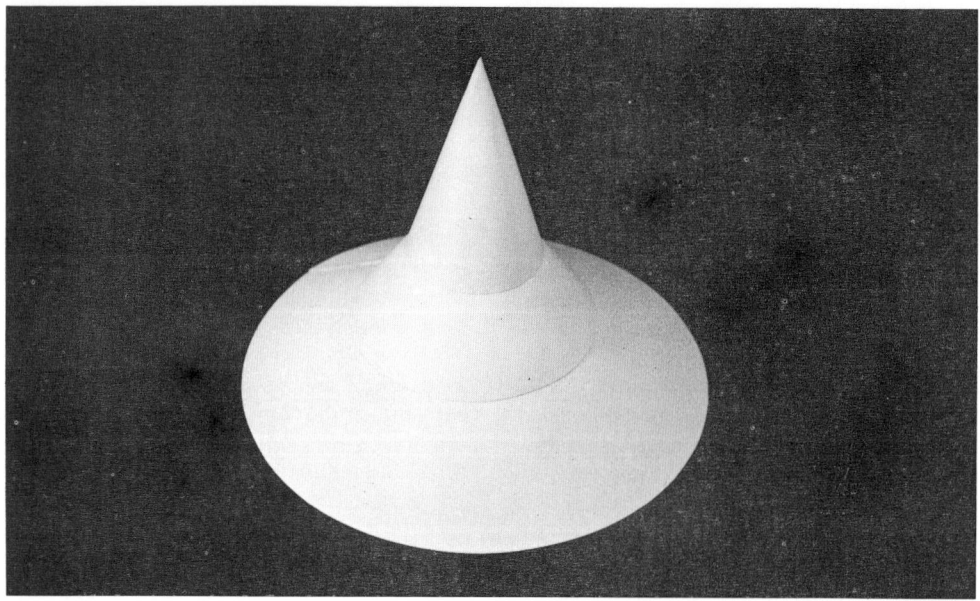

Creating with paper

Clearly paper strips can be used in many ways. What happens, for instance, if we fasten together a number of strips of different lengths? What happens if we contain this shape within a much larger coil, along with other paper strips and loops? What happens if the strips are of different widths, or of different colours? What happens if we fasten together a whole series of strips, fastened at different points, and containing other, larger strips?

The answer is that all sorts of things begin to happen. All sorts of shapes begin to present themselves. We find ourselves faced with a whole range of exciting possibilities. Ideas for screens, for abstract mobiles, birds, fishes, and imaginative creatures of all kinds. The illustrations show two kinds of model which might develop.

What is important, however, is sustained experiment. The trying-out of each and every possibility. Initial experiments such as these will not only provide necessary manipulative skills in the handling of paper, but will foster the ability to use paper creatively and imaginatively.

Experiment with paper strips used in profusion. Not one or two, but dozens, even hundreds. For this, any kind of paper will do. It need not be an expensive exercise. Used art paper, or newspaper would be quite adequate.

What happens if we begin to manipulate a large number of paper strips together? Fold

Paper strips folded into bundles and used in an open partition to diffuse the light from the window

a paperback book. What happens? In essence we create a multiplicity of mathematical curves. Curves that can be changed by pushing this way and that. Curves that suggest rhythm and texture: the bark of a tree, the motion of waves, and so on. Experiment first with strips of paper folded inside a matchbox. Now contain them within a circular coil. Try to record what happens.

One illustration shows the multiplicity of curves formed by containing a number of coiled and folded bundles of paper strip within a box lid. The same bundles could be used in an open partition to diffuse the light from a window. At other times, we can use bundles of paper strip quite freely, as with the paper bird.

As with all experiments, the act of experiment itself is tantamount, but experiment within limits. Experiment with new ways of artistic invention; for it is with the experience of experiment that our ability to create is made real.

A multiplicity of curves formed by containing a number of coiled and folded bundles of paper strip within a box lid

Cut and coil

Firstly, the use of coils. A strip of paper with the two ends brought together and stapled or glued.

Given a number of such coils, how can they be joined together to form a whole.

The first three photographs suggest just some of the ways. How many more ways are there?

The next step would be to experiment with the numerous ways in which the 'wholes' themselves might be put together. In other words, how can we utilize the strips of coils which we now have, to form a more ambitious whole.

Clearly, the combinations are limitless. Some combinations are less effective than others. Now we are beginning to learn through controlled experiment, and we begin to see more clearly, and are able to manipulate more readily, the very combinations which offer the most imaginative scope.

To use any material creatively demands a personal knowledge of the material. A familiarity with the 'feel' of the material; with its limitations and its possibilities. We acquire such knowledge by handling the material; using it in different ways. By experiment; by trial and error.

What follows is a programme of 'controlled' experiments with the use of paper as a three-dimensional medium. In a sense, the controls which I will suggest are arbitrary. Different teaching situations will require different kinds of control. What is constant is

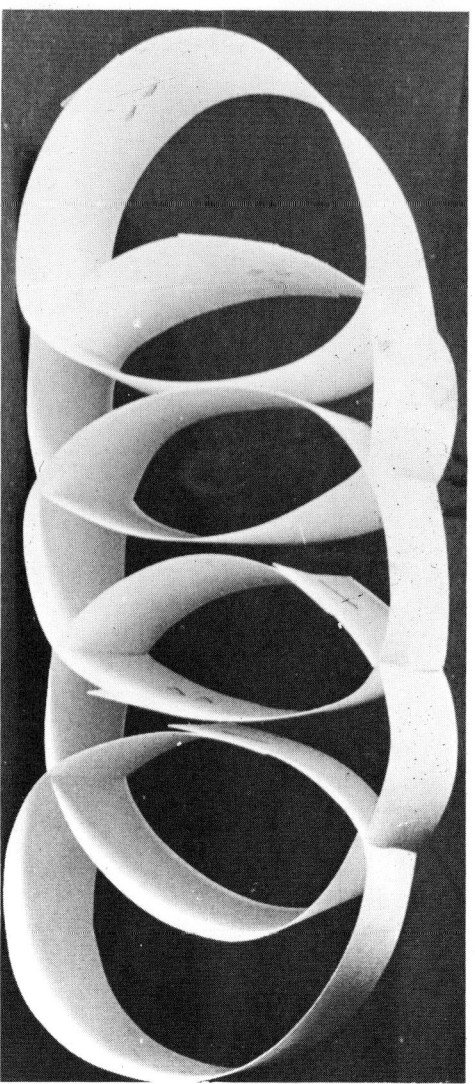

the belief that initial controls will foster subsequent skills; and that these skills will more readily facilitate creative approaches in time to come.

Suppose we limit our experiments with paper to the various uses of paper strips; and explore the range of effects which might be achieved.

An interesting experiment would be to create a screen or coils. These could then be filled with small balls of crumpled cellophane paper in different colours. Placed against a window or light source it could give an interesting effect.

How many other ways could your pupils create new combinations?

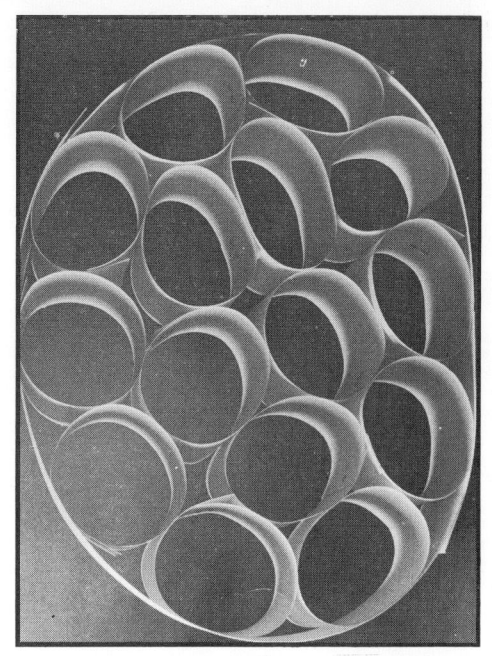

What other experiments suggest them-selves?

Firstly, the idea of containment. A collec-tion of small coils contained in a much larger coil. Here the coils are of uniform size. Much more interesting effects are obtained if we begin to vary the size of coils, and to vary the shape in which they are contained. Indeed, we can vary the size of coils in two ways.

Firstly in terms of diameter.

Secondly in terms of height.

Although the kinds of controls which we set are fairly limiting, the range of ideas which now presents itself is limitless. With this in mind, we should try to concentrate our efforts in an exhaustive study of the effects to be achieved.

Some projects could be very large, utilising the efforts of the whole class in the making of a large decorative mural or screen. Other projects might be quite small, arranging a set of paper tubes within a matchbox, or as a larger free-standing group.

We can further vary the scope of these controlled experiments by using different kinds of paper, different colours of paper, different textures and different weights.

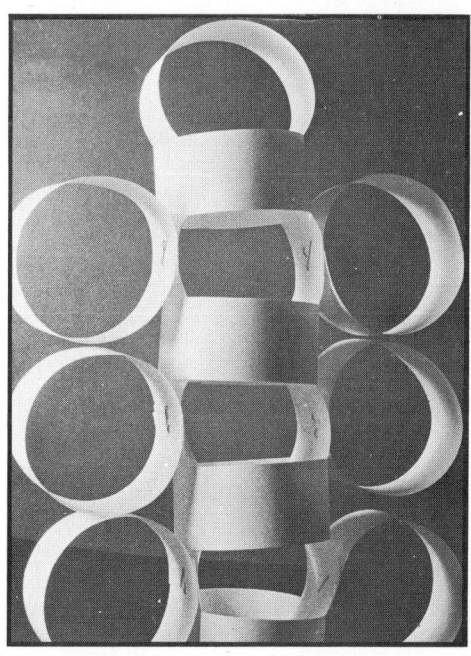

Silhouettes

Some historians trace the silhouette back to prehistoric man who darkened outlines of his prey on cave walls.

Silhouettes became popular as a form of portraiture during the eighteenth century on the continent, in England and in America. The Industrial Revolution made scissors and paper readily available and artists began to cut profiles of people from black paper. For the first time the common man could afford to have a likeness of himself. An oil painting was too expensive but a simple silhouette was not.

In fact, the silhouette got its name from the fact that it was cheap. Etienne de Silhouette was an unpopular penny-pinching Finance Minister under Louis XV. His hobby of profile cutting received his name after his quick demise. Before this, the silhouette had been called a "profile", "shade", "shadowgraph" or "shadow".

Profilists, as silhouette artists were called, used a variety of methods to obtain a likeness. The most talented cut directly from paper without even a guide sketch. Others used a "machine", perhaps some sort of projection equipment that reduced an actual shadow to the desired size. Some had the subject sit between a strong light and a paper and merely blackened the shadow cast by the light. Children today are fond of trying this method.

Most silhouettes were cut from paper using one of two methods: either the black paper was cut and mounted on white ("cut-and-paste" method) or the silhouette was cut out of white paper and mounted on black ("hollow-cut" method). Other silhouettes were painted rather than cut.

Some profilists cut only busts, that is face and neck in profile, but others cut full figures. Sometimes the whole family (even the dog) would have full silhouettes cut and these would be arranged on a pre-printed background and framed.

Many profilists travelled from place to place, setting up exhibits of their work and cutting silhouettes of all who wished. They moved on when business dwindled. Some of the more famous profilists attracted much attention as they toured.

August Edouart, one of the best known and finest of the profilists, toured extensively in Europe and America and cut thousands of full figure silhouettes averaging about 7 ins in height. He preferred these because he felt that only the entire figure revealed the true character of the subject.

Another profilist, John Miers, travelled throughout England in the 1780's making miniature profiles. Rosenberg became famous as a profile artist; he was a refugee profile painter from Germany and became attached to the English royal household.

Master James Hubard was considered a prodigy because he was cutting silhouettes at the age of twelve. He profiled Queen Victoria as a slender, young princess and after making his name in England he migrated to America while still in his teens.

In the mid-nineteenth century the invention of photography caused a sudden decline in the popularity of the silhouette as a form of portraiture. However, the silhouette did not completely die. Rather, it is still used today for a variety of purposes but only to a very limited extent for making portraits. Instead, its many other possibilities are being explored today as they never were before, when it was used mainly for portraiture.

Because of its simplicity, the silhouette conveys an impression instantly. Psychologists capitalize on this virtue in their ink blot tests. They use deliberately vague silhouettes and analyze the instantaneous impressions their patients receive from them.

Silhouettes are simple to make. They can be and are used in simple stitchery and art

Torn silhouette shapes from black porous paper

projects. Also they can efficiently convey the general impression of a new style and can be effectively used in fashion illustration.

Silhouettes are versatile and modern art is just beginning to tap their potential. Aubrey Beardsley employed distorted and convoluted silhouettes in his art. Norman Laliberté has obtained a variety of effects by making his paper silhouettes in various ways—tearing, cutting with pinking shears, razor blade, scissors, etc.

Children can also begin to explore the possibilities of the silhouette and with such simple equipment—black and white paper, scissors and a bit of paste.

A Polish cutout made by village folk. Guided by an almost instinctive decorative sense, young people, who frequently lack any skill at drawing, execute complicated designs using knives or scissors. Many of the patterns are traditional, originating in religion and in Polish folklore. (Illustration taken from 'Silhouettes, Shadows and Cutouts' by Norman Laliberté and Alex Mogelon, published by Reinhold

Folding paper

There are a number of ways to make folded paper patterns and they all add another dimension to picture-making. If the children are familiar with torn and cut paperwork this will be a natural extension.

Take some coloured sticky paper and experiment by cutting and folding strips and arranging them on a black or white background so that you create a raised surface. In this case, just fold the paper strips once, and arrange them closely, but at different angles; the pattern can be haphazard or regular, or better still, make two or three designs, using the same technique. Now fold coloured strips of paper into concertina shapes (three folds) and experiment with them, making a pattern by sticking down the end face of each. Again try different arrangements, as well as varying the colour combinations. You could also use this as a means of filling in areas of a picture, a furry animal, a forest scene, or a large expanse of sky.

An extension is to cut into the strips, about three or four times, a third of the way down the length, and score, or curl these pieces so that the overall effect when all the folded strips are attached is feathery and a good choice for bird pictures, or an elaborate Indian headdress.

The use of folds in paperwork for figures and buildings is also an interesting way to give depth and life to scenes of battles, soldiers and castles, a crowd or group picture. Simply draw and cut out your figures adding a fold down the centre and including either an

Unusual effects can be obtained by simply folding the paper strips once only, arranging them into patterns and sticking them on to a background of contrasting colour

extra tag on each side which can be folded back to be stuck or stapled to the background, or just staple near the edges of the figures, mounting them straight on to the wall—the background paper having been pinned up previously. For buildings simply draw the outline on card, cut out and fold in two sections, from each edge so that you have two flaps to stick down, and enough edge to make the castle or block of flats stand away from the background.

Try laying down blocks of colour with the folds all going one way so that an abstract pattern is achieved. The way the paper is folded affects this as much as the colours and, of course, the shadows also have a part to play in the design. Metallic paper will give a different effect.

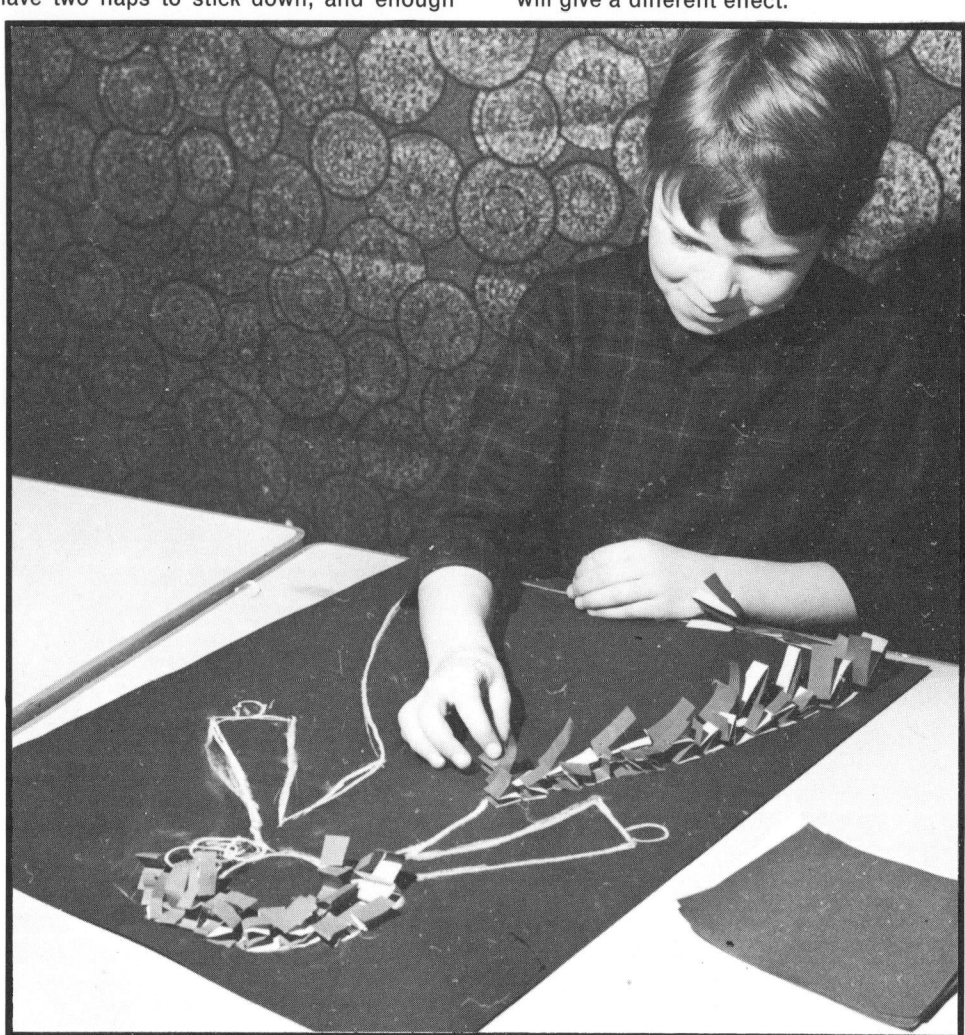

Coloured strips of paper are cut and folded into concertina shapes (three folds). Experiment by sticking down the end face of each into a variety of pictures and patterns

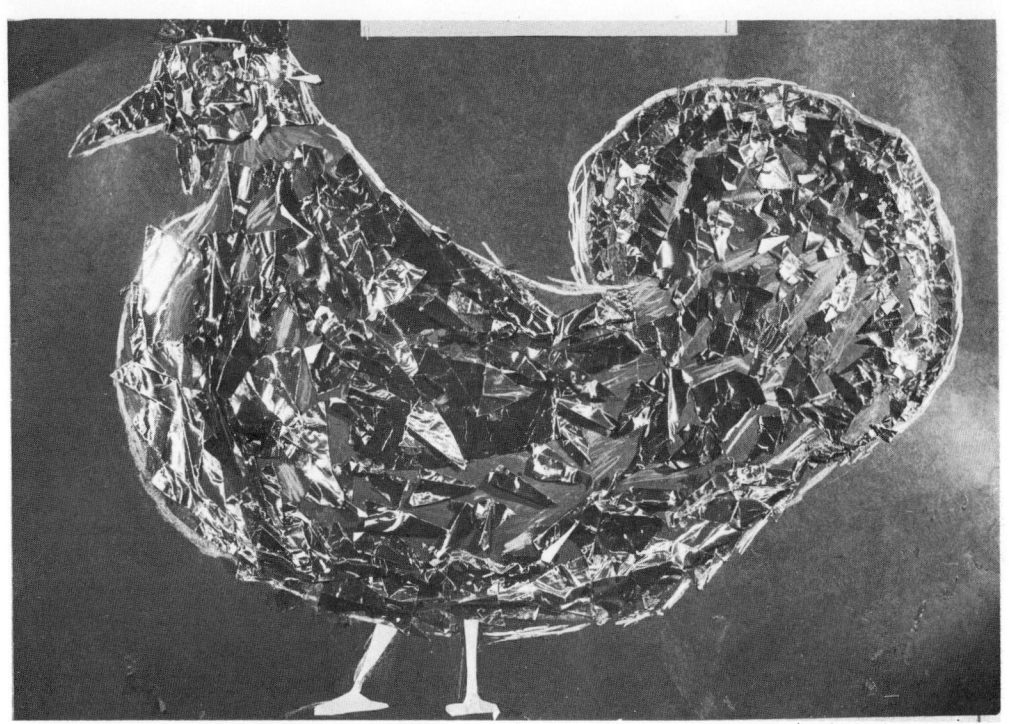

Cockerel made from folded shiny paper

Fabrics

Stitch a line

Mobiles for all

Flotsam and Jetsam

Decorative motifs for dresses

London folk

Fabrics

At the present time the possibilities in the manufacture of fabrics are endless. The basic construction of fabric, once confined to weaving and hand knitting, now may be found as machine knitted, woven in complicated textural patterns bonded without the appearance of thread at all, plaited, stitched, webb or sheet sprayed. All of which variety adds interest and spice to ideas in using them. The fact that a fabric is woven allows it to be frayed out to soften an edge or to gain textured thread to use for some other purpose such as embroidery or in a fabric picture. On the other hand, a bonded fabric will not fray but may be cut into any shape—sometimes very complicated ones—and still retain its sharp edge.

A rough textured fabric used with a smooth one will give a play of light and shade without any physical change of colour. It is this construction of the fabric and the nature and handle produced by this construction that governs the behaviour of any particular piece and, consequently, the ideas for its use. Inevitably, fabrics encourage the handling of them and the feeling of their texture, so developing an appreciation of their tactile quality, Fig. 1.

Requirements for play with fabrics

The bits bag. It is with the foregoing thoughts in mind that the first essential for play with fabric is brought into being—the bits bag. This can take any form as long as it is kept replenished and fresh. There is nothing quite so daunting as a bits bag which is just a bag of old rags two or three years old. They become chewed looking and crumpled to such an extent that all ideas are killed at birth. Personally, I find useful a large box or a cabin trunk, which holds a great deal and yet so much is seen when the lid is opened. A bag or sack is only a second best as the bits cannot be seen or handled easily without being emptied out each time.

All types of fabric should go into the bits box, particularly those with varied textures in weave or knit or other construction and varied textures in prints and colour such as stripes, spots and checks. Floral prints do not leave much to the imagination and are therefore not of such value.

Threads box. Going hand-in-hand with a bits box will be a collection of threads. Not only sewing cotton and embroidery cottons but heavy textural threads, perhaps frayed out from tweedy fabrics or curtain materials and knitting and weaving yarns. These, combined with fabrics, will often spark off an idea where fabric alone may not.

Other essential general equipment

Scissors. Sharp scissors are necessary—a large pair for cutting heavy materials and a small pointed pair for delicate cutting. An old pair, preferably fairly sharp, for cutting paper or templates.

Needles. Fine sharps e.g. No. 9 for sewing cottons or silks by hand. Crewel No. 5 for medium weight embroidery threads. Chenille No. 20 for heavy thread.

Threads for sewing types of fabric. Choose a thread to match the fibre; cotton for cotton fabric, silk for silk fabric, Nylon or Drima for man-made fibre fabrics.

Pins. Fine clean pins of steel or brass. Thick or dirty pins leave marks.

A sewing machine. Any type of sewing machine is useful, the essential thing is that the user is competent.

A sketch book of ideas.

A box of natural objects such as pieces of bark, shells, fir cones, water-worn pebbles etc.

The collecting of objects for these last two sections means that the collector has become aware of her environment, that nature and man-made constructions can be a source of design not to be slavishly copied but to be translated into ideas and used in combination with the sensual perception created by the handling of fabrics.

Sources of obtaining fabrics

Although the bits box will be the main source of the small pieces of fabrics used in building up a design, it is often necessary to buy a piece, for example for a background for a picture or other piece of work. Remnant counters are a source of wealth in this field, but one can be carried away by a beautiful piece of fabric and, on arriving home with it, find it is not quite right. So firm control must be exercised or the scheme may be spoiled. The soft furnishing department of a large store provides beautiful, coloured materials in wonderful textures and probably more

Fig. 1. A selection of the different textures found in fabrics

cheaply than its counterpart in the dress fabric department.

There is also a source of supply, not always realised, in areas where fabric manufacture is carried on. Many of the firms making cloth, knitted fabric in particular, find it difficult to dispose of cuttings and ends from the knitting machines if they are using man-made fibres. This scrap is not worth melting down and it is not suitable for paper, etc. and consequently the firms are very pleased to give the scraps of fabric to schools and educational institutions. Some of this type of scrap was used to make the doll in Fig. 2 shown opposite.

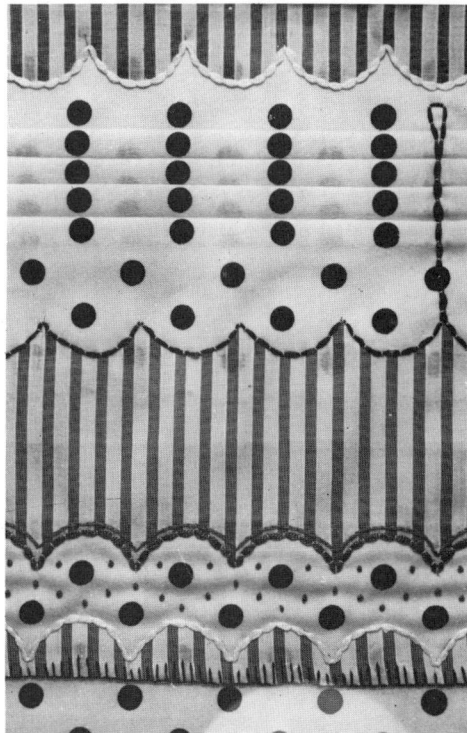

Fig. 2 (left). The plait for the body is shown on the left of the finished doll

Fig. 3 (above). Pleating and embroidering a spotted and striped fabric to increase the interest of a geometric pattern

Instructions for making the doll

Three strips of coloured jersey fabric 8cm wide the full 184cm width of the cloth. These strips are plaited.

If the edges of the strips are curled in the hand as the plait is made, this makes a smoother plait. If this is too difficult for children the plait without the curling will be quite satisfactory. A small neat tie on each end of the plait holds it from coming unfastened. Fold the plait in half. Do not cut it but fold over the doubled end for 18cm to make the body.

The four folds of plait are stitched together up the centre front, centre back and the two sides of the body as far as the arms. Some scraps of material should be pushed in to plump up the body before completing the stitching.

The arms are made from a plait approximately 43cm long made in the same way from three strips 61cm long. When this plait is made and tied it is pushed through the body from side to side. Make the arms even in length.

The head can be made from two circles of material with a neck. The circles will be 13cm in diameter, the neck 6cm wide and 5cm long. Stitch these two head pieces together, leaving open the bottom of the neck for stuffing with scraps of material.

Stitch on circles of white felt—smaller blue circles and still smaller black on top of each other—for eyes. Stitch on a mouth shape in red felt. A good plan is to look at the face of a doll to get the correct positioning.

The hair is made of pieces of the fabric 10cm long and approximately 1cm wide. Fold these pieces in half and stitch the folded edge on to the head firmly with three or four stitches.

Hands and feet may be added if desired.

For hands cut four pieces the shape of mittens 7cm long by 5cm wide. Make two bags of these to attach to the ends of the plait arms. Slip the end of the plait inside the open

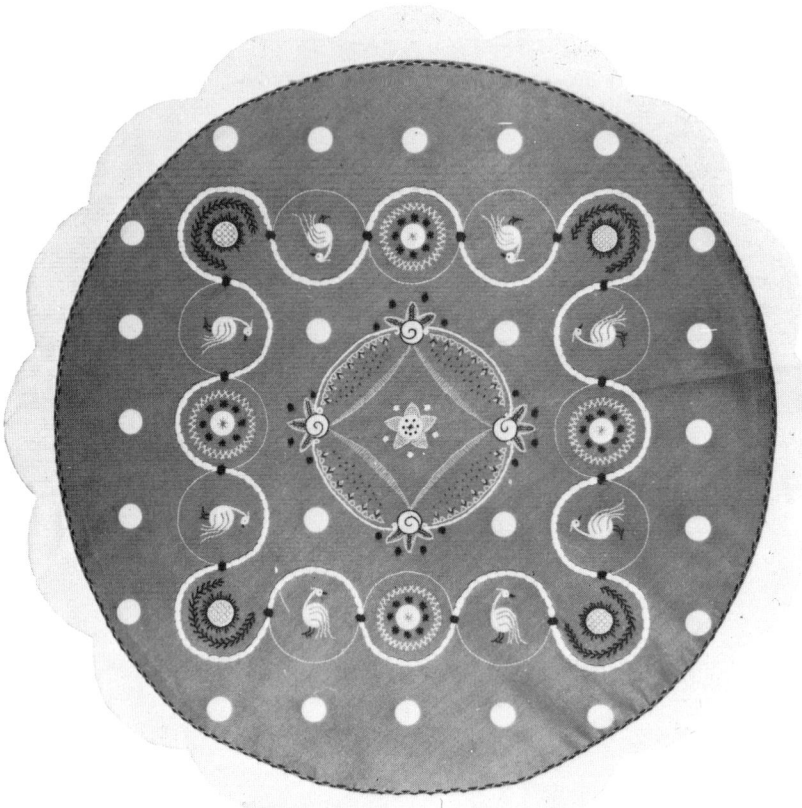

Fig. 4.

end of the mitten bag and sew round. Two ovals for each foot 7cm by 5cm stitched as a bag, leaving one end open. Place on the end of the plait and stitch on.

Sources of design—the fabric itself
When a printed fabric, for example a spotted gingham, is handled it appears to be uninteresting but when it is examined spread out, the spots can be seen to form designs.

Combinations of spots begin to make rhythm and can be worked with in embroidery or other crafts. Individual spots may be added to with stitchery to make birds or flowers, so increasing the interest of an otherwise geometric pattern, Figs. 4 and 5.

Another way of playing with spotted fabric to create design is to pleat out one line of spots and bring two alternate lines together so that the spots form bands instead of being

Fig. 5. Detail of embroidered tablecloth

Fig. 6. Detail of flowered gingham

alternate as printed, Fig. 3.

These suggestions show how simple pattern may be developed by handling the fabric and discovering its possibilities. Checked gingham and similar fabrics with squared pattern lend themselves to pleating out of one colour and to the change of pattern created by cutting on the cross of the fabric whereby a diamond is made.

The pattern of the fabric, Fig. 6, suggests pleating out the upright square lines to bring the flowers together and make solid vertical bands of them. Alternatively, the flowers themselves can be pleated out to show only the plain fabric.

Fig. 7. 'Bubbles' made from crystal nylon for dress decoration

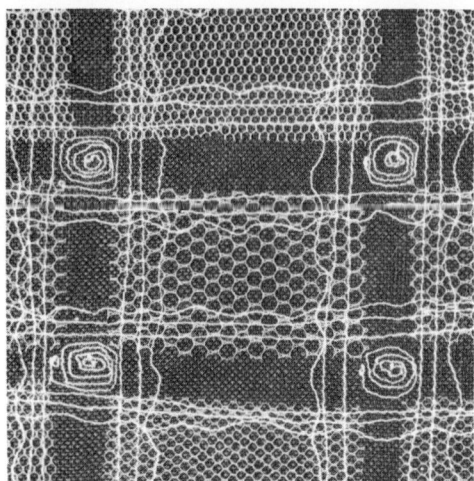

Fig. 8. Rectangular blocks of net machined in position

Dress decoration

Handling a piece of fabric is really the greatest source of inspiration as, for example, the idea of bubbles or balloons in the floating nature of crystal nylon. This is the origin of the piece of dress decoration in Fig. 7. Circles of nylon 7cm across, in different colours were cut out and a running stitch worked round the edge to gather up. These bubbles were then stitched on to the dress fabric very lightly (in this case by machine) here and there on the edge, leaving the nylon to stand out and bubble.

The second example, Fig. 8, is on a linen fabric and to keep the crisp effect net was used in rectangular blocks of colour and with a straight stitch just sewn on in vertical and horizontal lines to hold the net in place. Different sizes of mesh were used to add further interest.

The third example, Fig. 9, of decorating fabric shows how a heavy, woollen, plain coloured fabric can be made interesting by the addition of other colour in the form of cuttings of similar weight woollen fabric stitched on quite haphazardly by machine.

In this example the dress material is bright red and the cuttings light fawn and turquoise, making a brilliant and daring effect which is very successful.

Classifying materials

The sorting of materials into types by fibre content, texture or pattern may stimulate an interest which can be fulfilled by making articles in patchwork. This is a craft which has been carried on for centuries and requires careful workmanship. There is a gentle therapeutic quality about the working of it and it has considerable educational value, since it connects up many subjects. The drawing of templates may be done in the geometry class, the sorting of fabrics can be done in the science class and in the needlework session, where there is also required the knowledge of stitching, basting and seaming. The art lesson is also important in patchwork since the effectiveness of an example mainly depends upon the success or failure of the pattern and colour scheme. As a patchwork article is often washable the following points should be remembered:

Fig. 9. Attaching random pieces of fabric to the background

Fig. 10. A patchwork bag showing the use of patterned material. Above: Bottom view of the bag

1. The fabrics in a single piece of work should be of the same weight and, preferably, of the same type, although it is sometimes possible to use silks and cottons (e.g. lawn) together.

2. Wherever possible the grain of the fabric should run in the same direction in all the patches but, when using patterned fabric such as stripes, the design may be made interesting by the play of the stripes for an all-over effect. This is shown in the illustration of the bag in striped gingham and poplin. Fig. 10.

3. The sewing should be neat and firm enough to withstand wear and washing.

To begin the patchwork

Choose a selection of materials of similar weight. The greater the range of colour and texture the richer the finished work will be. Iron the scraps before starting.

The shapes of fabric will be cut out by means of a template, which must be completely accurate. The ordinary shapes for templates such as hexagon, pentagon, diamond, square, triangle, etc. can be bought from needlework shops.

If the templates and patches are not accurate and the sides of the shape not the same size the various patches will not fit together to make good work. From the key template copies should be made in firm paper. Thin metal templates are better than those in cardboard as frequent cutting or drawing round the shape tends to distort a cardboard template. The paper used for the copies should be firm enough to stitch through. Notepaper or pages from old periodicals are often suitable.

It is a good plan to draw the shape of the key template on the wrong side of the fabric in pencil to establish the position with regard to grain or pattern. Then the fabric shape can be cut out with 1cm turnings added all round. Each fabric piece is placed with the wrong side of fabric on to a paper copy, the turnings turned over the edge of the paper and basted to it to hold them in place. When the basting is completed the patches should be pressed to make them crisp. Many patches can be prepared in this way and eventually sorted out into colour, tone or design ready for assembling. Different layouts of the patches can be tried before the final arrangement is decided.

To assemble the work

Two patches are placed right-sides together with the edges parallel. Using thread to match the type of fabric and the colour, seam or oversew one side of two patches together with small, even stitches. It has been found that where a dark patch is sewn to a light one a darker thread shows less.

All the patches can be joined together in this way in the order of the pattern.

After all the seaming is finished, the basting and paper templates are removed and the work pressed. It is now ready to be made up into the finished article such as a cushion, bag, quilt, etc.

Appliqué patchwork

From the ideas box inspiration for a design for a cushion cover came when a piece of driftwood was found. A design was drawn using the rhythmic lines of the wood grain as the basic idea. From the design a tracing was made and used as a pattern for the cutting-out of the fabric shapes. These were in a poplin material in tones of brown and fawn to white. They were cut true to the straight grain as drawn on the design and cut with great care to ensure an exact fit of all the pieces.

A piece of cotton material was prepared as a background by ironing on a piece of Bondina fusible fleece. This can be obtained at most shops which sell interfacing fabrics and instructions for use are included in the pack. The patches were cut out and assembled on this background true to grain and fit. They

Fig. 11. Design inspired by a piece of driftwood

were then ironed on, using a steam iron as required by the instructions. Finally, all the edges were stitched with a swing needle sewing machine. The finished fabric was made up into the cushion cover, Fig. 11.

Crochet and patchwork

Crochet as a craft is a form of fabric construction but, as a method, can be used in conjunction with other forms of work to decorate, finish or assemble. An example of

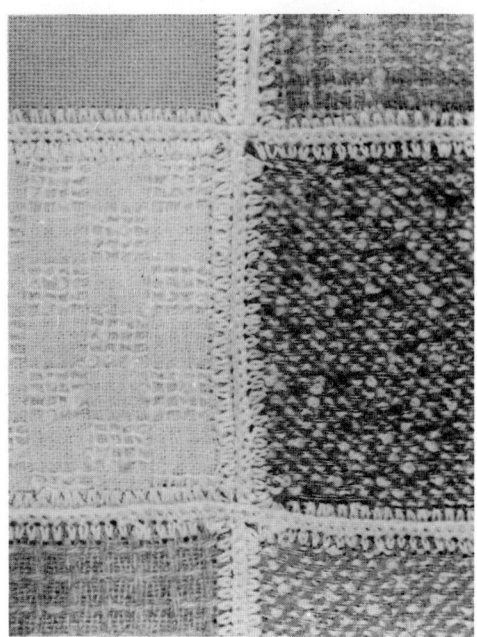

The scraps of tweed are from old out-of-date fabric swatches, but could be cut from left-over dressmaking scraps. These were too bulky to have the edges turned in to assemble and frayed too much to leave raw. So each piece was worked with double crochet stitch all round in four-ply wool, Fig. 15. All the patches were then sorted into a pattern of colour and joined together with double crochet on all the lines. In the main, the wool used for the crochet was dark purple as this colour was most suitable for the majority of the patches but white was also used to give a tonal effect to the centre of the cover.

Rug making

Fabric pieces can be used in conjunction with many other crafts, one of which is weaving. Where a solid block of colour is required without its being cut up by the texture of the warp or weft, a piece of fabric woven in, as a wide shape, will provide the required effect.

Fig. 12 (above). Blouse designed and made by Susan Lee, Crochet worked by Elizabeth Hope of Kielder Crafts

this can be seen in the skirt and bedcover where numerous small pieces of woollen fabrics have been put together by crochet, Figs. 12 and 13.

Fig. 13 (above). Bedcover made from small pieces of woollen fabric. (left) Detail of the crochet stitch used to join the pieces

Fig. 14 (below). Wall hanging using pieces of fabric and felt to give solid blocks of colour

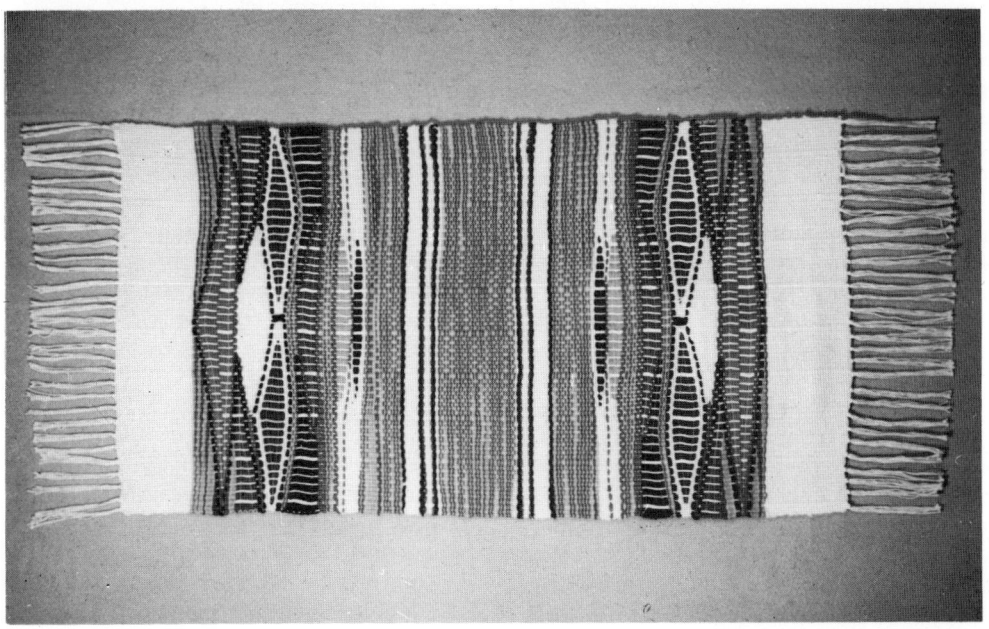

Detail of hanging shown in Fig. 14

The wall hanging in Fig. 14, reminiscent of a Navajo blanket and designed with a traditional blanket in mind is brilliant in colour with red, rich purple, black, turquoise and green on a white background of tapestry weaving. To give strength of hue undiluted by the white warp, the coloured patches were woven into the weft using pieces of fabric and felt.

A simple rug frame can be made by knocking nails, 6mm apart, on two opposite sides of an old picture frame and winding the string for a warp backwards and forwards across the frame and round the nails.

The weft can be made of strips of fabric approximately 2·5cm wide. The fabric can be cut up in a continuous length, backwards and forwards across the material and wound into a ball ready for use. Old sheets, dyed, make good strips or the nylon waste that can be bought by the pound in bags is a good source of supply. This can be woven in plain weave across the warp by means of a flat strip of wood or thick card 38cm by 8cm with V shapes cut out of each end. When the

weaving is finished and taken off the picture frame the ends of the warp can be knotted to make a fringe.

A third method of making a rug from scraps of fabric, preferably woollen fabric such as suitings, is the old method of a pegged rug. A piece of hessian is used as a backing and the work done from the underside. The pieces of fabric are cut approximately 13cm long and 2·5cm wide. The tool is a broken wooden peg sharpened to a point.

With a piece of cloth rolled sideways in the fingers of the left hand the end of the strip is pushed through the hessian with the peg, to half-way. Near the hole, two or three strands of hessian away, the other end of the strip is pushed through in the same direction. All the strips of cloth are pushed into the hessian very close together in rows, to a previously decided pattern. The closeness of the working holds the fabric pieces firmly in place. By rolling the strips in the fingers a curled effect is imparted to the appearance of the surface. When completed the rug should be backed with a second piece of hessian for neatness and strength.

Fabric dyeing

A plain coloured fabric can be hand printed or dyed in many different ways to create something personal. One method is the use of tie-and-dye and by this means individual backgrounds for embroidery or hangings can be produced. The fabrics most suitable for tie-and-dye are silk and cotton as both of these will iron out successfully after dyeing. Fabrics of man-made fibres retain creases if a boiling dye is used.

Method

The simplest form of tying the fabric is to take a bunch of the material and, after smoothing it down in the hand, begin tying. Lay one short end of the string up the bunch to the pointed end and proceed to wrap the

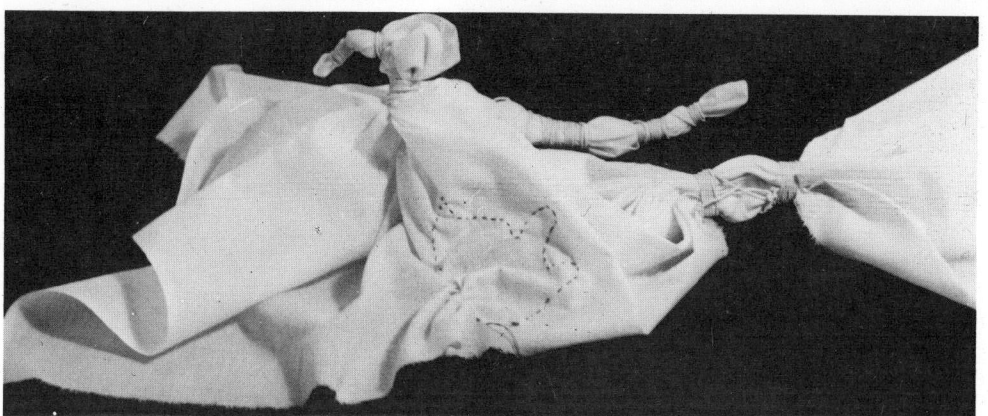

Fig. 15 (above). Different methods of tying the fabric

Fig. 16 (below). The pattern after dyeing

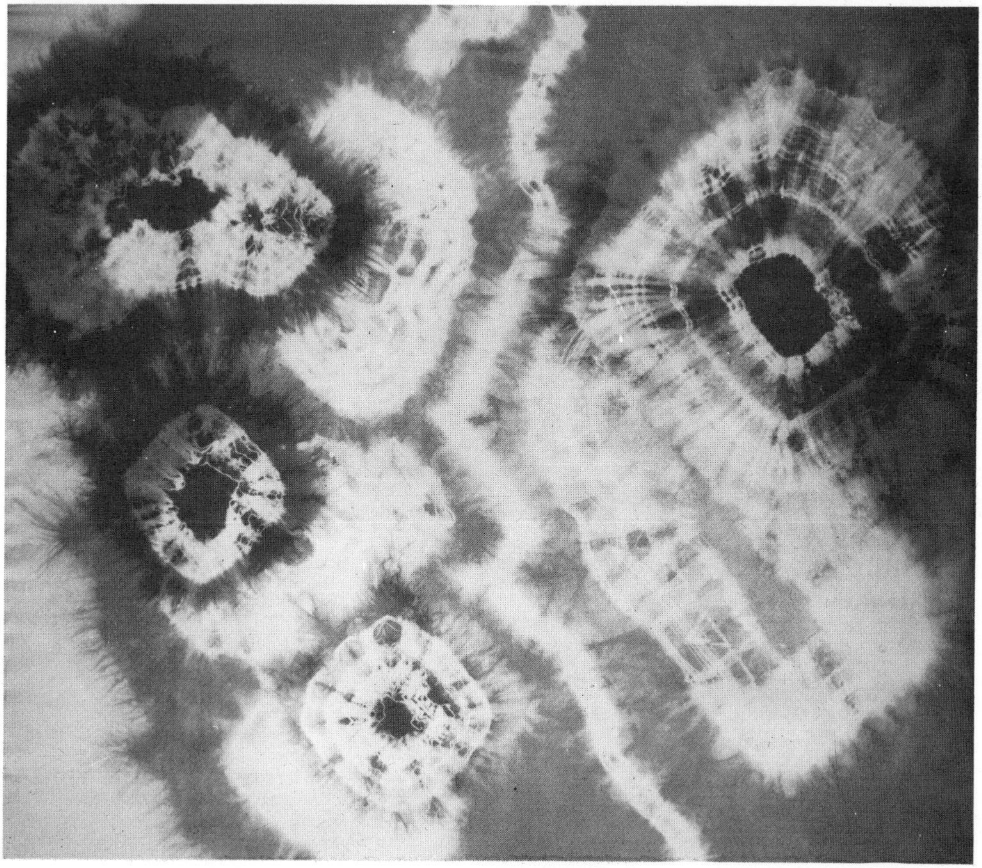

string round the material tightly down the bunch. When the bottom is reached the two ends of string are tied. Where the string is tied the dye does not penetrate. Many knots can be made in this manner all over the fabric, although this gives a haphazard effect. A more controlled pattern can be obtained by pleating the fabric and tying or by stitching in a pattern with strong thread and then gathering it up, Fig. 15.

After the fabric has been knotted or tied it can then be dyed. Household dyes are very successful and either the cold or hot method can be used. Instructions are provided with the tins of dye. Other colours can be added by repeating the tying and dyeing. When the dyeing is finished the material is rinsed and the strings carefully removed, so revealing the finished pattern on the fabric, Fig. 16.

Using the fabric

The illustration of the embroidered panel in Fig. 17 shows how a tie-and-dye fabric can be used as a background to machine embroidery. The dyed pattern suggested a garden with herbaceous border slightly out of focus, similar to the effect given when one specific flower is being looked at. The marguerite was made from applied patches of white sail cloth and the background machine-embroidered to give form and extra colour.

The detail of coral beds under the sea, Fig. 18, shows how a tie-and-dye background was emphasised by machine stitching with the top and bottom tensions altered, the top being tightened to 9 and the bottom slackened so that the bottom thread pulled up to the surface to give a spikey effect.

The machine embroidery in both cases was worked on a straight stitch domestic sewing machine with the foot removed and the work stretched on a frame as in Fig. 19.

Fig. 17. Using a tie-and-dye background as the basis for an embroidered picture

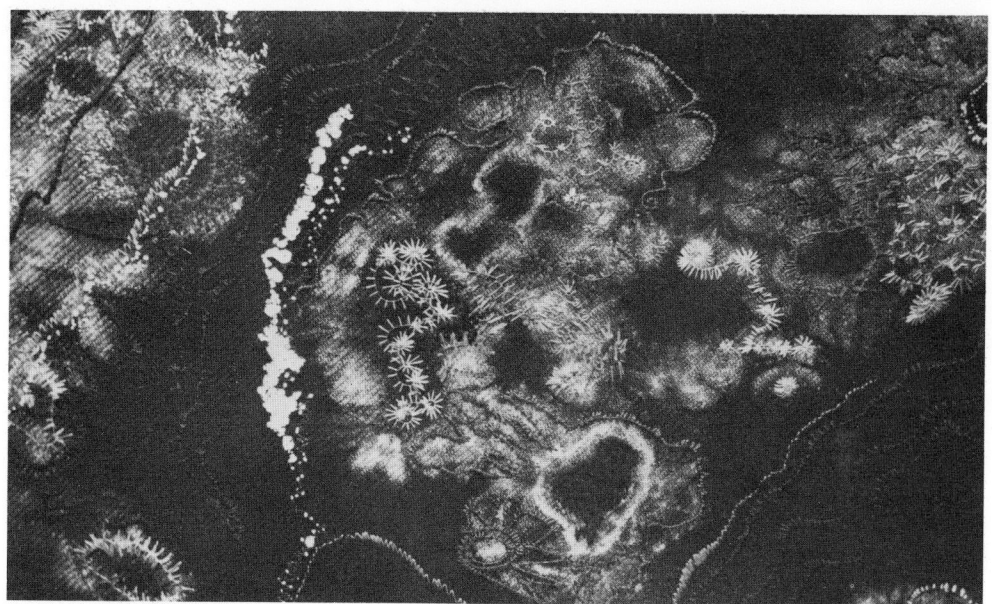

Fig. 18 (above). Detail of machine embroidery on a tie-and-dye background

Fig. 19 (below). Note the position of the hands on the frame with the first finger of the left hand holding the thread before beginning the embroidery. The tension lever must be engaged as shown

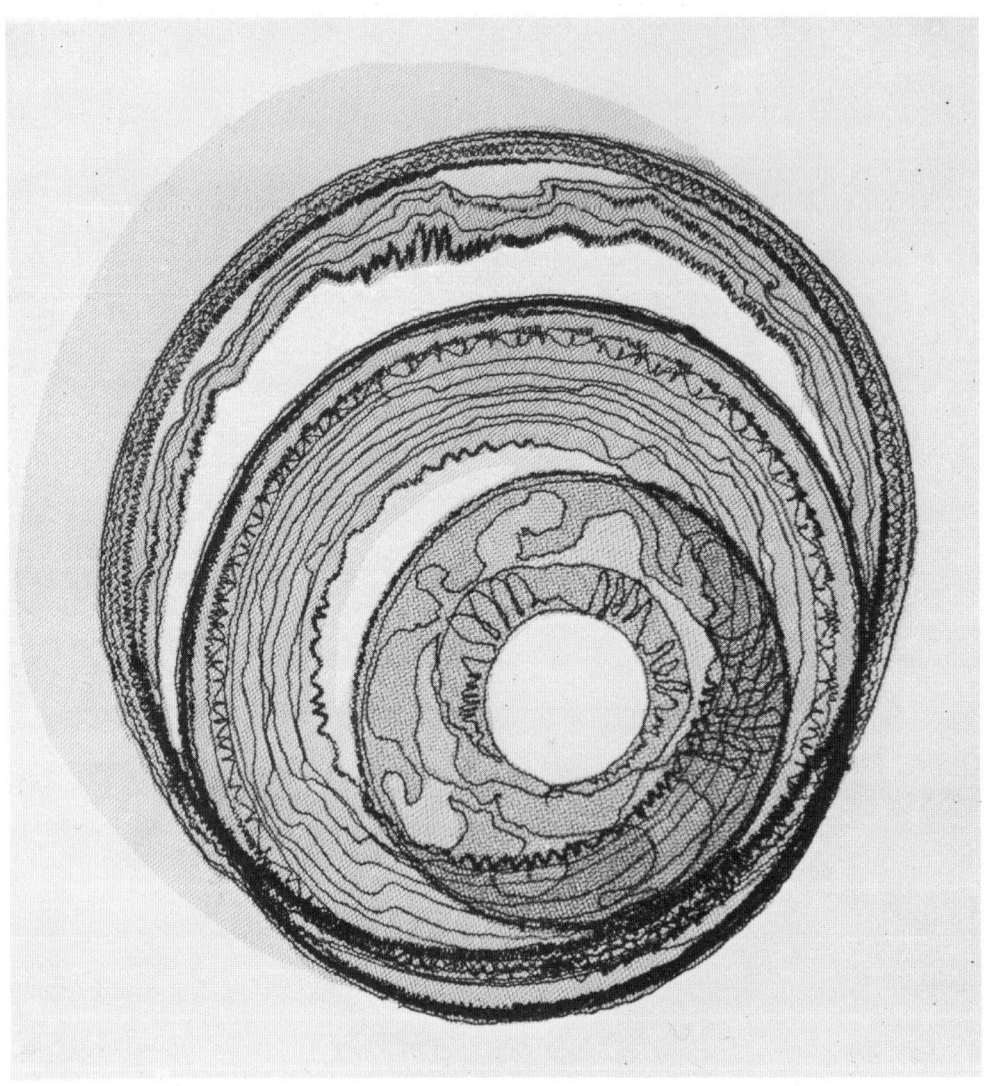

Fig. 20. A window mobile, machine stitching on net

The use of other fabrics for machine embroidery

Most fabrics will make backgrounds for embroidery and machining. Experiments with modern fabrics have great educational value and many unexpected effects are discovered. Thin fabrics such as net can be used where the background is required to be practically invisible, as the window hanging, Fig. 20 where the machined pattern is the important thing and the mechanical processes unimportant. The embroidery mounted on a sheet of perspex becomes transparent and suitable for a window mobile.

176

Fig. 21 (top). The use of fabric in picture making with (below) a detail of the cloud effect

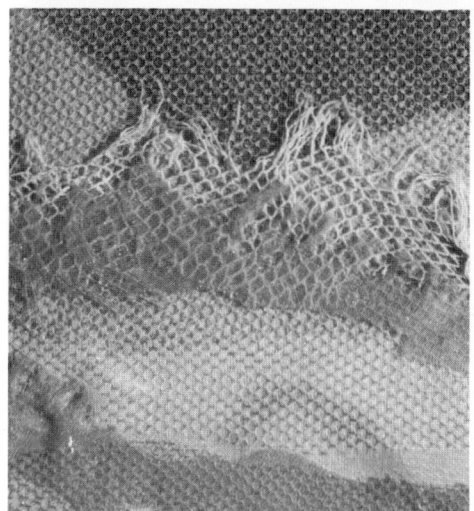

Fig. 22.

Fabric pictures

The most exciting use of fabric, however, is to exploit it as an alternative medium to paint in the making of pictures. Every possible colour and tone and every possible texture and effect can be obtained in fabric. The limitations are few. This very fact imposes a need for restraint by the artist because care and discrimination must be used in the choice of fabric to ensure that the impression created is not more natural than nature. The quality and freshness of the idea, the simplicity of shape obtained by the handle of fabric and scissors, the control of colour and the searching for the exact tone required, can all contribute to an aesthetic awareness of a new medium. Texture is also important and can represent visibly, something understood or imagined such as a cloud effect made by ragged cotton net, bulky in appearance over the different texture of dress net, Fig. 21.

Quite a different type of picture is the portrait in Fig. 23 because in this case fabrics have been used in the way that paint would be laid on in washes to obtain the right colour. The cheek has four layers of transparent fabrics of different colours to give the effect required and is finished off with a piece of nylon stocking to make the shadow. The hair is made from frayed tweed, net and lining material. The fixing of these fabrics created a problem. Sewing the pieces would have given the effect of a contour map so they had to be lightly stuck on with glue to hold them where necessary.

It is apparent that, as a medium in craftwork, fabric is indispensable.

The suggestions made in this article only introduce the craft and should lead to experimentation in the many other ways in which fabric can be used.

On handling a particular piece of fabric the worker should be aware of all its qualities— its colour, texture, weight and the way it reacts to other fabrics. In this way a perception of the possibilities of fabric as a medium is developed. On its own, fabric can be used in the making of many household and personal articles but it can also be closely linked with other crafts and arts not usually associated with fabric. Further it can be examined, handled, draped and manipulated for itself alone.

Fig. 23. A more intricate fabric picture

Stitch a line

The tactile quality of fabrics is their main attraction and is a quality little enough explored by teachers in general.

To provide an environment in which certain discoveries can be made is generally accepted in the Primary school and to some extent in the Secondary school. Interests can be aroused and many textile skills learnt through creative play with fabrics and threads. Crochet, knitting, knotting and weaving are a means of fabric construction; tie-dye, batik, printing and embroidery a means of fabric decoration.

It is more valuable to develop an attitude of mind than always to dictate set ways of using this fabric with that thread with a particular group of children or students. The actual quality and behaviour of the materials themselves will suggest ways in which they can be used.

Fabrics can be compared with paint as large areas of colour; threads compared with pen or pencil as giving lines of varying thickness. Immediately the advantage of fabrics over paints will be clearly seen. The infinite variety of colour, matt, shiny, transparent or opaque already mixed and in a multitude of shapes and sizes waiting to be torn, cut, crumpled, rolled or folded and manipulated into different shapes and forms.

Fabrics and threads need not be used flat. Clothes are worn upon the body, rags put upon a scarecrow, curtains hung across a window, flags fly upon a pole. Fabrics can move thus giving a change of shape, pattern

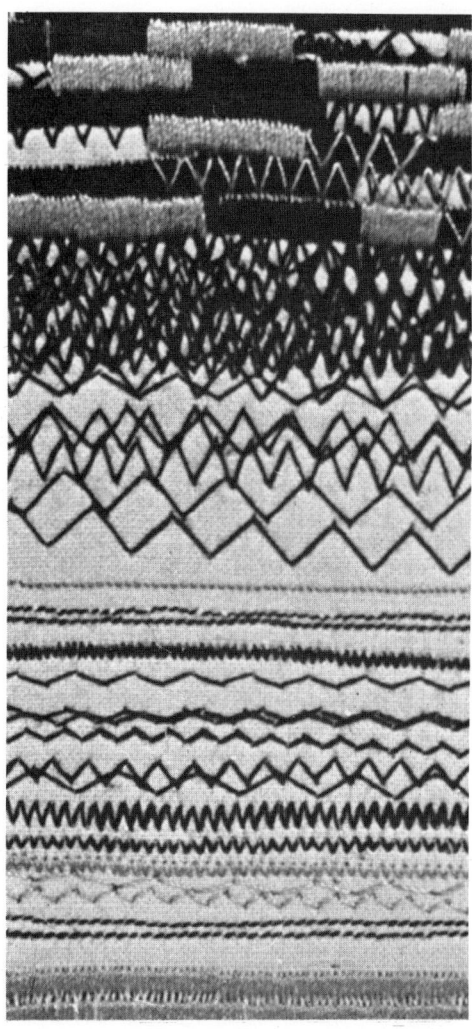

and colour. The change can be caused by atmosphere, by sun and shadow as well as by the movement of air or the movement of the wearer if the fabrics are in the form of clothing.

Fabrics and threads can be used to obscure a view or to enhance a view. They can be assembled to record or create an impression of something seen or something imagined.

The sight of certain colours and the feel of different textures will evoke memories in some children and stimulate the imagination of others thus providing ample opportunity for original creative work.

The influence of environment cannot be overlooked and will greatly affect the thinking and doing of both pupil and teacher. Local traditions, crafts and industries should be fully explored where they relate specifically to textiles. Visits could be made to factories and work rooms concerned with the clothing and soft furnishing industry; to mills producing and decorating fabrics and threads and to local craftsmen. These craftsmen should include as wide a range as possible, from fishermen mending sails and nets to retired ladies repairing church vestments and furnishings. The skill and enthusiasm of these people concerning their work or hobby can prove of real value to teacher and pupil alike and is a contact to be cherished. It also provides a valuable means of establishing a relationship, a sharing of a common interest, between different age groups.

The needs and skills of the individual must be seen and respected and allowed to develop. Likewise there should be the opportunity to use fabrics for fun for the sheer joy of handling them as well as for function.

This gives invaluable training in the consideration and awareness of design through

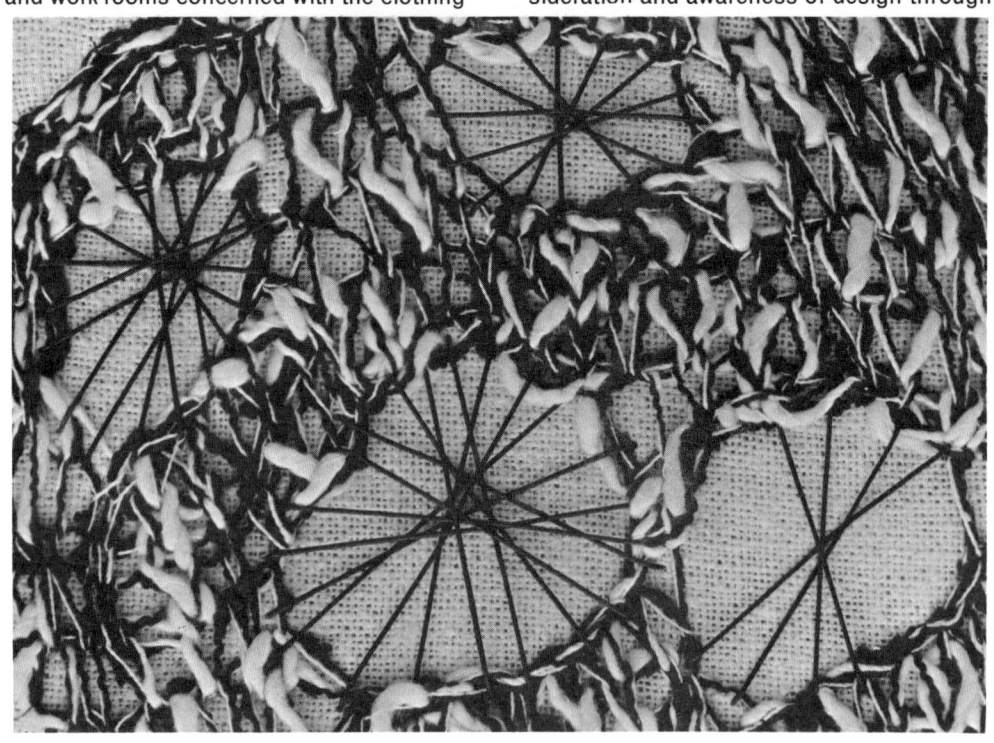

first hand experience of actually designing and making something whether it be a toy, a dress, a cushion or a school flag.

Many people can be involved, opinions given, experiments made, time and cost of materials estimated and the work undertaken with the knowledge and enthusiasm resulting from previous experience in the handling and use of fabrics and threads.

As a result of a visit to an exhibition of modern murals in needlework, we were interested in those done in machine em-

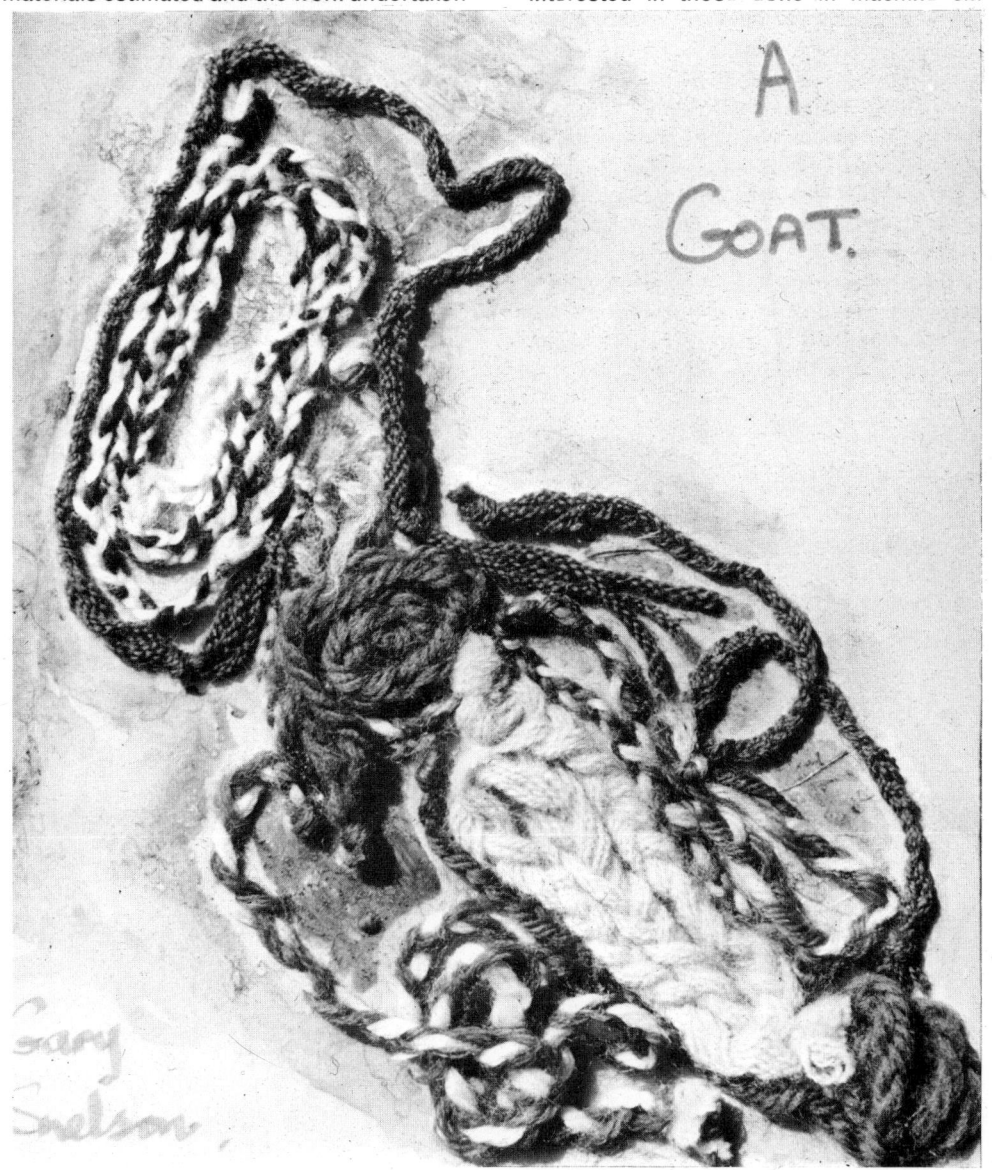

broidery. It was not possible to do this in school and we worked out the following idea as a substitute for it. We found that this was a better method for children as it gave more scope for basic craftwork and more pliability in design.

Strips of wool or other yarn were plaited. Children experimented with types of plaits—multiples of three strips, mixed numbers, plain colour, mixed colour. When the children had a collection of plaits they began to arrange them on cardboard to make designs or pictures. These were either stuck down piece by piece and the picture or design allowed to "grow", or the whole piece of cardboard was covered and then the design was stuck down. The pictures reproduced here were built up gradually. In most cases the picture was finished and then the title chosen by the child.

Alternatively a picture could be drawn first and then outlined by plaits and other plaits coiled to fill in the spaces.

Plaits of different thicknesses add interest and dimensions to the work. Different yarns can also provide contrast that may be needed in the picture.

A better base than cardboard is a polystyrene tile or part of a tile. If a tile is cut it is advisable to use a very small saw—the edges are neater than if it is cut with scissors or a knife.

String for hanging up the picture when finished is fastened on the back with Sellotape. Those made with tiles could be affixed to the wall to make a mural.

Some children after plaiting the yarn, stitched a picture or design on to material. Ordinary running stitch was used and coloured cotton to match the colours in the picture. Again for the most part the design or the picture just "grew". When finished it was pressed, then stretched over cardboard and either folded and stuck down at the back, or each side joined at the back with long stitches. This method could also be used to make cushions, mats, purses, etc.

Children could join in a group to make a small mural, planning the design, choosing the colours. This would be a useful project in which the draughtsmen of the class could draw the picture and the rest do the plaiting, all joining in the planning of the colours and arranging the plaits.

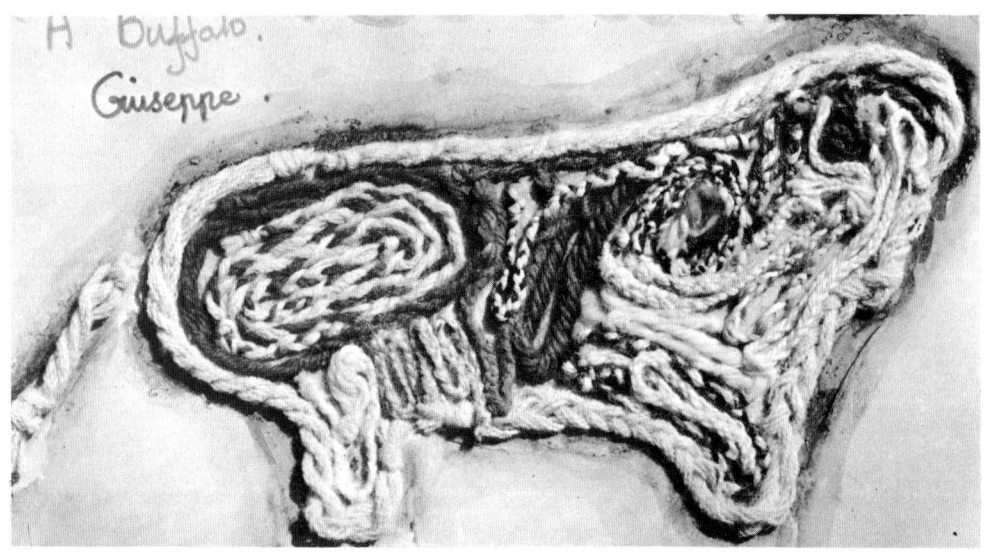

Mobiles for all

The first mobile discussed in this article brings together three sections of the craft class.

The units are motifs worked in machine embroidery. These are mounted in frames of cane twisted into rings and are then strung as a mobile on a fish shape made from thicker cane.

Free embroidery on the sewing machine gives the two-sided effect required in a mobile since the stitch is the same on either side of the material. To make these units transparent the ground material used is net in two units and tarlatan in the third. To obtain a painted effect pieces of different coloured net may be attached to both sides of the ground fabric. These are tacked in place and where an outline of the shape to be embroidered is desired it may be put on in running stitches which should be taken out when the embroidery is finished.

The ground material should be stretched tightly in a tambour frame with narrow rings, which will slip under the needle of the sewing machine when the presser foot is removed.

One of the main factors of good technique in machine embroidery is correct tension of the material in the frame. The fabric should be drum-tight and the grain should run straight, with warp and weft at right angles to each other. The frame should be screwed up very tightly to prevent the material from slipping.

Other requirements helpful to a beginner

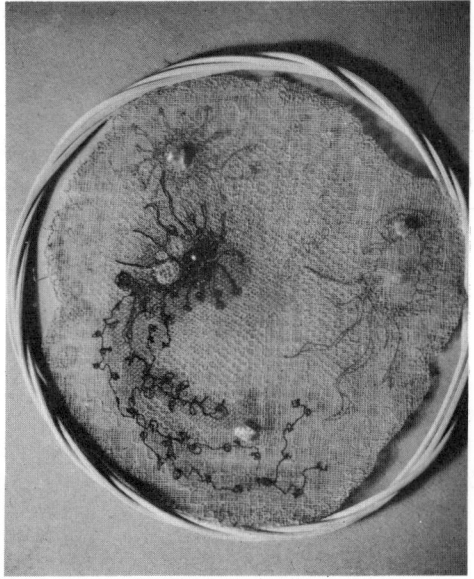

Detail of first mobile. Free machine embroidery mounted in cane frame

in machine embroidery are a fine needle in the machine and a suitable thread used both on the spool and for the top thread.

When the frame is dressed with the ground fabric and is placed under the machine needle the presser foot lever should be lowered so that the top thread is held at the same tension as it would have been had the foot not been removed. This point is important and should never be overlooked.

At the start of the embroidery the lower thread should be brought to the surface and held with the other until the first stitch is completed.

Some line work is useful in a design and this can be done by moving the frame in the direction necessary at a speed coordinating with the speed of the machine to make a suitable length of stitch. To control the frame the hands should be placed lightly on the top of the rings as shown in the photograph of the process on page 175. Fillings in the design may be solid like the granite filling done by taking the needle round in tight curls or may be lighter in effect like the granulating and vermicelli. Experiment with these fillings will demonstrate the different effects obtainable with different types of thread and varying tensions. So the complete design is gradually built up. When the work is taken from the machine beads and/or sequins can be stitched by hand on both sides of the fabric to give extra sparkle.

The motifs on their transparent ground materials are trimmed to shape and attached to the cane frames by stitches or with glue. In this mobile each frame is made from a piece of No. 6 centre cane about 2½ yards long twisted round itself three times in the form of a ring, but other materials can be used. Frames can be cut from polystyrene sheet or can be simple metal rings or wrought iron framework.

When the units are finished thought must be given to the hanging of them—the stringing, the design of the completed mobile and the position in which they will be displayed. Because the units are framed in rings of cane the hanging shape will also be of cane. It has been found that No. 15 centre cane makes a good medium for the frame work from which to hang units. A simple twist of cane makes the shape of a fish which is in keeping with the fish motif in one of the rings and invisible thread was used to suspend the rings from three points

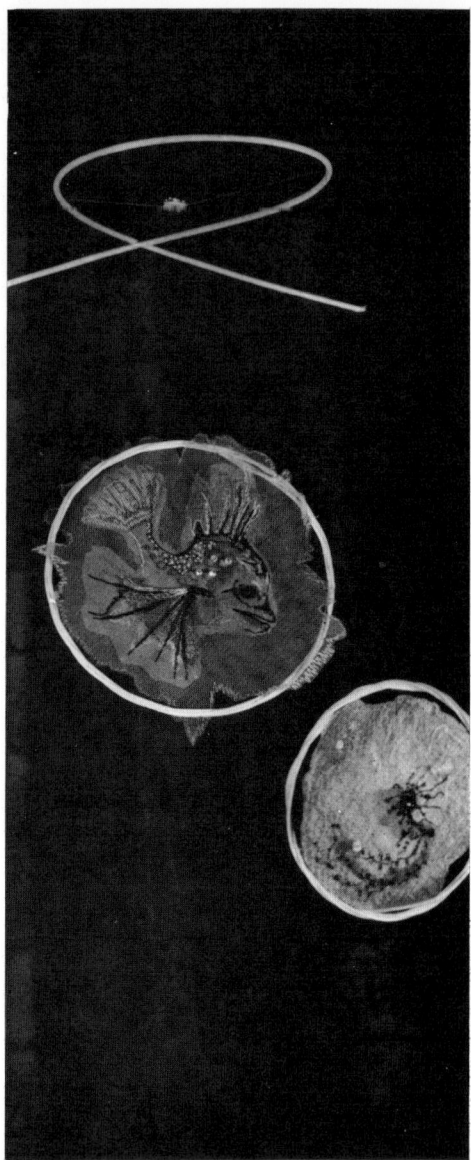

Units worked on net and tarlatan grounds in free machine embroidery

on it. A well strung mobile is obtained only by testing and experimenting with the balance of the units and the suspension of the completed arrangement. In this case a good balance was obtained when invisible thread was tied to cross the body of the fish from the framework to make supporting threads for the ring to hang from the centre. This also gave a position where the threads crossed on which could be fixed an eye. Any interesting detail such as a bead or jewel will fulfil this purpose. The suspension of the whole arrangement is worked from a central point on invisible thread or any thread desired so long as it is pliable and well twisted.

The second mobile shown has not the transparent effect of the first already described but the method of mounting allows the embroidery to be seen from all sides. The machine embroidery has been worked with the patterns from a fully automatic swing needle machine, which have been used to attach various textures of material e.g. fur, suede, date stones, glass etc., on to a coarse hessian ground, in the form of appliqué work. The finished embroideries were then mounted on cylinders which when hung would turn and show different phases of the embroidery in different combinations with each other. Five different sizes of cylinders were made, each embroidery combining a different set of textures and colours, but worked in combination with each other to make a satisfactory group.

The stringing of the five units was done on thin copper wire. The balance of them was tested and experimented with until the wires hung level and horizontal and until all the units hung freely without touching as they moved around.

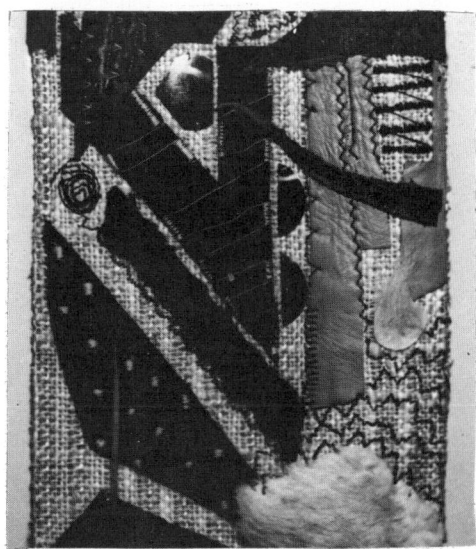

Above. Unit of second mobile before mounting showing embroidery stitches produced by an automatic machine

Left. Machine embroidered applique on a hessian ground mounted on cylindrical shapes

Flotsam and Jetsam

Ideas for mobiles are often inspired by the odds and ends brought home after a visit to the seashore.

Both the mobiles described and illustrated in this article were made from objects picked up on a beach. The theme of sea and sand was kept appropriately by working in natural-coloured string, linen thread and similarly coloured yarns of differing textures.

The first mobile is composed of three units in the form of beads hanging from a twist of wire. The beads are nothing more than bits of sea-washed glass of varied colours found on the beach, but to preserve the transparency and brilliance they had when wet they were coated with clear polyurethane varnish. Nail varnish could have been used as an alternative. When the varnish was dry the beads were chosen so that each unit would be made up of pieces similar in colour, shape or other likeness.

Since the bits of glass were solid, as would be the case if pebbles were used for a similar mobile, a form of mounting them had to be worked out. The method decided upon was that of using brass rings of appropriate sizes to form crowns on the top and bottom of each piece of glass. These rings were covered by buttonhole stitching in natural-coloured coton perle DMC No. 5 thread. Linen thread No. 25 of a similar colour to the coton perle was then threaded into a crewel needle and a framework of thread made by stitching through the knotted edge of the buttonholing on the rings crowning the pieces of glass. The framework was knotted

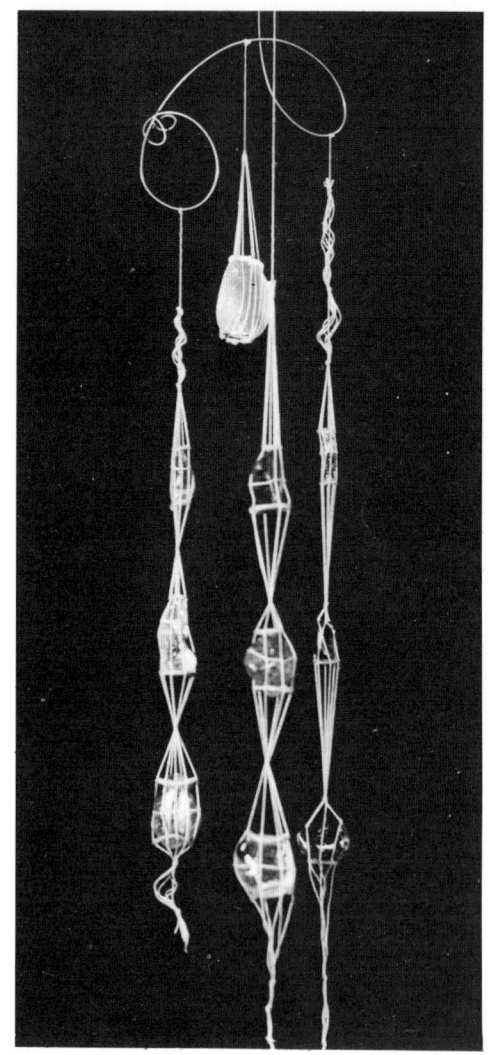

where necessary to hold the rings in place and to make a decorative pattern extending up the unit as shown in the detail photograph. A mobile of a similar pattern could have been made with thicker thread or string and different objects but the delicate effect of the glass and thin thread makes this mobile especially suitable for hanging in a well-lit place such as a window or beside a white wall which can show the shadows and coloured reflections thrown by the sun. The units were strung from a length of coppered welding wire, which had been obtained from a garage, bent into an abstract shape. Although the second mobile, like the first is made from bits and pieces from the beach and string and thread of varied textures, its effect is much rougher and heavier, the result of its being an experiment in string weaving. The theme of the mobile is ships' sails. Three shapes reminiscent of sails were made in wire to form frameworks for the string-weaving. The warp threads making the base of the fabric were wrapped round the wire

shapes in one direction after the wire had been given a thin coating of glue to keep them in place. The warp having been laid, the weaving was begun by threading a long, big-eyed needle with a considerable length of thin string and working in and out between the warp threads in the manner of darning. Two or three rows of tabby or plain weave were used first to hold the warp, spaced in position on the wire, and then the experimenting began. The threads were grouped, leaving large holes and this resulted in a pattern of heavy and light design effects. In places, in order to give emphasis or heavy texture, flat stones, shells, twigs and knots of wood were woven in, using them as a thread in the shed of the warp. When this is done the pieces of heavy texture should be woven in carefully in conjunction with tight, regular weaving of the string to prevent them falling out of the warp.

A different selection of textures of string was used in the three units but the basic theme and technique was maintained in all units.

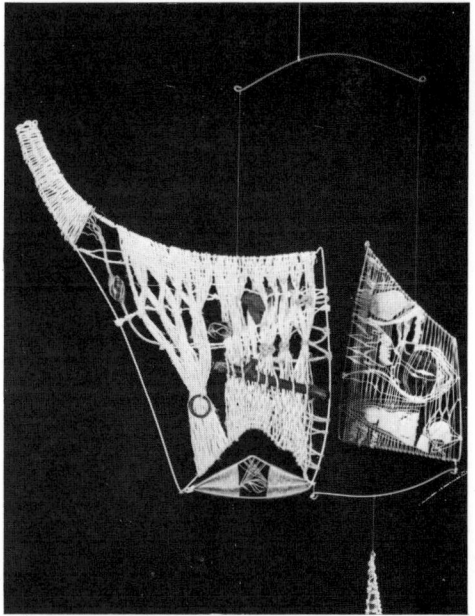

Decorative motifs for dresses

In this article I would like to suggest a rather more practical use for your ideas in exploring the great scope of this medium as a means of decorating dress. This is, of course, very much tied up with fashion, at times surface embellishment is in vogue, such as was the case during the reign of Elizabeth I, while at others plain unadorned garments are worn. At the present decoration has a certain popularity so that I would like to put forward various ideas for simple motifs which could transform a plain dress or jersey into an exclusive one.

For my first idea I have taken a landscape theme. Even using only one simple tree motif quite a striking effect can be achieved. By altering the size of the motif and placing a number of them around the hem or midriff of a dress an impression of pattern and distance is created. Here, as you will see in the illustration, I have cut a tree shape out of a material with a small floral print, the tree trunk is cut from brown corduroy. Another tree shape is cut from a piece of lace with a coarsely woven hessian for the trunk. By placing different areas of fabric around the tree it is even possible to extend the area and suggest a landscape. Pale delicate green or blue to depict spring or deeper, richer colour in summer, stark simple branch structures in winter.

One may place a single motif directly on to a garment with a few well-concealed stitches, but if a whole area such as the landscape described is being used, then it may be wiser to work on to a suitable piece of material. This whole area may then be easily removed when the garment needs washing. There should be only one area of major interest on any garment. Scattered areas of decoration lose emphasis and are best omitted, whereas a concentrated area of pattern gives richness and has purpose. Some areas are obviously more appropriate for this than others, for example the midriff, the hem, sleeves and pockets, rather than neckline, cuffs or a motif too near the waistline.

A more popular and even simpler motif is the flower. An attractive and simple flower may be cut out of material and perhaps enriched in the centre with another smaller flower from a different fabric or with beads or sequins. These individual flowers may then be grouped together into an arrangement of one or two placed on the outside of a sleeve or used as a central motif on a bodice.

There are many traditional and well-known symbols and shapes, all of which can be found by doing a little research in books at your local library. Looking carefully, observing details then simplifying the shapes of birds, butterflies, animals should give you many further ideas and enable you to transform some dull garments into more exciting ones.

Right. By placing different areas of fabric around the trees it is possible to extend an area and suggest a landscape

Tree motif cut from small floral print and brown corduroy

Tree motif cut from lace and woven hessian

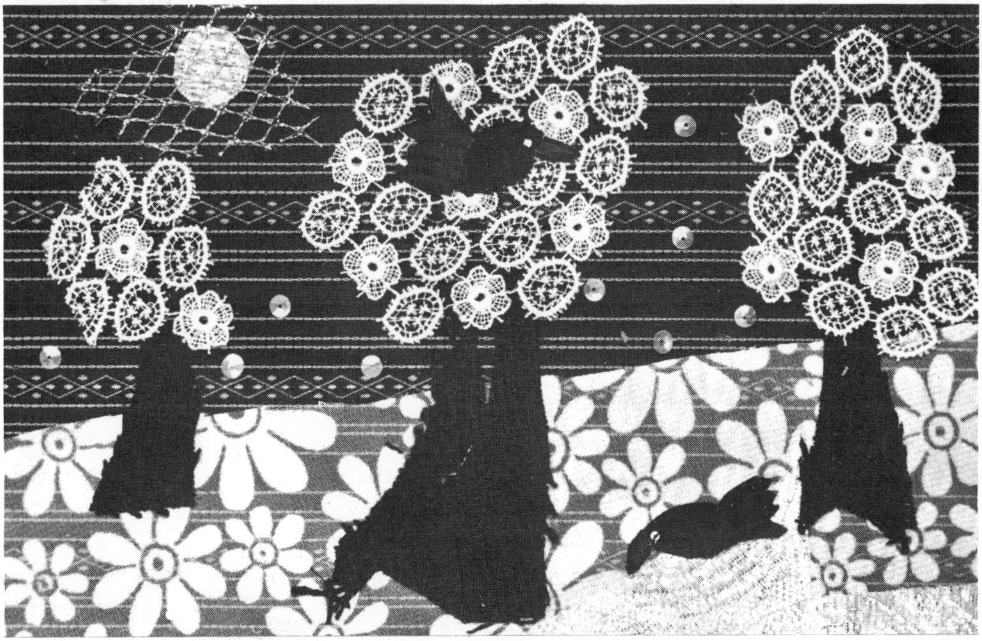

London folk

There is, of course, no limit to the subjects one might use in fabric collage. It is a unique medium in which one can contrast the densest, thickest of forests using wools and heavy tweed material with the most delicate of mists on a river by using a semi-transparent material such as net.

A story, a poem or a landscape, all these could inspire you but in this article I would like to suggest a city, like London, as being a rich source of inspiration.

The first and most important step is to collect your ideas: that is, in this case to go and visit places in your city. Make notes and sketches trying to find what really interests you most in a place. It is useful to keep a scrap-book which includes reproductions, written descriptions of colour and texture and perhaps odd pieces of appropriate fabric and threads. Small sketchbooks are the best means of recording first-hand information. These can easily be carried so that anything of interest can be noted down on the spot. Photographs in newspapers and magazines are often excellent so long as they are not regarded as a substitute for reality, but rather as a supplement to it.

Let us consider first the Tower of London and the legends which surround it. Most people know the story of the ravens in the Tower. It is said that when there are no more ravens left at the Tower the British Commonwealth will come to an end. These evil looking birds seem well suited to live in this place where so many heads have rolled off the block and so many ghosts are

said to walk still. Imagine the pictorial possibilities here, the bird itself and the richness of dark fabrics which one could use to depict its blue-black sinister quality; sequins and beads, velvets, satins and thick wools.

It is possible that the shape of a building itself is what interests you. Remember, if this is so, that although you might want it to be recognisable there is no need to strive after an entirely realistic image. Slavish copying is neither advisable nor suitable. Try to develop a simple approach so that basic forms and essential structures are understood better. Once having grasped the basic structure look carefully at the patterns made on turrets, chimney pots or at the decorative brick work found around the edges of doorways and windows.

The building itself, for example, the Tower

Sequins and beads, velvets and satins, and rich dark fabrics depict the sinister quality of the ravens at the Tower of London

of London, Hampton Court, St. James' Palace may be only as it were the stepping stone for your imagination. You may picture the court of Henry VIII with the nobles and their ladies all in richly decorated robes. Perhaps knights in armour, an Elizabethan lady or some ghosts who are said to still haunt in filmy transparency.

Tower Bridge could also be a fascinating subject with all its sombre industry. These are only a few ideas, and as you will see from the illustrations, the ones which have interested me particularly. There is an infinite variety of subjects from which to choose and you will, of course, find your own easily.

Having decided on a theme and collected ideas together in a notebook you can really begin to enjoy yourself. Choose those fabric pieces which look right on your background and suit your purpose. If you have difficulty regarding the choosing of colours remember that it is always best to restrain the impulse to use every colour to hand.

Using your sketches as reference, cut or tear the main shapes in paper and lay them on the background until they fit well into the area. Once having decided on these main shapes use them as patterns for your fabric. Large fabric areas may then be glued down with a rubber-based glue. It may be

necessary to secure the fabric to the background, it is unnecessary to embark on complicated embroidery stitches. You may wish to include stitchery to add richness and texture to your design and this can be very exciting, but do not feel bound to do so. The inclusion of other materials such as matchsticks, string, glass, beads, sequins can all add to the interest and three-dimensional quality of your picture.

In this short article I can give you only a few suggestions but even from these few an inexhaustible number of ideas may be worked out. You will find that once having begun to observe, ideas will multiply. Of course, you can adapt this idea to any city.

Puppets

Puppets from peculiar sources

Candle marionettes

Jumping Jacks, Jills and
Jollyboys

Puppets

Puppetry is one of the performing arts, primarily visual and concerned with performances and audiences, having elements of the other arts. Craftwork is involved: no puppets, no puppet shows—unless, as with notable French puppeteer Yves Joly, the human hands themselves become animated puppet creations. The craftwork involved is functional, serving the requirements of performance.

Unlike paintings and sculptures, performances are ephemeral, but are the only justification for puppet-making. The only valid test of the craftsmanship, whether at the most elementary or most advanced level, is effectiveness in performance. In fact, puppets are not really complete until on their stage and in action.

Twentieth century renaissance

Since its mid-twenties' renaissance the puppet art has successfully invaded the realms of film, television, advertising, education and therapy. In each of these areas it is always performance that matters. There are thousands of newcomers to the practice of puppetry every year: teachers, students in college, art school, drama school, young people in clubs, children in Nursery, Primary and Secondary school. *Given the right approach,* all can enjoy becoming actively involved in this branch of drama.

Books on puppetry

There is an unending flow of new books about puppetry: historical, technical. educa-

Hanuman the Monkey General; articulated shadow puppet from Andhra Pradesh, India. Figures cut from animal hide (known as Tholu Bomalatta) vary in size up to 1·5 m tall, height related to importance of character. Traditional plays are based on religious epics the *Ramayana* and *Mahabharata*

tional. An American publisher is issuing a six-volume Bibliography (Scarecrow Press, New Jersey). The Library of the City of Munich Puppet Theatre Collection has some 4,000 volumes from international sources. Technical works by experts do not always allow for the problems of beginners, and often assume too many prior craft skills. It is best to begin with the simple—with basic principles—mastering the simple before moving on to the more complex forms and methods.

String puppets (Kathputlis) of Rajasthan, India, are usually legless; those of Orissa sometimes have legs; minimum stringing: one from top of head passes over performer's hand and down to the back of waist; second string controls both hands of puppet

Puppet history

Puppetry has its own history, part of the history of mankind, and this might well be introduced into the conventional history lesson. In some parts of the world, notably India, Indonesia and China, puppets are mentioned in the earliest literary records. The history of the English puppet theatre alone is an inch thick, George Speaight's impressively documented *History of the English Puppet Theatre* (Harrap, 1955). The second edition of Paul McPharlin's *The Puppet Theatre in America: a history: 1524–1948* (with a Supplement "since 1948") (Plays, Inc. Boston, 1969) is 2 ins. thick, and has a chapter on the aboriginal (pre-

Columbian) puppets and much on the immigrant puppeteers from Spain, France, Italy, Germany and England.

There are books on puppetry in Europe, Asia and elsewhere, and on contemporary puppetry (part of the historical process) such as *The Puppet Theatre of the Modern World,* with some 240 illustrations, compiled by the editorial board of UNIMA, the international puppetry organisation, issued in eight language editions (English: Harrap, 1967).

In 1929 UNIMA (Union internationale de la marionnette) was founded, re-constituted in 1957, and now has members in over 50 countries, national sections including one in Britain. There have been outstanding and world-wide developments since World War II. National and international events are held each year, festivals, congresses, conferences (at which the themes for discussion often relate to the educational aspects).

It is of course not necessary to know all the historical background before starting practical puppetry, but teachers should certainly know enough to be able to answer the questions bound to be asked about puppet origins. Bill Baird's *The Art of the Puppet* (Collier-Macmillan, 1967) is a magnificently-illustrated survey of traditional and contemporary puppetry. Two of the present author's works supply basic data: *Dictionary of Puppetry* (Macdonald, 1969) and *Let's Look at Puppets* (Muller, 1966), the latter aimed at Juniors upwards.

The realisation that puppetry in education, at all levels, is part of the historical process can be an extra incentive to the practice of the art. The standard book for educationists is *The Puppet Book,* edited Wall, White & Philpott (Faber, 3rd edition, 1965) compiled by a committee of the Educational Puppetry Association.

Scope of puppetry

Puppet shows can be for—or by—the very young or any age-group up to adult. There can be solo or group performances. Shows can be very simple, naive, highly sophisticated, avant-garde, or outright revolutionary. *Space Age Puppets and Masks* (Harrap, 1969) by two craft teachers, M. C. Green and B. R. H. Targett, has topical inspiration and illustrations of authentic children's work.

Puppet shows can be in different *styles*— realistic or naturalistic, surrealist, symbolist, abstract, pop, auto-destructive (an Yves Joly item needs new puppets for each performance) and out and out fantastic.

Different methods of construction and control of puppet action continue to evolve.

Puppet repertoire

The repertoire of the Puppet Theatre is of an extraordinary range, as can be seen at any of the international festivals. Some shows reflect live theatre, some burlesque live theatre, some are unique to the puppet theatre. Productions include: high and low drama, classical and contemporary comedy, tragedy, farce, slapstick, pantomime, fairy tale, fable, satire, musicals, opera, circus, folk dance, ballet, underwater ballet, space travel. Types of production possible in the classroom, college, club, etc., are for those involved to decide (teacher, instructor, students, children).

Techniques

Teachers and others who fight shy of the word "experiment" should look afresh at the learning process by which *any* technical skills are acquired: always and unavoidably personal experiment is involved, the individual handling of tools and materials. This is still true if one of the step-by-step and infinitely detailed type of textbook is used as the starting point. *Discovering answers for oneself is one of the major "educational values".*

Puppetry stimulates observation, the learning about the nature and use of materials, of textures, colour, the effect of light, of movement, weight, co-ordination, and of team work.

There are no technical problems whatsoever— until it has been decided what specific end-results are desired, what type of puppet is to be used, what form and style of production is to be achieved. The very real and much publicised "educational values" of puppetry derive from individual thinking, active imaginations, the joy of creating and the social value of performing to audiences. Satisfaction comes from finding the answers

Nozacek (Pinocchio) from the Central Puppet Theatre, Prague, Czechoslovakia. Rod puppet with string controlled legs. Operator: Violet Philpott

for oneself and in giving pleasure to others. I recall the noticeable change in social outlook of a group of boys on probation when in their own eyes they became "showmen".

Puppets in education
Results of real worth do not follow automatically when puppetry is introduced into the curriculum, from the making of a few puppets simply as a craft exercise, or from "doing" puppetry merely for speech training or any other teacher-motive. *Puppetry in the Curriculum,* a Bulletin published by the Board of Education of the City of New York, as far back as 1947, includes an analysis of results obtained by the various grades of

children using all types of puppets—listed under Language Arts, Social Studies, Science, Music, Arithmetic, Health, Art— but it must be appreciated that maximum results depend on *how* the art is introduced, at each level, and the importance of the appeal of puppetry *for its own sake*. Used as a teaching-aid (e.g. in the teaching of French in the Primary school, or of English with immigrant children) the proper under- standing of *the dramatic use of puppets* is essential.

Beginning puppetry

Ideally, beginners should first see some good shows and demonstrations of making and handling puppets—but all too often the opportunity is lacking. Courses are some- times held locally but unfortunately they are not at all common enough. The majority of beginners, however, are obliged to consult books or leaflets, these having the dis- advantage of being unable to demonstrate movement-control.

The watching of puppet films, fictional or documentary, can help visually, but is no substitute for handling puppets and dis- cussing technical points with experts. A *List of Puppet Films* for hire in Britain, with addresses of distributors, is obtainable from the Educational Puppetry Association. A high percentage of newcomers to puppetry are therefore obliged to begin experimentally anyway. This has the advantage, however, that originality is called into play and exciting discoveries displace any tendency to mere reproduction of examples from books.

As with all the arts, puppetry should be judged by the best. There is alas plenty of bad puppetry, which could well put off the newcomer for life.

There is even an anti-puppet brigade—in- cluding the magistrate who lumped puppetry in with other educational innovations to which he attributed present day juvenile delinquency. A principal of a college, who should have known better, allegedly told a student who wished to make a special study of the art, that puppetry is "dying". People are dying, all the time, yet we also have a population explosion. In India puppets are even being used to promote the use of the Pill. Certainly there can be no real doubt that puppets are experiencing their own all-time-high population explosion, as reflected in international events.

There are also the myth-makers who decry the use of one type of puppet and extol the virtue of their own pet type, whereas in fact *all types* have their particular possibilities and limits. The world-famous Russian puppetmaster Sergei Obraztsov, during an appearance at the Toynbee Theatre in London, when asked if it were true that the marionette type was now "out" in his Moscow puppet theatre, replied: "Not at all. The choice of type depends on the par- ticular production." His reply was the more significant in that he uses hand (glove) puppets in his brilliant solo performances, and his development of the rod puppet techniques (in large-scale productions) has influenced world developments.

Any type of puppet, then, can be experi- mented with by any age group—so long as the beginning is with simple forms and methods of control. Children and adults will discover for themselves the constructional and performing limits.

Puppetry fundamentals

Some percentage of the readers of this will already have the necessary preliminary grounding in the subject. The discussion of *fundamentals* which here follows is for the benefit of the newcomers, the fresh and

Tulukutu figures from Zambia. Operator: boy at Hoxton Hall, E. London. Puppets activated by performer slapping his thighs, tightening and slackening strings looped around his big toes. Rhythm may be chanted by group

eager minds, and perhaps for those who may already have begun on conventional or haphazard lines and are a little frustrated by results so far. Once an understanding has been gained of the nature of *the puppet itself* and of what puppetry is all about, the practice of the art will be rewarding to all concerned, teachers, pupils, audiences.

Puppet Function A puppet is not a doll, which is a private plaything; and it is not "an actor". A puppet is (physically) *a theatrical character;* it is created to perform on a stage before an audience. A puppet requires a human actor to animate it (give it life: which is *more* than mere manipulation). It has been called "the complete mask". Off-stage it remains the same character. The actor on the human stage uses his own body as a kind of puppet and it is an amusing and useful exercise for the would-be puppeteer to "become" a puppet controlled by imaginary strings or rods, or with co-actors controlling the movements of his head, arms, legs.

Puppetry A term covering the complete art of creating puppet characters, acting with them, designing and making the puppet stage (improvised or permanent), scenery and props, providing lighting (simple or complex), music, sound and visual "effects". *Range of parts* Because he is not seen, the physique and physiognomy of the actor-with-puppets do not limit the range of parts he can play as they may on the human stage. The actor-with-puppets can play human, animal or completely fantastic parts, may be required to play *several* parts in the *same* production. A solo performer plays *all* the parts as well as taking care of all back-stage activity. Puppetry provides universal opportunity for every child or adult who wishes to act (even the physically handicapped), one of the major 'educational values' of this art.

Performing As in the human theatre, the actor-with-puppets has to "identify" with each character he plays—but has the *extra* problem of *acting through the puppet*. Acting the part off-stage is wasted effort unless transferred to the puppet. If the characters are to speak, the actor must provide the appropriate voices.

In some complex forms of performance, where very elaborate and detailed movement of puppet hands, heads and body, is required, the handling of the *same* character may need two or more animators, these collectively identifying with the character. Mastery of the traditional Bunraku puppets in Japan, requiring three actors each, means years of dedicated experience.

Character range In addition to the obvious human character types—hero, heroine, villain, clown, and so on—many animal

Author introducing junk-box puppets to children at Prior Weston School

characters (naturalistic or humanised), from mouse to elephant, can appear on the puppet stage—and more effectively than on the human stage. Kipling's *How the Elephant Got His Trunk* is pure puppet material. Some "personality puppets" such as Muffin the Mule and Sooty the Teddy Bear have become world famous, and others will doubtless appear. Birds, fish and other underwater creatures and those of the fairy kingdom and myth, fabulous monsters (converted egg trays!), strange outer space inhabitants and, as seen in therapeutic puppetry, those of the *inner* fantasy world, extend the range. *Objects,* apart from being used in puppet construction, may have a life of their own on the puppet stage: a broom may sweep by itself (aided by a concealed rod or a string) and may even talk; flowers may grow visibly; a balloon play hide and seek with its owner.

Puppet Theatre This is the trendy term for the genre rather than a reference to a building or auditorium. There are enough puppet theatres to justify the publication of an international directory (enlarged edition in preparation)—but there are only two professional puppet theatres in Great Britain: *The Little Angel,* in Islington, London, and *The Harlequin,* at Rhos-on-Sea, North Wales.

The Harlequin has twice been the centre of international festivals.

The term "puppet theatre" in the title of a company does not of itself indicate possession of a theatre building. Most companies are mobile, including those with theatres.

Types of Puppet The distinguishing feature of each type is technical: *the means of control.* The hand or glove type is animated by the human hand inside it. The rod type has a main central rod supporting the head, with other rods to the hands. The string type (marionette) may have any number of strings attached to the moveable parts of the puppet and to some sort of handling device held by the animator. The shadow puppet, usually controlled by rods, is, however, distinguished by the fact that the puppet itself is not seen, only its shadow on an illuminated screen. There are hand-rod and other hybrid types.

Hand or Glove Puppet The first thing to study for this type is *the human hand itself:* the hand is part of the anatomy of the puppet which is "the hand dressed up". As well as Yves Joly's (white gloved) hands becoming a sea anemone and an octopus, there are performers content with a ball on a finger and a bare hand as a character. A Hungarian does a spectacular cock-fight with net gloves plus small heads on his thumbs. A teacher created a brood of chicks from cut-wool on a net glove, a head on each finger, watched over by a hand-puppet hen.

The arrangement of the fingers should be related to the type of character and construction: human, animal, fish, etc. The traditional "three finger" method of the Punchman is not suitable for group work, the fingers not being interchangeable from left to right hand of the performer (a factor important where several actors share a stage, with puppet entries and exits right, left and centre). For human (or upright animal) characters the modern use of index-and-middle fingers in the neck, thumb in one arm, ring-and-little fingers in other arm, gives a body shape permitting use on either hand. The three-finger method is practical with small animals such as tortoise or squirrel.

The wrist is the natural waist-line for hand puppets of the human kind: it gives the performer a guide to the right height for holding the puppet. The costume should reach almost to the elbow. Wrist and forearm movements also come into play with animals and monsters. A variant of the hand type is the arm (or sleeve) type: with arm-length bodies, usually monsters.

Another variant is the two hand puppet (forearms crossed) as with the fish or crocodile with head and tail movements. Some puppeteers use larger puppets with both thumbs inserted in the neck, the remaining fingers being the arms (restricting performer to one puppet at a time). With the hand puppet the performer is below stage; the top of his head should be just below the playboard level (acting area). In solo performances the puppeteer can sit or stand; the kneeling position should be avoided, being exhausting! In group work it is essential to stand and be mobile.

Rod Puppet The central head-supporting rod is also the spine of this type. Experiments with rods of different lengths and thicknesses are advisable: gripping too thin or too heavy a rod imposes hand strain, affecting performance. Some writers stress the "majestic" possibilities of rod-controlled puppets, but it will be discovered that they have in fact a very wide range: they can move at speed, swirl about, can even be tossed into the air. A shoulder-piece can be added to support the costume and for attaching arms (which may be lengths of rope, or sections of thin cardboard tube). The head-rod swivels freely in a hole in the shoulder-piece. Hands can be of card, wood or foam rubber. Garden canes, thin plastic rods or stiff wire (preferably with hand grips) attach to hands or wrists.

Usually the stage for rod type is similar to, but wider than, the hand type stage, with performer's head reaching to just below playboard level: but short performers may use longer rods.

Mixing the types

Usually the performer's hand is inside the puppet, holding a short head-rod, with external rods to the puppet hands. A variant employs the live hand as puppet hand—whether related to size of puppet head or not.

Balloon-head rod puppet

Two-man rod puppet with balloon head

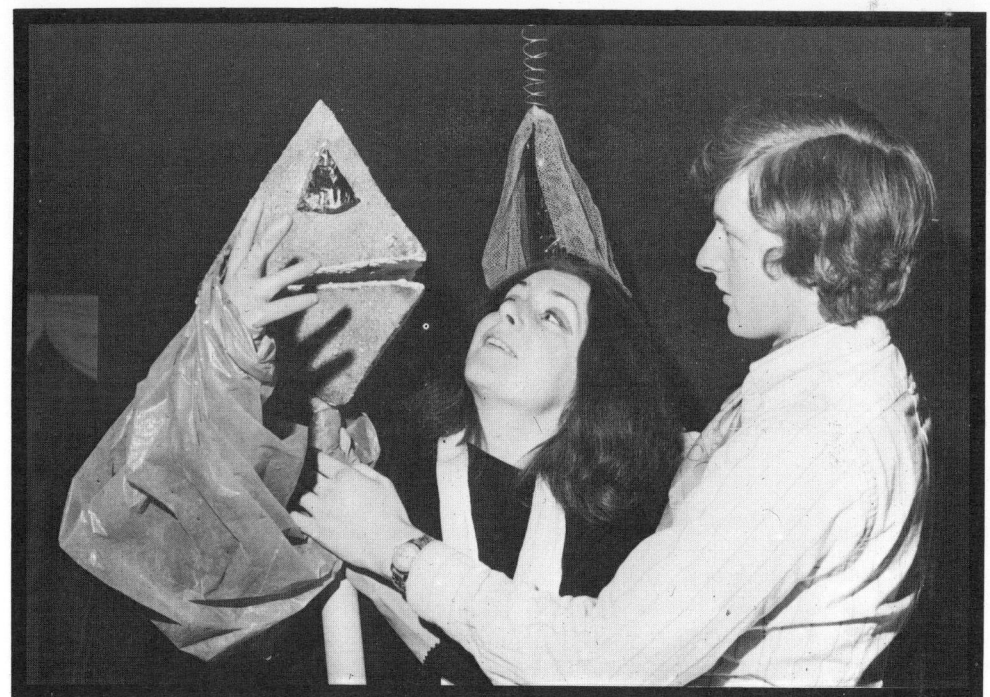

Rod puppet Space creatures. Science fiction lends itself to the puppet stage

Rod puppets

Often used for animal characters. Some sort of spine (e.g. coiled wire spring) is attached to the tops of the two rods, then details added. A cat, very flexible, on examination may prove to be a feather boa or other material. The front and back legs of a horse can share a rod each. Just as study of the hand puppet begins with the live hand, so it is discovering the possibilities of the rod or rods which can lead to interesting and original creations of the rod type.

Shadow puppets

Here it is essential to start with the three ingredients: a translucent screen (e.g. white sheeting stretched taut over a glass-less picture frame, with wooden feet added), a source of light (even strong daylight), and some flat cut-out shapes. Experiments with materials and objects such as fern fronds, cake doilys, coloured toffee-papers, coloured balloons, strings of glass or wood-beads, etc., will give ideas for developing shadow scenes. Methods of control depend on kind of movements desired—short rods or strings. The operating position can be at rear, below, above, or sides of screen. Light from hand torches with colour variations can be explored. The simplest demonstration of shadow possibilities can be given by holding a sheet of white paper in front on a light source, then putting the other hand behind and close to the paper. The closer the hand or object to the screen, the sharper the silhouette. Experiments can be made with plain silhouettes and with outline figures and coloured effects. An excellent book on modern techniques is *Play with Light and Shadow* by Herta Schönewolf (Studio Vista, 1969) with illustrations related to the delightful and technically interesting items demonstrated by German art-teacher students.

String puppets or marionettes

The first term is clearer as to technique. In French "marionette" is the equivalent of English generic "puppet": other words being added to distinguish the various types —important to remember if reading French puppet literature. This type is operated from above stage—by anything from one to sixty strings (India and Burma respectively) or average of nine (Europe and America).

Instead of copying the joined human figure of most textbooks, then adding strings, it is more instructive to *begin with a string* to which some object is attached—an old tennis ball, or perforated plastic ball used in Infant schools, a bunch of keys, a handkerchief . . . anything. The performer can stand on a table, a low platform, or the floor, trying different lengths of string (thin twine, carpet thread) and discover the range of movement possible. The ball can be made to bounce, jump, climb a chair, fly. The ball can then be given arms and legs, dressed up, turn into some fantastic creature. A solo performer can use two handkerchief puppets—or even more if the strings are attached to a horizontal stick; two or more performers can perform a handkerchief ballet to music.

By adding a *second* ball, free running on the string, with an extra string to control it, the principle of creating certain "trick" figures is realised (the popular "dissecting skeleton" has a double set of strings). The Rajasthani marionette has a single string from the head (passing over the performer's hand) to the

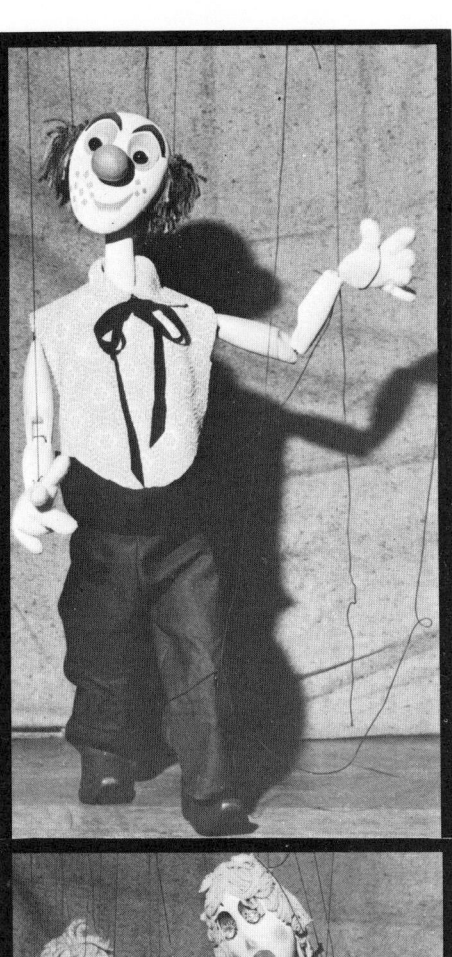

Carved wooden marionettes by John Thirtle

rear of the waist, with another running down to the puppet hands, and remarkable dance movements are achieved.

Usually when the strings exceed two some sort of handling device (control, controller, perch) is usual, to which the strings are attached. The control itself may have moveable parts. With a control (the simplest form being a single stick) some movements can be obtained merely by tilting the stick. What is important is to realise that the control is an integral part of the marionette, just as the human hand is of the glove puppet. Two sticks can be used separately or joined to form a cross. A vertical stick can have various cross pieces added (e.g. a detachable leg-bar) and various wire or tape extensions for special stringing.

As manner of movement is part of the characterisation of each puppet, the control design should be related to the needs of each character—not standardised. In group work, where the animators may be very close to each other on the "bridge" of the stage, the *size* of the control needs considering. In the famous Salzburg Marionette Theatre where productions of opera and ballet are given, compact controls are used. A solo performer, such as Albrecht Roser from Stuttgart, sometimes has quite large controls.

Rod and string puppets

Variants of the rod and string types. Sometimes rods may be used *downwards*—as in southern India, where strings supporting the puppet are attached to an iron band around the performer's turban, the puppet hands being controlled by downward rods. The heavy Sicilian armoured knights (paladins) are supported by a strong head rod *downwards;* a lighter rod controls the sword arm; a cord controls the shield arm. Fights are spectacular! The puppeteers sell small replicas as souvenirs—about a foot high—with tin armour, a stiff head wire;

these might well be made by juniors in school.

Mixing the types

Given the necessary staging facilities, it is sometimes feasible to use *two or more types* in the *same* production. A shadow screen, for instance, can be used to present a dream sequence in a hand-puppet production. The Hungarian puppet company from Budapest use a translucent tent (screen) in their version of the *Petroushka* ballet; the hero and the Blackamoor appear as shadowy figures "inside" the tent, and three-dimensional forms outside.

A Polish show used three different *acting levels* in a large-scale production in which an old violinist is kicked out of Heaven for disturbing the work of the Angels (*Zwyrtala the Musician*) and returns to his beloved mountains. The Hungarians also used all types of puppet in a version of *Midsummernight's Dream*. The drama blocks found in most schools would lend themselves to building various acting levels.

Toy theatres

There has been something of a revival of interest in this form since the appearance of the second edition of George Speaight's impressive work on the Juvenile Drama (*History of the Toy Theatre,* Studio Vista, 1969). Mr. Speaight himself performed at Pollock's new premises (1 Scala Street, London, W.1) the Mecca of J. D. enthusiasts, 'when the publishers gave a party to launch the book. Flat cut-out figures a few inches high are pushed on stage from the wings by means of simple horizontal wire controls. This is drawing-room scale, but (even if the purists shudder at the suggestion) it is possible to produce a *large scale show* with figures 1 ft. or 2 ft. tall, moved in on long wooden battens on a hall platform or trestle tables. I recall a beautiful version of *La Belle Dame Sans*

Merci done in this fashion, with some harp music in the wings.

Toy puppets

Very simple to construct, the traditional "Jumping Jack" of the German woodcarvers is making a come back. Flat figures, some times with shaped arms and legs, head and body in one piece, supported by a short head-string, the four limbs controlled by a single string from below. Good illustrations in *Make Your Own Dolls* by Ströbl-Wohlager (Batsford, 1968). Lindie Wright (of *The Little Angel* theatre) has produced gay modern figures about 20 ins. high. Jumping *Jills,* too, and *animals* make jolly variations. Pollock's still have some of the early French "pantins"—printed sheets for cutting out and mounting on card, operated in similar manner to the Jumping Jack.

Tulukutu

Small whittled figures with lion-skin loin-cloths, from Zambia, operated by performer seated on ground, legs outstretched, short strings (horizontal) from the figures to the performer's big toes. Fun for infants and juniors! The two figures share a single pair of arms (split cane). Before World War 1, very similar "clothes peg puppets" were known in Britain, one string tied to leg of chair or table. The Zambians say Tulukutu is indigenous to their region, but there is a possible relationship with earlier European

Jumping Jacks (German and Italian) and Finger Puppet made of felt (Czechoslovakia)

marionnettes à *la planchette,* of which there are reproductions from French lithographs and a Hogarth engraving (*Southwark Fair*) in various puppet books. With these a horizontal string passes through the chest of one, two or more figures (of simple articulation) and is attached to a short post at one end of a plank on the ground (the "stage"). The other end is looped around the performer's knee, leaving both hands free for playing pipe and tabor or bagpipes. Tapping with the foot induces amusing puppet action. Well worth reviving in school, perhaps.

Head puppet
A sophisticated type consisting of a large puppet head perched on the performer's own head, held by a chin strap, possibly with a moving-mouth control. The puppet hands are the actor's live hands. Something for seniors to try out!

Multi-puppet stage
Although experiments are being made in the production of puppet shows without any formal stage, for many performers the anonymity of a stage (*something* to hide behind, even a blanket pinned across a

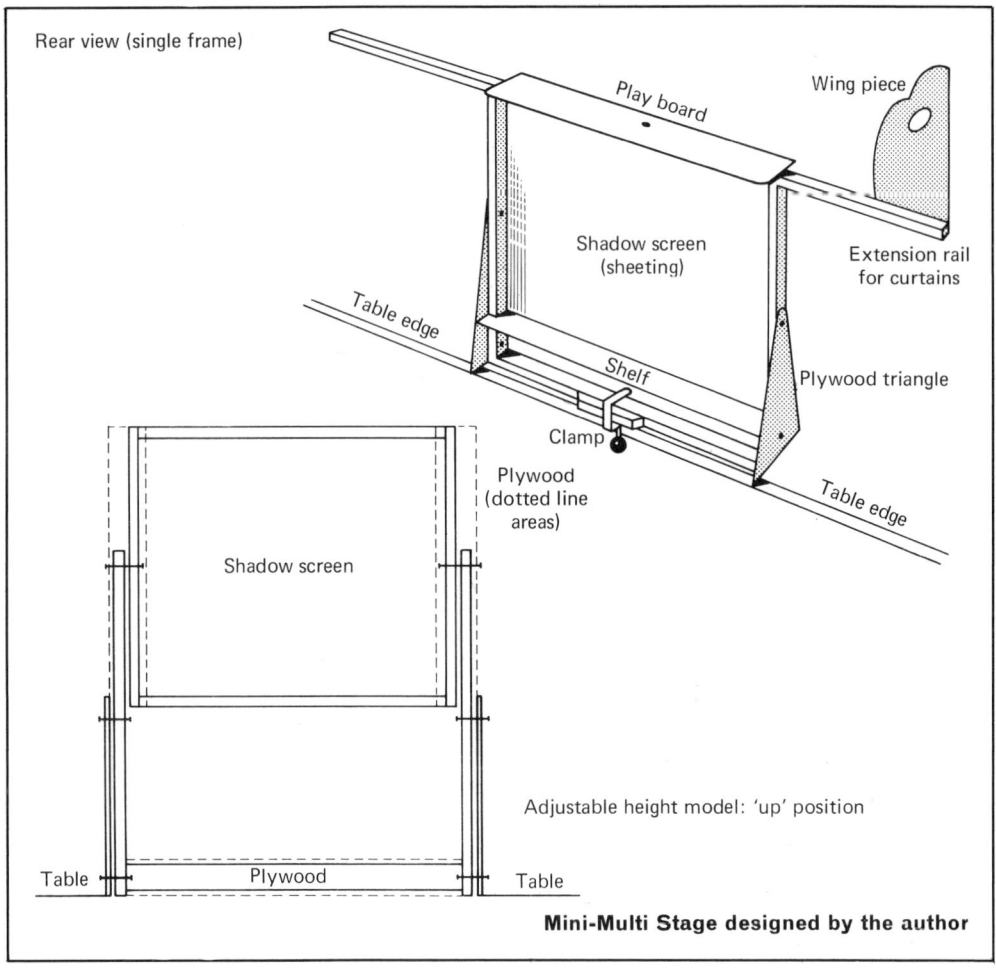

Rear view (single frame)

Play board

Wing piece

Shadow screen (sheeting)

Extension rail for curtains

Table edge

Shelf

Plywood triangle

Clamp

Table edge

Plywood (dotted line areas)

Shadow screen

Adjustable height model: 'up' position

Table

Plywood

Table

Mini-Multi Stage designed by the author

doorway) releases their innate acting ability. A simple multi-purpose classroom stage should be available from the beginning. The model here illustrated was designed for demonstrations in African colleges, on a tour sponsored by the British Council. It can freely be modified as to size and proportions to suit individual needs.

Easy to construct, compact, ready for use in minutes (simply clamp to edge of table), minimum storage space, ideal for classroom use for all types of puppet. Dimensions,

proportions, adapted to individual needs. A variable-height model can be used by groups of differing heights or where used on tables of different heights.

Basic structure is a single frame, square or oblong, made from 1 in. by 1 in. (planed) wood, the corners fixed by triangular plywood plates held in place by an impact adhesive and then $\frac{1}{2}$ in. panel pins. For extra strength a 2 in. nail is driven through each corner (through the verticals into the cross rails, after gluing). A further cross

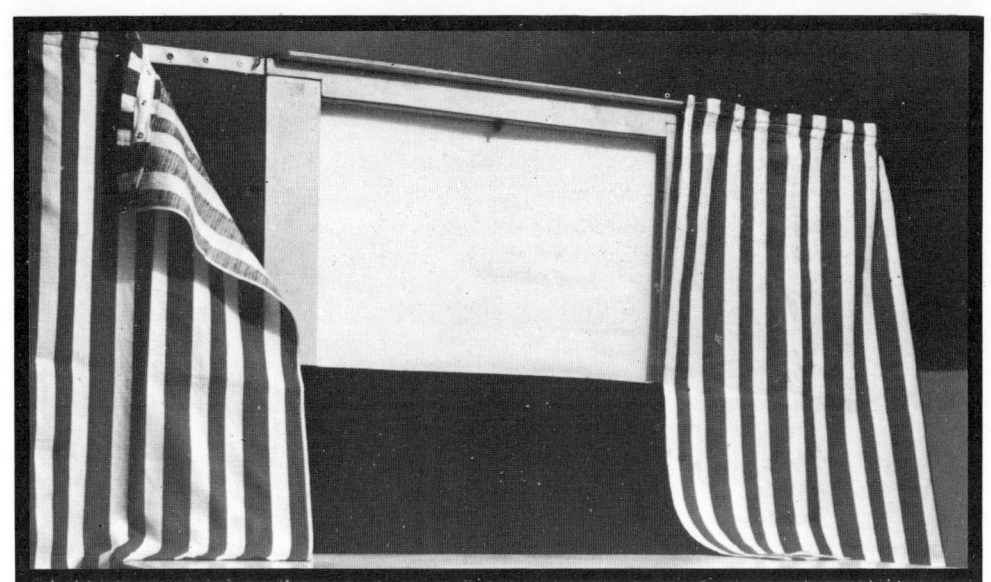

rail is fixed about 4 ins. above the bottom rail, this area being covered in by plywood on the face side of the stage. The open area above this is covered by white sheeting stretched taut and fixed with drawing pins (at rear) forming the shadow screen. A narrow plywood shelf can run the width of the extra rail (screwed and glued along the underside) extending about the width of a matchbox, to support standing shadow figure or scenery.

The framework is clamped to edge of table top (4 in. clamp) and a better grip is obtained if a short block of 1 in. by 1 in. (4 in.–6 in. long) is screwed and glued to rear-centre of bottom rail. For rigidity, counteracting the tendency to push forward on the stage during performance, a long plywood triangle is bolted to each of the verticals, giving the effect of a buttress. When the stage is of one fixed height, these buttresses are positioned by a short piece of $\frac{1}{4}$ in. dowel projecting from the vertical 1 in. below top of the plywood, with corresponding hole in the latter.

In the variable height model a second bolt may replace the dowel, or may be used in addition to the dowel, to fix the frame (shadow screen section) when raised to higher position. Bolts are of the hexagonal-head type for easy handling, with wing nuts; diameter $\frac{1}{4}$ in., length 1$\frac{1}{2}$ in. or 2 in. to 2$\frac{1}{2}$ in. according to need.

To extend the playing area of the stage for glove or rod puppets (or to hang a back-cloth for marionettes) a length of 1 in. by 1 in. (not less than 4 ft.) is bolted to the top of the frame and may optionally have wing pieces at each end, so that puppets do not need to appear from below stage. To prevent movement of this extension bar, a length of plywood 2 in. wide is attached to the side of the bar, running the width of the frame and overlapping the top cross rail, only one bolt is then necessary.

Finally, a "playboard" (on which to place props—box, basket, etc.)—consisting of a shelf 4 in. wide and 1 ft. long, can be held by the same bolt. A short piece of 1 in. by 1 in. fixed to the underside of the playboard, pressing against the rear of the top rail, prevents movement.

On the original model the curtain was attached to press-stud tape glued to the extension rail (removable for packing) with a centre section of two draw curtains on a taut, concealing the shadow screen until required. For the variable height model the length of curtain should allow for maximum height.

The variable height stage consists of a simple square or oblong frame—similar method of construction—preferably with plywood the full length of the verticals and 3 ins. wide, overlapping the supporting (outer) frame, acting as a runner when changing height. The supporting piece consists of two verticals, a bottom cross rail, a second ditto, but *no top rail*. Additional bolt holes will probably need to be 3 ins. or 4 ins. apart. The maximum height determines the length of the verticals of the supporting frame; a 6 ins. overlap is desirable to ensure rigidity. The illustrations clarify technical points. Individual makers may vary method of construction (e.g. if part of a formal carpentry project).

If a second table is used as a "bridge" on which the performers stand, marionettes can be used *in front of* the stage. Another possibility is to have a backscreen clamped to a second table, two or three feet to rear of stage, and of appropriate height: two uprights of 2 ins. by 1 in. batten and a connecting top batten, with a neutral colour back cloth.

In classroom work no special lighting need be provided except for shadow shows, for which one of the flexible arm clamp-on lamps will suffice, attached to the rear of playboard and focusing on the screen. Experiments with large torches can be made.

Puppets from peculiar sources

Much of the waste material which is normally thrown into the domestic dustbin could be diverted to the classroom for puppet purposes.

Any puppet-minded teacher (or student concerned with visual aids for use in school practice) could easily assemble an impressive display of convertible basic shapes—the various forms of empty egg-boxes, cheese-boxes, squeezies and other plastic containers, picnic plates, ice cream cartons, paper pulp flowerpots, cones from cereal carton card, the humble toilet roll, postal tubes, milk cartons—which have inspirational as well as economic value.

Alongside these basic shapes for heads put a colourful array of samples of materials for puppet hair—as many textures as possible: string, rope, plumber's tow (hemp, jute), strips of crepe paper and felt, raffia, garden twine, feathers, fur, fur-fabric offcuts, and what have you. Some could be home-dyed for extra variety.

A large sheet of perforated hardboard (peg-board) makes a good assembly area for mounting everything. Some space can be allocated to puppet eyes (mounted on a piece of black card): beads, buttons, bottle-tops, coloured drawing pins and map pins gummed paper shapes, self-stick labels (stationers carry wide range of colours and sizes), cardboard badges, sequins, marker pens.

This nowhere near exhausts materials with puppet potential: foam rubber offcuts and old sponges; plastic, rubber, or cloth stuffed balls; bottle mops; lengths of metal tape (from tea chests), bendable, fine for tails (covered with fur, felt, etc.); cotton reels, floral wire, galvanised wire, pot scourers, fish line (nylon) and guitar strings for animal whiskers.

Storage boxes and plastic laundry and food bags, all clearly labelled, economize time in the search for most effective materials. Sleeves from old pullovers and legs from pyjamas make fine arm-length bodies for monsters with egg-box heads. Socks convert easily to lesser monsters, with or without stuffed feet. Tops of socks (especially coloured, striped footer types) make sailors' knitted caps.

Puppet bodies should vary with different characters and shape of head to which to be attached; do not have fixed "patterns". A vital factor in performing is to have the *inside* measurements right for the hand of the performer; variations in external shape can be made by stuffing with foam rubber offcuts or other fillings.

The greater the total range of basic shapes and disguise materials, the greater the range of inspired creatures which will emerge—many of which could have been visualised by the experienced puppet-maker eyeing the rubbish heaps.

Tubes of quick stick adhesives (for cloth to cloth); push-through paperclips, sticky tape, needles and threads, scissors and rigid-blade craft knives, should be available. Then sheer experiment can commence.

Time enough when the possibilities of the

Display board showing basic shapes, hair materials, eyes, etc.

214

basic shapes have been exhausted to switch to the slower processes of modelling or carving.

It is not necessary to 'design' puppets on paper first—and this could only be done satisfactorily by a designer already familiar with many textures and colours. Simply by handling materials the puppet-maker will invent characters.

Experiment includes trying all available hair materials and all eyes on each head, to find the "right" combination before finally attaching these.

All details must be effective *at a distance*— and so should be tested across the classroom. The principle is the same as for stage "make up"; it must look right *to the audience*. This is why it is advisable to have some form of simple classroom stage on which to try out puppets *during the making*.

A factor all too often overlooked and which considerably affects quality of performance is the comfort of performers. There are *two* 'acting areas' in all puppet stages (1) that where the human actors move about (2) that where the puppets are seen in action. Performers squashed together, having to stretch or crouch, tire quickly as well as limiting the action range of their puppet characters.

It is futile to talk about the "educational values" of puppetry if these are defeated by ignorance of essential technical requirements; this is true from the nursery upwards. The teacher or student who will assemble the initial display of materials and makes two or three finished puppets to show in action, lets the children handle and play with them, will usually be surprised by the speed with which the children then take over and produce their own creations.

The child is struck by the accent on inspirational materials stacked on shelves or in boxes (including some lucky-dip assortments). It is found that even adult students sometimes need such starting points, having no clear mental picture of the puppet characters to be made.

Candle marionettes

Candles, with a string wick firmly set in easily-carved wax, are an excellent base for marionette making. The wicks provide a ready-made means of "jointing" those sections of the marionette's body where movement is desired. The wax itself can be marked and shaped with a blunt knife or metal ruler. Mistakes can be easily corrected by dropping melted wax on a broken or badly carved section and recarving the new wax once it is cold. The wax marionette, perhaps surprisingly, does not break easily but can, anyway, be simply repaired. The basic raw materials are cheap and easily obtainable. The final result is dependent on the skill of the class, but the technique is appropriate to both Primary and Secondary school pupils.

Materials
1. One large candle from which the trunk and head will be made. (The authors used a candle 6 ins. in height by $2\frac{5}{8}$ ins. diameter).
2. Four thinner candles from which the limbs will be made. (The authors used four candles $6\frac{1}{2}$ ins. in height by $\frac{7}{8}$ in. diameter).
3. One candle with which to weld limbs to the body and, where necessary, to effect repairs.

Method
Flatten the front and back of the candle. Place a previously prepared paper pattern against the flattened sides of the candle and

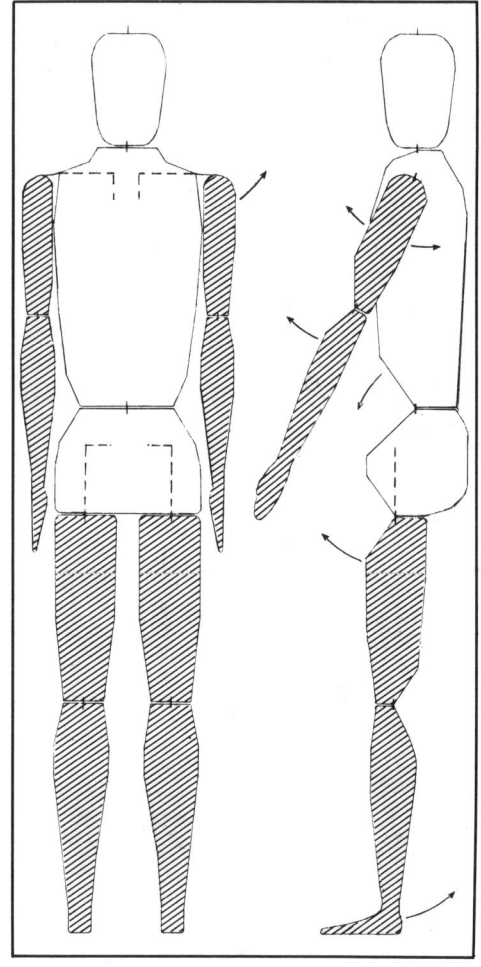

Diagram showing movement of limbs

mark the candle accordingly. Now begin to cut the wax to the markings made from the pattern. Actually, scraping with a metal ruler or other blunt instrument allows greater control.

Carefully flatten the remaining two sides of the candle, mark to a pattern as before and cut away in the same way. Cut as thin a slice of wax as possible from the waist and neck so as to allow movement. *Take care not to*

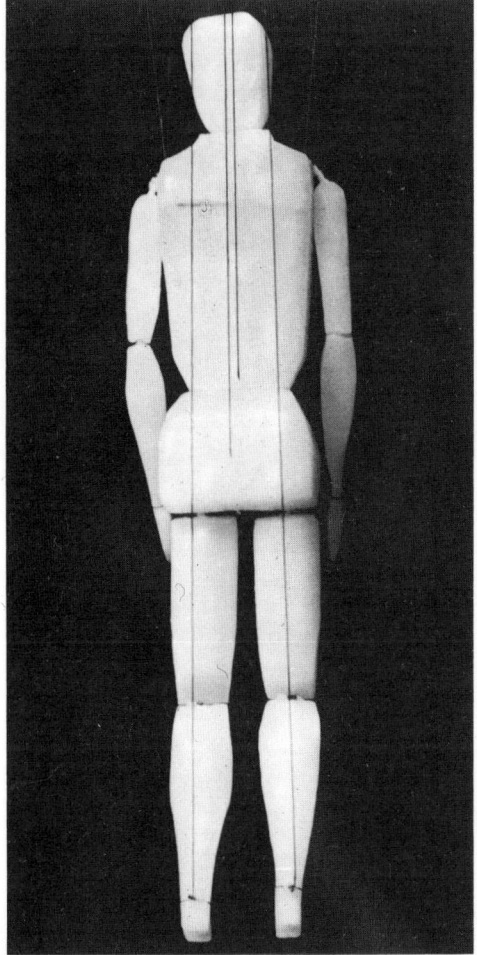

Candle marionette showing stringing

cut or damage the wick. Repeated scraping with the corner and thin edge of a metal ruler makes just about the right sort of "slice" and does not damage the wick. Take care to keep the wick in the middle of the sculptured wax.

Limbs The arms and legs are made in the same way. It is more satisfactory to restrict "joints" to elbows and knees and to keep wrists and ankles rigid, as this strengthens both hands and feet. Movement of hands and feet add little. Leave about $\frac{3}{4}$ in. of wick at the top of each limb. Later, this is used to attach the limbs to the body in the way described below.

Attaching limbs The limbs can be firmly attached by embedding the $\frac{3}{4}$ in. of wick at the top of each limb in the wax which forms the marionette's trunk. (An L shaped bend in the trench gives added 'holding' strength.) After a drop of molten wax has been dropped into the trench, the $\frac{3}{4}$ in. of wick is firmly pressed into the trench and held in position by the filling of the trench with molten wax.

Moving "joints" This design limits the marionette's movements to those "joints" judged to be the more important in its performance, in a more or less anatomically "realistic" way. For example, the marionette can bend forward at the waist because the wax was cut away at an angle but cannot bend backward. In the same way the design "limits" other movements: the "knee" will allow the lower part of the leg to bend backwards but not forwards or sideways; the hip joint allows the leg to move forward but restricts other movements; finally, the "elbow" will allow the lower arm to bend forward but not backwards. The shoulder allows unrestricted movement.

Readers may wish to simplify this process. This could be done by carving the wax directly, without making or using patterns and by replacing "angled" joints with simple $\frac{1}{8}$ in. to $\frac{3}{8}$ in. gaps. Once attached, the strings support and work the marionette, keeping the limbs and trunk facing the right way. The erratic twisting at the waist can be prevented by adding points of wax on to the top half of the trunk which fit into corresponding sockets in the lower half.

Stringing The wax marionette is strung in the same way as other marionettes. Certain strings, including the main support strings attached to the shoulder, are embedded in the trunk in the same way as the wick from the limbs. There is nothing to prevent more elaborate "sculpturing" of the marionette. Wax is very suitable for detailed carving. Nuns in Spain have produced carvings of great delicacy in wax.

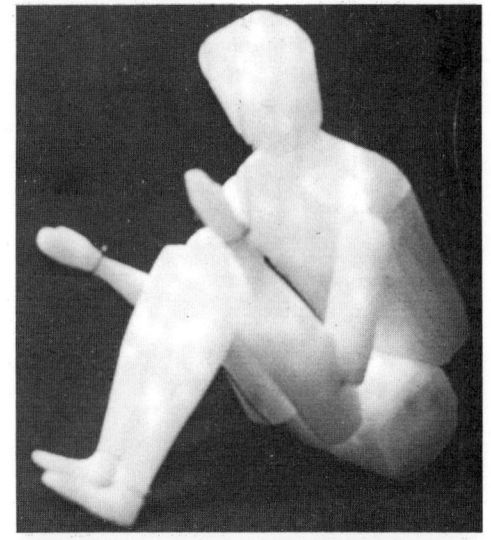

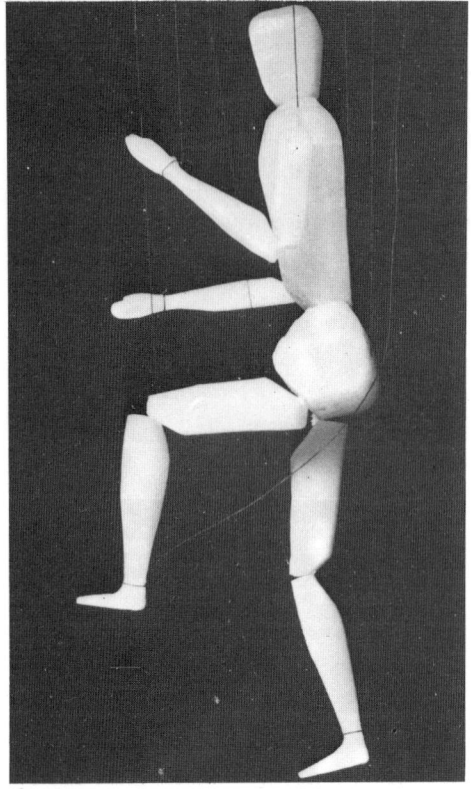

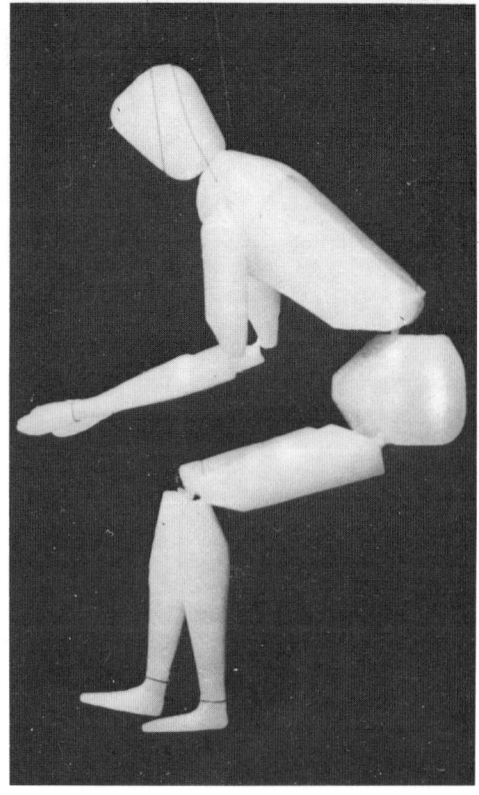

Jumping Jacks, Jills and Jollyboys

Toys or Puppets?

Both! *Toys* because they are for self-amuse-ment; *puppets* because they can perform for the amusement of others, an audience. Construction-wise they can make a nice introduction to the marionette family; their action is more in the line of variety turns (rather than drama) but such items are among the traditional forms of puppetry.

Flat figure marionettes are occasionally to be seen in professional shows—limbs moving sideways as with the Jumping Jacks and Jills. The limbs of Jollyboys move backwards and forwards as with the more usual marionettes.

In addition to Jacks and Jills there can be Owls, Clowns, Ballet Dancers, fantastic creatures with extended limbs—whatever individual imaginations suggest. These can also be used as *shadow figures,* performing behind an illuminated translucent screen. The latter can be an old picture frame, minus glass, with a tautly stretched piece of white sheeting fixed with drawing pins. A pair of wooden feet can be added so that the screen will stand on a table. The method of making the joints is similar to that for jointed shadow figures (thin twine passed through the over-lapping parts and knotted each side; a dab of tube glue on the knots gives security).

Any of these can be converted into marion-ettes by attaching individual strings to the head and moving parts, then taking the strings *upwards* to some form of control.

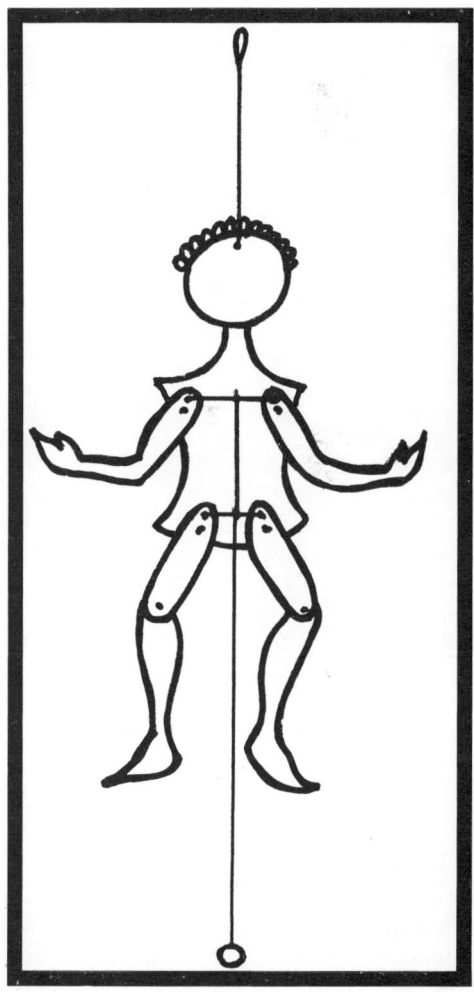

Pantins

The first experiments can be with stout card, making cut-outs with scissors or rigid blade craft knife, using thin twine for joints. Historically these will be similar to the *pantins* popular with French society in the eighteenth century and later with the gentry in London. Coloured sheets of costumed parts—a variety of characters—to be cut out and mounted on card, were sold. These card figures can have features and costume added with crayon or paint or waterproof inks.

The principle of stringing is simple. A short piece of twine (or carpet thread) connects the top end of the arms, another at the tops of the legs. Knotting-off is done with the limbs in the "at-rest" position. A string is then attached to the centre of the arms-string and hitched around the legs-string, dropping to about 6 ins. below the feet, with a large bead at the end (to give a grip). Pulling the string operates the four limbs. A single string is attached to top of head, held by the other hand. When not in use the figure can be quite decorative on a wall,

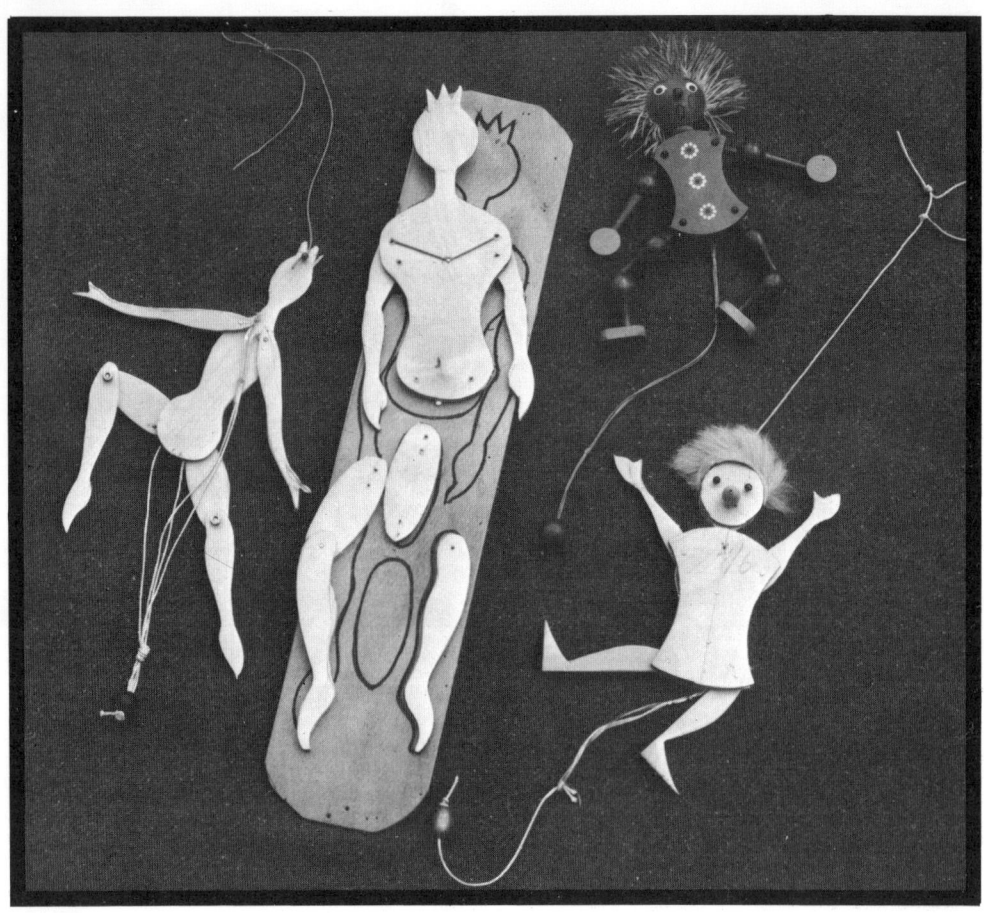

Jumping Jacks and Jills in plywood. Struwwelpeter (top right) has ball head and rounded limbs, double body. (see page 221)

suspended from a nail by the head string. In the classroom a whole array of figures could enliven the scene.

Plywood

More durable figures can be cut from plywood by fretsaw. (They could be mass-produced with a jigsaw, cutting a number of duplicate parts simultaneously.) Body and limbs are cut with the grain of the wood running lengthwise. Joints must be free-moving (experiment with panel pins, tiny bolts, rivets, as well as knotted twine). Painting of features and costume should be done *before* assembling the parts, using tempera colour (with coat of clear protective varnish), oil colours (over ground coat of flat white) or acrylic paints, water-proof inks or dyes. Fantastic characters might have psychedelic colouring!

Even for large-scale figures most of the parts can be cut from off-cuts of ply—and part of the fun is seeing how much can be cut out from each piece (as also with Jollyboys). Figures can be of geometric design or drawn freehand. Technically, the important point is in allowing for the overlaps of parts to be joined (shoulders, hips, knees).

Some of the traditional German figures have a double body concealing the stringing (picture page 220 top right: Struwwelpeter; lower right, unpainted figure). To ensure free movement the front and back of this type are separated by a small piece of wood or by square or tubular beads through which pass small bolts.

Multiples

Taking an idea from the marionette multiple-control dance items, there can be *groups* of Jacks and/or Jills (or what have you)— say three or more figures—their head strings attached to a horizontal rod (dowel, curtain rod), their control strings hitched to a second rod. These could perform over a

table, an operator at each end, holding ends of both rods. Action could be to music, e.g. percussion instruments, with varying rhythms. Dancer figures could have small bells attached to wrists and ankles. Or a number of individual puppets could be used by a group of children.

Jollyboys

Although a professionally-made figure will have joints similar to those of the marionette, this is not essential. In fact a lot of amusing movements come from having joints of very simple construction. Arms and legs operate on the pivot principle; the pivots can be small nails. The holes in the limbs are made with a bradawl (preferably square sided) or an archimedian drill. If of plywood this needs to be at least five-ply. Figure on next page is $\frac{1}{2}$ in. thickness. Shelving can also be used as in picture on page 223, $\frac{5}{8}$ in. thickness. Parts should be smoothed with

Jumping Jill by Lindy Wright

221

glasspaper before painting and painted before assembly. As with the Jacks, the head and body are usually in one piece, the arms have no elbow joints (but could have), the legs are jointed at knees and hips. Halving joints can be used as in photograph (below left).

Performance

Jollyboys perform on a springboard, a length of thin ply, 4 ins. to 6 ins. wide and at least 2-ft. long. One end is placed on a chair and the operator sits on it. He taps board with spare hand to induce movement. The puppet is supported by a horizontal rod (thin dowel) inserted in a hole in middle of back. It would be possible to attach a string to front end of board, make a loop at end to go over operator's foot.

Planchette

The horizontal method of control of the Jollyboy is reminiscent of some earlier forms of puppet, e.g. the *marionnettes à la planchette* (fourteenth to seventeenth century, France, Italy). There are reproductions of these in von Boehn *Dolls and Puppets,* Baird *The Art of the Puppet,* and other puppet books, from old lithographs. A Hogarth engraving, *Southwark Fair,* shows an itinerant showman using this type. On the ground is a short plank with a post at one end. A horizontal string passes from post, through the upper chest of one or more puppets, and is looped around the knee of performer. Tapping the foot induces puppet action. The hands are free to hold pipe and tabor or bagpipes to provide dance tunes.

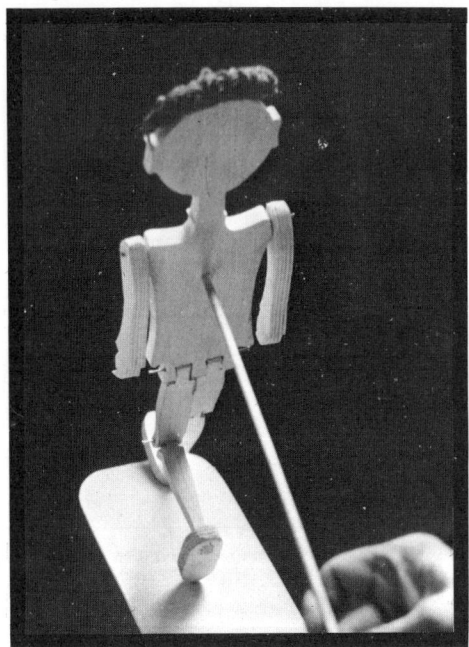

Jollyboy in action on springboard ($\frac{1}{2}''$ ply figure; board of three-ply, cross grain)

Planchette puppets

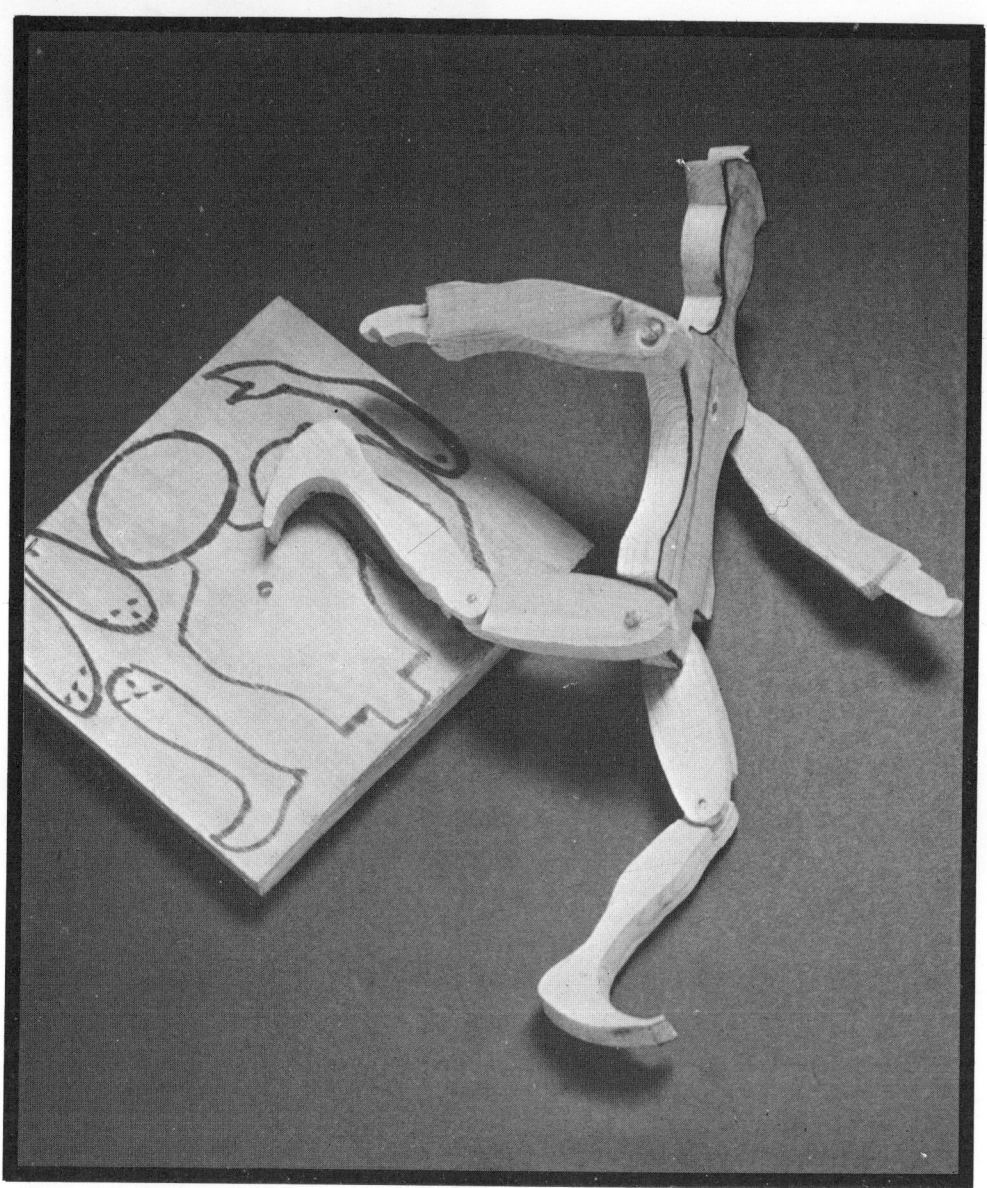

Jollyboy from $\frac{5}{8}''$ shelving, and lay-out for another figure